ROUTLEDGE LIBRARY EDITIONS: LIBRARY AND INFORMATION SCIENCE

Volume 85

SCIENTIFIC JOURNALS

SCIENTIFIC JOURNALS
Improving Library Collections Through Analysis of Publishing Trends

TONY STANKUS

LONDON AND NEW YORK

First published in 1990 by The Haworth Press, Inc.

This edition first published in 2020
by Routledge
2 Park Square, Milton Park, Abingdon, Oxon OX14 4RN

and by Routledge
52 Vanderbilt Avenue, New York, NY 10017

Routledge is an imprint of the Taylor & Francis Group, an informa business

© 1990 The Haworth Press, Inc.

All rights reserved. No part of this book may be reprinted or reproduced or utilised in any form or by any electronic, mechanical, or other means, now known or hereafter invented, including photocopying and recording, or in any information storage or retrieval system, without permission in writing from the publishers.

Trademark notice: Product or corporate names may be trademarks or registered trademarks, and are used only for identification and explanation without intent to infringe.

British Library Cataloguing in Publication Data
A catalogue record for this book is available from the British Library

ISBN: 978-0-367-34616-4 (Set)
ISBN: 978-0-429-34352-0 (Set) (ebk)
ISBN: 978-0-367-43267-6 (Volume 85) (hbk)
ISBN: 978-0-367-43268-3 (Volume 85) (pbk)
ISBN: 978-1-00-300222-2 (Volume 85) (ebk)

Publisher's Note
The publisher has gone to great lengths to ensure the quality of this reprint but points out that some imperfections in the original copies may be apparent.

Disclaimer
The publisher has made every effort to trace copyright holders and would welcome correspondence from those they have been unable to trace.

Scientific Journals: Improving Library Collections Through Analysis of Publishing Trends

Tony Stankus, MLS

The Haworth Press
New York • London

Scientific Journals: Improving Library Collections Through Analysis of Publishing Trends is monographic supplement #6 to *The Serials Librarian*. It is not supplied as part of the subscription to the journal, but is available from the publisher at an additional charge.

© 1990 by The Haworth Press, Inc. All rights reserved. No part of this work may be reproduced or utilized in any form or by any means, electronic or mechanical, including photocopying, microfilm and recording, or by any information storage and retrieval system, without permission in writing from the publisher. Permission does not extend for any services providing photocopies for sale in any way. Printed in the United States of America.

The Haworth Press, Inc. 10 Alice Street, Binghamton, NY 13904-1580
EUROSPAN/Haworth, 3 Henrietta Street, London WC2E 8LU England

Library of Congress Cataloging-in-Publication Data

Scientific journals : improving library collections through analysis of publishing trends / Tony Stankus, [editor].
    p. cm. — (*The Serials Librarian*, ISSN: 0897-8409; #6)
    Includes bibliographical references and index.
    ISBN 0-886656-905-7 (alk. paper)
    1. Libraries—Special collections—Scientific literature. 2. Science—Periodicals—Bibliography—Methodology. 3. Scientific libraries—Collection development. 4. Acquisition of scientific publications. 5. Acquisition of serial publications. 6. Periodicals, Publishing of. 7. Science publishing. I. Stankus, Tony. II. Series: Monographic supplement . . . to the Serials librarian: #6.
Z688.S3S34   1990
025.2'75—dc20   90-40988
                                                                                                                                     CIP

Dedication

Readers often ask if my books and articles are done in pen, pencil, or laser print. I tell them in all honesty they're done largely with late night pots of Irish tea, tins of Balkan pipe tobacco, and tons of encouragement, all brought tenderly by my wife of eleven years, Mary Frances (Doyle) Stankus. This book is dedicated to her. She deserves much more.

This book also serves as a memorial to my second son, Peter, who since the writing of my last book, has joined his little brother Andrew in Heaven.

CONTENTS

Acknowledgements   xi

Introduction   xiii
    Barbara A. (Rice) Lockett

THEME ONE

Knowing Success Stories When We See Them, and Realizing We Can Use Them to Our Advantage   1

High Yields on an Expensive Investment in Science Journals: Career Histories of Known Undergraduate Users Ten Years Later   5

The Scientist Is Appointed an Editor: Adjusting the Journal Collection at Stages in a Client's Career   19

The Academy Award Without Oscar: What Happens to Your Client's Journal Use After Election to the National Academy of Sciences and Guaranteed Acceptance into Its *Proceedings*   29

THEME TWO

What Do Shifts in World Science and World Publishing Mean for U.S. Librarians?   51

The Rise of Eurojournals: Their Success Can Be Ours   55
Tony Stankus
Kevin Rosseel

How Vulnerable Is the European For-Profit Sector Within U.S. Science Journal Collections? Comparing Its Staying Power with that of the American For-Profit Sector in an Incremental Cancellations Trial, with Special Attention to the Subspecialty Journals of Both Sectors   69

Is the Best Japanese Science in Western Journals?   91
Tony Stankus
Kevin Rosseel
William C. Littlefield

Asia's Other Sci-Tech Dragons: The International Publishing Patterns of Hong Kong, the People's Republic of China, Singapore, South Korea, and Taiwan   105

Greater Familiarity Will Not Breed Contempt: Canadian Scientific Journals as Economically and Professionally Attractive Outlets for U.S. Researchers and the Libraries that Serve Them   129

The Producer of the Article as Its Distributor: The Competitive Status and Prospects of the University Sector of U.S. Science Journal Publishing   143

THEME THREE

Technology and Competition are Improving Today's Science Journal   159

Desktop Publishing and Camera-Ready-Copy Science Journals   161

Competition as a Force in the Evolution of Science Journal Format and Publishing Schedules: A Case Study from Cell Biology 173

Index 199

Acknowledgements

This book could not have been done without extraordinarily capable assistance. I wish to thank the following:

BILL LITTLEFIELD, coauthor of a paper, my current assistant, and Simmons Library School student. He now teaches me more about management and computing than I was ever able to show him about journals.

KEVIN ROSSEEL, coauthor of two papers, my past assistant, currently with United Technologies. His thoroughly cosmopolitan outlook awakened me to patterns of global competition.

JOHN LITTLE, Associate Professor of Mathematics at Holy Cross. With great forbearance he plays the role of "bad cop," finding errors of calculation or logic in my manuscripts before they can be seen by my readers.

ROBERT GARVEY, Associate Professor of Physics at Holy Cross. He plays the role of "good cop," after Dr. Little plays "bad cop." He finds whatever is salvageable in my papers and encourages me to finish, reminding me that otherwise I'd have no readers.

JOEL VILLA, Coordinator of Audiovisuals at Holy Cross, Master of Computer Graphics. If one picture is worth a thousand words, Mr. Villa is worth more than a thousand pictures. All the good graphs in this book are owing to him. The poorer ones are my attempts.

DIANE GALLAGHER, Periodicals Librarian at Holy Cross. Without a real serials librarian like Ms. Gallagher, I would have no serials about which to pontificate.

BARBARA LOCKETT, Director of Libraries at Rensselaer Polytechnic Institute. Sci-tech author, editor, administrator, organizational leader, kind contributor of the Introduction.

My thanks go to Pergamon Press, the copyright holder, for the permission to reprint the paper "The Scientist is Appointed an Editor: Adjusting the Journal Collection at Stages in a Client's Career," *Library Acquisitions: Practice and Theory,* vol. 11, pp. 113-118, 1987. Thanks also to the Office of Copyright and Permissions of the American Library Association for permission to reprint the paper, "The Rise of Eurojournals: Their Success Can Be Ours," from *Library Resources and Technical Services,* vol. 31, no. 3, pp. 215-224.

Introduction

Can it be that Tony Stankus has already written another book? Using material developed largely in 1988 and 1989 he has amassed another volume of collected papers on the relationships among scientists, publishers and journals. This material is extremely useful to all who must deal with acquisitions budgets and, like his former work, can substantiate journals selection/deselection decisions to library users and administrators. How does he do it, when we lesser librarians groan under the strain of getting out one or two articles a year?

Tony labors 40 hours a week, 48 weeks a year at Holy Cross' Science Library, a one-professional operation. There he deals with the intricacies of circulation, reference, collection development, student staffing, etc. He has no faculty status. For him there is no tenure, promotion, or sabbaticals. At quitting time he reflects on the meaning of his day, and then writes on the more heady, philosophical and sociological and economic aspects of the scientific journal as in "The Academy Award Without Oscar: What Happens to Your Client's Journal Use After Election to the National Academy of Sciences . . ." or "The Producer of the Article as its Distributor . . ."

Why does he torture himself this way? Why not leave work and go to karate class to ease the tensions of dealing with demanding patrons and unpredictable journals? I can see only one answer. Tony is in love with the scientific journal. He finds it exciting, attractive, challenging, and important. He wants to know and savor its every nuance.

Tony's writing is sometimes hurried and sometimes an analogy is tortured. Always, however, the reader senses Tony's intense involvement and fascination with his material, his desire to explore another facet of journal publishing or compare characteristics of different subject specialties. His research is sound, and he is always able to back up his conclusions with analyses of use, citation and publication data. Tony's works are never dry reading.

My association with Tony Stankus began in 1980, when I was science bibliographer at SUNY Albany and I saw one of his early articles in the *Sci-Tech News*. The journal had omitted the tables, and I wrote asking for them. This began a correspondence and led to two coauthored articles, one of which is the much cited "Handle With Care; Use and Citation Data for Science Journal Management." The "Handle With Care" part of the title came from Tony—the dry part from me. I am very pleased to again be participating in a small way in Tony's work by writing the introduction to these odes on the scientific journal.

Barbara A. (Rice) Lockett
Director of Libraries
Rensselaer Polytechnic Institute
Troy, NY

THEME ONE

Knowing Success Stories When We See Them, and Realizing We Can Use Them to Our Advantage

Today librarians in the United States have a choice of two visions concerning science journals in libraries. Which they choose depends on who they decide are the real experts. Librarians can accept the dark vision presented by much of the library literature: that science is too complicated for librarians and that it is too expensive for libraries. Or they can look into the faces of their science journal users for enlightenment.

In your library this very day there is likely someone who was a "boat person" with no English five years ago. Now that student somehow manages tough papers in top technical journals. No expert had told her that the scientific literature had become unmanageable! Then there's the professor from another poor country. He doesn't think that there are too many journals with which to keep up. His method in the old country involved long bus rides to several libraries twice a month in the dry season. Shouldn't a real expert convince him how badly off he is today! In yet another corner of the library, a doctor is looking for the latest "Instructions for Authors." The physician has concluded a study that shows that a conservative treatment saves lives and involves fewer hospital stays for the patient. Shouldn't a real expert warn him or her that there are already too many papers published and that this is driving up the price of his favorite journal? The vision of science journals in American libraries derived from these insights is one of bright success. The rest of the world would dearly love to be in our predicament!

The choice of the dark or light vision affects the way librarians and libraries function. The librarians of the first vision focus on the monotony of their own routines: they check "those damn things" in and they pay the bills. They lack a larger context for their work. Their internal gauge of success has become some combination of greater speed, accuracy, and account balancing. They fear an intellectual overture to the material. They have a sense of being overwhelmed by its sheer volume. They are aware of their political powerlessness in defending the material before angry treasurers, should they form any sort of attachment to it, at budget-cutting time. The librarians of the first vision are tempted to let the science journal situation slide down into darkness. Their attitude is in effect a prediction of doom; and this prediction can become at least locally self-fulfilling. Cancel the journals and be done with them! Maybe then the treasurer will relent.

But there are those librarians who choose the second vision. The librarians of the second vision transcend an introspective view of what constitutes work and success. They handle the same operational problems and the same problematic treasurers, but don't measure themselves as successful primarily on incremental improvements in little procedures and turf wars. Rather, they see themselves as a small but real part of hundreds of personal success stories in science. They put up with the annoyances because there's a lot of science to be uncovered, and the scientists need their help to do it.

Librarians dealing with these two visions are probably confused as to a choice. They need a sense of direction. The three essays that follow will help. Emotionally, librarians need to be bolstered by some success stories. Politically, librarians need to identify the scientifically successful and cultivate them for an alliance against the treasurer – no mean feat given that the cultivation must proceed on soil that is not too rich just now. But the smart librarian manages the available resources with a hope for better later, once the alliance is firmed.

Colleagues, it is time to choose your experts and your vision. You can be as miserable as you want, or you can sign on with the winners.

High Yields on an Expensive Investment in Science Journals: Career Histories of Known Undergraduate Users Ten Years Later

SUMMARY. Many librarians at small colleges feel that the high cost of science journals represents a disproportionate part of the budget given the small number of users typically found today. This is a short-sighted, inappropriate application of popularity-based thinking. The minority that use science journals may in fact, be critically important for the technological and medical future of the majority. A group of 470 students clearly involved with scientific journals as coauthors in the mid to late 1970s is shown to have contained a high number of exceptionally promising scientists and physicians. Access to a good assortment of science journals was a part of the process that set them on their way to success, and making such access possible must remain our commitment to future generations of scientists.

IS ANYTHING THIS PROBLEMATIC THAT NECESSARY?

Serials librarians are strongly tempted to cut science journals, particularly at financially hard-pressed small colleges. A number of reasons make this category of material vulnerable to such adverse action:[1]

- Science journals, from whatever source, are habitually the most expensive material within the serials budget.
- Many of these journals come from strong-currency nations such as West Germany, the Netherlands, and Switzerland, at a time when the dollar is particularly weak, and this inflates their already unattractive base prices.
- Some librarians feel strong resentment at the large number of

for-profit sector publishers in the sciences. Many librarians are attuned to the notion that free or low-cost information is "everyone's right." They consider people who make a healthy living from information to be "gougers." As one industry representative puts it privately: librarians expect everyone involved with the literature to live on what librarians have come to accept.

— Handling science journals involves a great deal of extra work. They often come in many confusing subsections. Issues frequently arrive late or out of sequence. The many issues cost a good deal to bind, and they gobble up shelving. Claiming is constant, and there are fewer back-runs available for replacement in these days of the *Thor* decision.

— Very few serials librarians have a background in the sciences or a strong personal interest in technical topics. Serialists may well support the most obscure little magazine of poetry or alternative lifestyles out of a personal affinity for literature or ecological awareness. Few librarians have such an interest in partial differential equations or quantum mechanics.

— Relatively few librarians willingly involve themselves as authors in their own professional literature. While the amount of library research published today seems overwhelming when one tries to read it all, there are probably more papers published in biochemistry in one week than in a year of library science. Instead of being humbled by this insight, some librarians suspect that scientists publish so frequently for reasons of ego or salary aggrandizement. They argue that libraries can no longer afford to indulge these disordered passions with expensive science journals.

Whatever their sentiments, many librarians try to arrive at a fair, professional way of making cuts in the serials collection. Since there is a lingering suspicion in the literature that citation data is not a decisive measure,[2] and that when it is, it tends to unhappily indicate that the journals that are highly cited are often highly expensive,[3] they turn to studies of local use. Use studies afford the librarian a certain sense of democratic procedure. The idea is that the journals that are most popular should be saved, and that the least popular should be cut. Unfortunately, this approach will almost certainly cause a loss of science journals in most institutions. The reasons are clear with a moment's reflection:

— Enrollment in the sciences at general purpose universities has been falling precipitously. The number of students attempting to major in the sciences has fallen by 50% in the last thirteen years, down to about 5%.[4]
— Students who do enroll are often poorly prepared and require remediation. They are either delayed in their approach to sophisticated journal literature, cutting off a year or two's use of that literature, or they switch to majors in the arts and social studies, before ever reaching for it.
— Students in the sciences generally have far less free time for study in the library because of extended hours in the laboratory. It is entirely typical for a chemistry major to take the same number of courses as a history major, but to spend twelve hours less in the library because he or she is in a lab. This does not mean that the young chemist is not using the library with a sense of mission. It means that he or she has less time for the serendipitous and coincidental use of materials promoted by the longer spans of time within the library that humanities students enjoy. Those are uses that would be counted in use studies along with all the weight of required reading.
— Science is heavily dependent on noncirculating materials, the use of which is difficult to count. The most common approach is to flag a check-off sheet onto current issues of journals on display. This has some validity for science faculty use, although their intense use of computerized alerting services has made random scanning as opposed to cued scanning less common. (The faculty need just as wide an assortment of journals to retrieve pertinent papers, but they need not flip through as many issues before finding papers of interest since they have prior warning of the specific issues that contain them.) By contrast, science instruction is dependent on bound volumes of back years. Students initially get their cues from assigned instructive readings, textbook references, and retrospective searches of indexing-abstracting services. Indeed even in their

initial duties as collaborators with the faculty, they are much more likely to start as retrievers and interpreters of older materials than as scouts for the newest items. They build up a sense of the present importance of an idea by tracing what has gone before. They get their ideas of the roles of differing journals in the publication process by handling those with an emphasis on their theme. Only after this process can they make sense of the array of current journals before them in the display area. How many libraries are going to tag 10,000+ back volumes to trace this important use?

If quantity is not going to be present in use studies can there be a qualitative argument involving the users? The answer is yes. In this study we propose to trace through their publication records what happened to a known group of student science journal users—students who coauthored papers with chemistry faculty while attending a small undergraduate liberal arts college. We will argue that although their numbers were relatively small, even in the small colleges from which they graduated, a disproportionate number of them have gone on to make a mark in science and medicine.

TRACKING DOWN THE STUDENT JOURNAL USERS AND ONLY THE STUDENT JOURNAL USERS

From an initial group of over 1,000 authors listed in a directory of chemistry researchers at small liberal arts colleges,[5] 420 were ultimately chosen for the study. The essential qualification was that the subject be both an undergraduate student and an author or coauthor of a paper in a nationally circulated, scholarly, refereed journal between 1974-1977. The operating principle underlying this approach is that these students were in fact science journal users.

Students with common last names, particularly if they lacked two initials were generally excluded since their tracing involved too many opportunities for error. Sadly this excluded many women who married and assumed their husband's surname, although the growing habit of retaining maiden names or using compound last names reduced this loss. Also excluded were virtually all students whose later work gave an affiliation outside the United States and

Canada, unless the address was of the foreign affiliate of an American firm. The goal of all this stringency was to avoid any charge of inflating statistics through assigning to these students the achievements of others with the same name. Librarians following this approach at their home institutions should get even better yields. Through working with alumni records there can be less exclusion of students with common names and initials, and one has access to marital status updates.

The question then becomes, what became of these early science journal users whose serials costs have become such a burden?

SUBSEQUENT EDUCATIONAL ATTAINMENT OF STUDENT JOURNAL USERS

Entries in *Dissertation Abstracts* yielded a highly gratifying result. Even though no credit was given to students who took doctorates in non-scientific fields (and counting them as not gaining a degree but not dropping them from the pool), a surprising 30% of the 420 went on to earn Ph.Ds. Lacking a national, uniform, inclusive directory similar to *Dissertation Abstracts*, of those earning M.Ds, we were forced to analyze the clinical medical literature for works by our group. This undoubtedly lost us a large number of M.Ds who did not publish. Nonetheless, we still uncovered a minimum M.D. attainment rate of 19%. Even after rigorous exclusion we found that at least 49% of our journal users earned scientific, technical, and medical doctorates. See Figure 1. These figures are all the more stunning when one compares them to average rates for all U.S. college graduates. See Figure 2. In sum, our group of journal users were ten to twenty times more likely than average to earn these hard-won degrees.

An argument can be made that since there are many vacancies in science graduate programs these days, just about anyone can get into a program and earn a degree if the person stays long enough. To test this we examined the ratings of graduate programs published by the National Academy of Sciences.[6] We derived a list of the top 20% of programs, and asked what proportion of doctoral students enrolled at these schools. As Figure 3 indicates, a remarkable 60% of our journal users took their degrees from this top group. The list

Educational Attainments of Known Early Science Journal Users

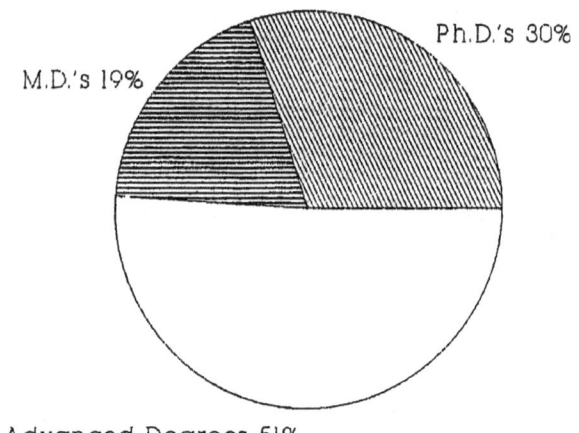

FIGURE 1

of the favorite schools of our group reads like the roll call of elite American institutions of science. In descending order among the top five are: Berkeley, Illinois, Chapel Hill, Harvard, and Cornell. Twenty-six of the top twenty-nine schools had these journal users among their Ph.D. alumni during the period of this study.

Doubters may still argue that those who stay long enough at these schools will ultimately earn their degree through persistence if not talent. We therefore determined that the national median average time for earning these degrees was 5.8 years,[7] and asked ourselves how many of our special group were numbered among those in the fastest 10% (essentially anyone completing in four years). The answer once again demonstrates the special nature of our journal users: 29%. See Figure 4. This is three times the expected proportion.

The question of the quality of the M.D. granting schools remains. Reporting for this group was frustrated by badly incomplete data and a change in the medical school recruitment situation. Nowadays a reputation for high quality does not draw in medical school

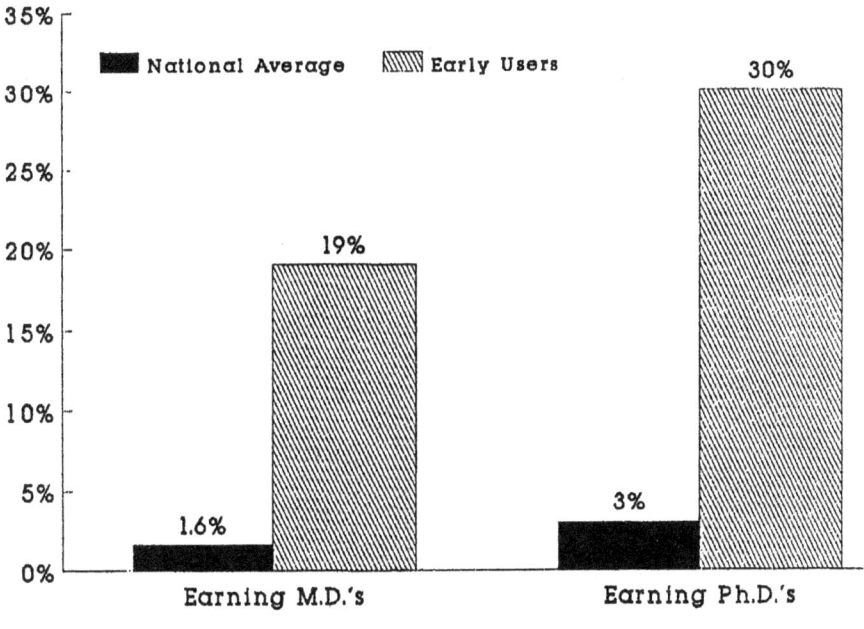

FIGURE 2

students as strongly as it does in Ph.D. programs in the sciences. Money has become an extremely important modifier of the urge among students accepted into more than a single program to go to the medical school with the highest rating. By contrast, virtually all U.S. Ph.D. candidates in the sciences are substantially underwritten by grants, fellowships, research assistantships, part-time teaching, and genuinely low-cost loans. This is true of both rated and unrated graduate programs, although the former will usually make somewhat better offers to promising new students. There are, however, few medical school students today who are not paying the bulk of their much higher tuitions bills directly or through expensive loans. This includes students at both rated and unrated medical schools. Virtually the only reliable financial breaks apart from some limited minority, military, or governmental service programs come from choosing a state university school at a cost of less than $10,000

Elite Nature of Ph.D.'s Earned by Known Early Science Journal Users

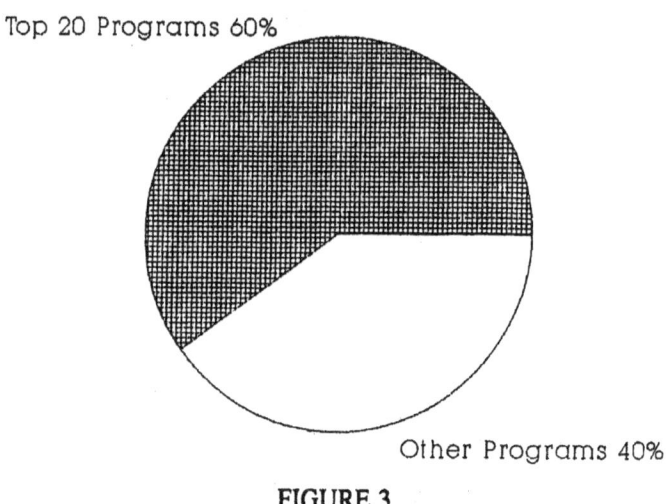

FIGURE 3

annually as compared to a private school at over $30,000. Consequently, fewer conclusions can be drawn about the academic quality of our journal user group — as opposed to its financial resources or risk-taking behavior — on the basis of medical school enrollment. This situation may not be as plausible in a state like California or Michigan, where state medical schools are members of the elite group, but is entirely possible in the East, where a student may bypass an Ivy League acceptance for an unrated state school. We have chosen to consider as more reliable the status of the teaching hospital or research center where the M.D. is currently affiliated.

WHERE THEY'RE WORKING TODAY

Critics may suggest that our special group of journal users are essentially pampered people who have been given special treatment and perhaps even sheltered from the real world of work. We decided to check into their current employment as indicated by affiliations on recent papers. We were able to trace approximately 75% of

Percentage of Fast-Trackers Among Known Early Science Journal Users

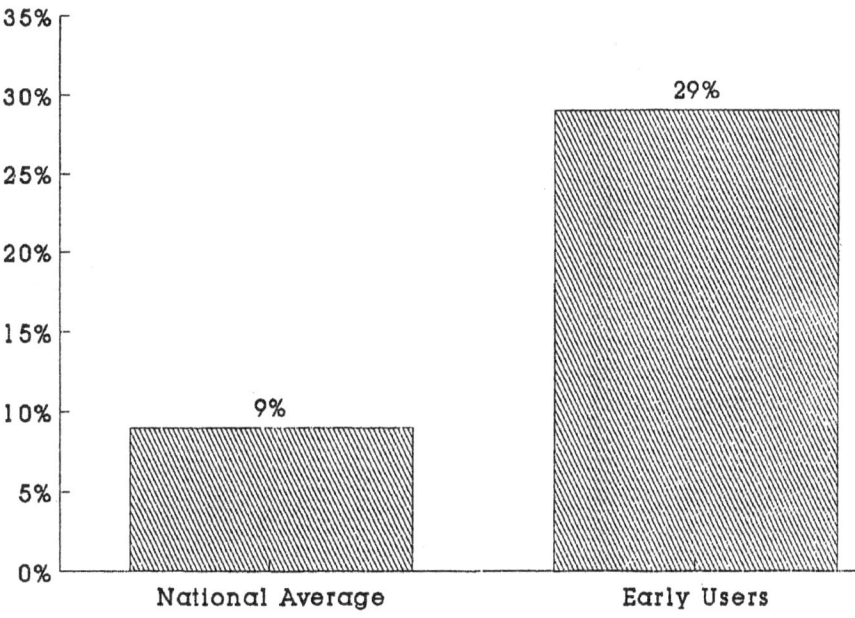

FIGURE 4

the entire study group. The result is again gratifying. While it is understandable that the largest sector represents university careers, there is substantial representation in clinical medicine, government service, and the corporate sector. See Figures 5 and 6.

The argument may be made that virtually everyone has to get a job sooner or later and that persons with advanced degrees stand a better chance of being employed. We responded by analyzing the employers. With little surprise we note that America's most scientifically and medically elite centers are frequent in most cases.[8]

In medicine 17 elite medical school affiliation networks out of a possible 120 account for some 37% of the physicians and surgeons. The five most common among our group in descending order are: Harvard, Cornell, the Mayo Clinic, Illinois, and Stanford.

In university teaching and research, 56% of the group are at top 20% schools. The most common are: Berkeley, Caltech, Cornell,

Employment of Known Early Journal Users by Sector

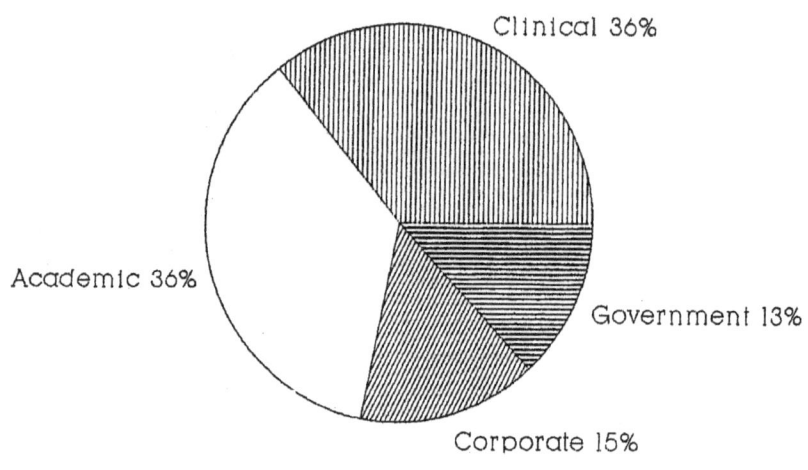

FIGURE 5

Harvard, Duke, Wisconsin, Purdue and Washington University of St. Louis. (The last four are tied for 4th-8th place.)

In terms of governmental service, 45% are at elite centers. Approximately one third of these are at either the National Institutes of Health or the Centers for Disease Control, with two-thirds at major Department of Defense weapons development centers, most notably Los Alamos.

In industry, four world-class firms actually employ three-quarters of our corporately affiliated journal users group: AT&T Bell Labs, DuPont, GE, and IBM.

ULTIMATE ARGUMENT:
THE COUNTRY NEEDS THE TALENT,
THE TALENT NEEDS THE TOOLS

While the elite nature of this small group should be abundantly clear by now, some within the library community will still argue that the financing of its "tools" or "toys" — expensive science

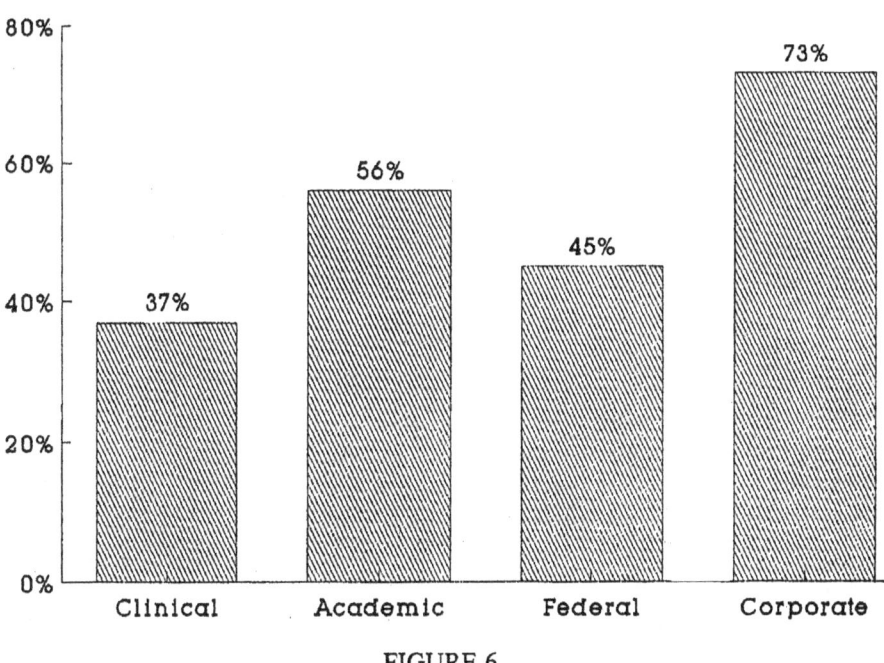

FIGURE 6

journals — on the backs of all the rest of the students remains unfair. This is incredibly short-sighted from this author's viewpoint — indeed this anti-elitist argument strikes him as akin to that of the Maoist Red Guards during the Cultural Revolution. Perhaps a new viewpoint, a new analogy, is needed to put the situation into perspective.

Consider the Olympics. Hundreds of countries, great and small, send thousands of athletes to a city from among many world-class cities that has literally begged for the opportunity of hosting the events. Within each country people have pulled together to set up whatever national training centers are possible. In much of the free world support is voluntary from individuals and corporations. People have pride in their heroes. They are not jealous of them because they do something that most people can't. For the most part these athletes are not an elite because of inherited millions but of developed merit. While I am sure that I can answer reference questions far better than Greg Louganis, I am equally sure that I have neither the talent nor the guts to dive ninety feet into the water. While I might wish that librarianship attracted the attention and respect of Olympic diving, I do not fault the diver for what he wins through years of training, and I do not pretend that my talent is as rare or that my level of achievement as high.

And yet I feel that even Greg Louganis needs me. When I buy my bottle of beer (a portion of the proceeds goes to the Olympics) or give to an amateur athletic association I feel that I am enabling my country to show off its best. I'm buying people like Mr. Louganis a piece of the stadium in which they will do their best to fulfill all our hopes.

So must it be for the journal collections for our best and brightest young scientists. They can do the math, physics, chemistry, and biomedicine that the overwhelming majority of humanities and social studies students — including most eventual librarians — are quite frankly incapable of mastering. These mental athletes are undemocratically few. Their needs are undoubtedly greater than those with more commonplace interests and skills. But their promise and performance have been tremendous thus far. The gold medals of achievement in beating back disease and ignorance have been earned by their sweat, and rightfully belong draped around their necks. Can it be that we are too mean-spirited to back them when they really need it?

REFERENCE NOTES

1. The complaint literature mounts every year, price is the most common concern, but all the others surface regularly. See Stankus, T. "The Year's Work in Serials, 1987," *Library Resources and Technical Services* 32, no.3 (July 1988):217-232. Refs. 37, 38, 43, 62, 63, 74, 93, 110, and 143 are typical of last year.

2. Wallace, Danny P. "A Solution in Search of a Problem: Bibliometrics and Libraries," *Library Journal* 112, no.8 (1987):43-47. Represents a recent critical viewpoint. Interestingly, critics of bibliometric measures generally assign much more influence to the stand-alone power of citation data than do its proponents, who have long regarded it as a tool to be used alongside others.

3. Houbeck, Robert L. "British Journal Pricing: *Enigma Variations*, or What *Will* the U.S. Market Bear?," *Library Acquisitions: Practice and Theory*

10, no.3 (1986):183-197. Some of the journals with the steepest price rises have some of the best citation rates, making their cancellation highly problematic.

4. The bulk of the educational statistics concerning enrollment and attainment are derived from data and graphs in Carrier, Sam C., and Davis-Van Atta, David. *Maintaining America's Scientific Productivity*. Oberlin, OH: Oberlin College, 1987, p.9-29.

5. Andreen, Brian C. *Research in Chemistry at Private Undergraduate Colleges*. Minneapolis, Council on Undergraduate Research, 1979.

6. Jones, Lyle V., Linszey, Gardner, and Coggeshall, Porter E., Eds. *An Assessment of Research Doctorate Programs in the United States: Mathematical and Physical Sciences*. Washington: National Academy Press, 1982.

7. *Ibid.* p.52.

8. Our notion of elite employing institutions and firms comes primarily from the many lists found in Zuckerman, Harriet. *The Scientific Elite*. New York: The Free Press, 1977. Her work stresses the educational and occupational backgrounds of U.S. winners of the Nobel Prize. Her lists are constantly reinforced by data showing employers of authors of highly cited articles, found in Eugene Garfield's continuing series in *Current Contents*. Interestingly there is a remarkable agreement and stability in the membership of institutions regarded as elite in training or hiring elite scientists in the physical sciences. Perhaps the greatest change in the last twenty-five years in the academic sector has been that some Texas and western schools have taken over a few slots from older eastern universities. There are some schools with a higher standing in the life sciences and medicine that are no longer among the Chemistry elite — Johns Hopkins and Washington University of St. Louis, for example. When an early journal user took a degree in biochemistry or was clinically employed at these institutions, he or she was regarded as having joined the elite as well.

The Scientist Is Appointed an Editor: Adjusting the Journal Collection at Stages in a Client's Career

SUMMARY. A study of 66 biomedical scientists showed that few (four) maintained a level research output after being appointed to journal editorial boards. They were much more likely to have demonstrated a significant drop (-31% average) or rise ($+70\%$ average) in the number of papers when three-year and pre- and post-appointment periods were compared. Yet it is argued that these fluctuations do not justify either precipitous journal cancellations or freewheeling additions to the collection. In the 32 cases of declining output, editors maintained much (73%) of their original journal assortment even if this meant fewer repeat appearances in some journals. In the 30 cases of increasing output, the tendency to add new journals ($+37\%$) with each new paper was tempered somewhat by repeat appearances in their original assortment. Nonetheless, for those times when the budget either demands or allows, most adjustments can be made involving two types of journals identified as swing outlets for these editor/authors.

AN INTRODUCTION WITH THREE SCENARIOS

What happens to a customer's demand for science journals when he or she is named to the editorial board of a research journal? Three scenarios are possible. Two suggest possibilities for collection adjustment.

In the first scenario, the sometimes onerous duties of the added job cause a decline in the scientist's own level of library use and research output. While screening incoming manuscripts, assigning

---

Reprinted with the permission of Pergamon Press: Tony Stankus, "The Scientist is Appointed an Editor: Adjusting the Journal Collection at Stages in a Client's Career," *Library Acquisitions: Practice & Theory* 11(2):113-118; (1987). Copyright Pergamon Press Ltd., 1987.

reviewers, handling correspondence, and dealing with publishers, the formerly productive scientist takes time away from the classroom, laboratory, and library. Most librarians are willing to give the new editor deference in the short run. But in the long run some consider the editor's own output to be the principal determinant in his journal allocation. If the editor no longer has time to produce, some of his journals may be vulnerable.

In a second scenario, the appointment may signal your customer's arrival as a "hot" scientist. The increased contacts the editorship brings seem to stimulate the flow of even more papers. The editor's increased visibility may make his or her manuscripts highly "acceptable." Invitations to contribute to new journals or to write survey papers in established reviews begin coming in. Such an increase in output of papers may well merit additional journal titles in your collection.

In a third scenario, the appointment comes at a time when your scientist is able to make the transition with little disturbance in output. Library subscriptions seem to need no adjustment.

More than just the number of papers is likely to be affected by this change in the scientist's career. The number and category of journals in his or her customary assortment of journal outlets may also change. Will the scientist increase or decrease the number of papers sent off to the journal he or she now edits? To what degree will the scientist contribute to the journals which directly compete with his own? Will the new editor have more involvement with prestigious multispecialty journals? Will the scientist publish in fewer journals in allied fields or new subspecialties, or in more of them?

This paper, then, is a study of two types of change coincident with becoming an editor: shifts in output and assortment.

BACKGROUND

This study is part of an ongoing author's series on stages or events in a scientist's career and changes in this may engender in their involvement with—and demand for—scholarly journals. Earlier work[1] argued that scientists were scarcely born knowing which journals to follow; rather, they tended to develop in their graduate school years a pattern similar to that of their thesis advisors. Further work[2] showed that a majority of midcareer scientists were receptive to the flood of new subspecialty titles, usually at the expense of more established titles that had become a little less exclusively devoted to their specialties. The most recent study[3] showed that some academic scientists had a virtually predictable decline in output after tenure, and that waiting longer than four years for further activity was fruitless. The librarian was advised to cancel those expensive specialty titles taken exclusively on their behalf.

A second motivation for this study is a rise in interest by sociologists of scientists and higher education in the "gatekeepers of science." "Gatekeepers" are intellectual leaders who exert control over the progress and quality of research programs, funding and individual careers. Not surprisingly, journal editors are prominent among "gatekeepers."[4-7] Librarians should be alert to efforts by their prestige-conscious institutions to either recruit editors, or otherwise encourage their current faculty to accept editorial board memberships. Librarians must develop a feel for their journal demands.

METHODS

Biomedical journals were studied because of their widespread occurrence in a number of library types, their high cost,[8] and their comparability with some of the author's earlier work.[9-11] Editorial boards of over 100 titles were examined for changes in membership reported in 1981. Working with a somewhat larger pool initially, 66 new editors were eventually identified. Added criteria included choosing new editors with publication records in the three years prior to and post-1981, and convenient traceability in the "Source Index" of *Science Citation Index*.

LOOKING AT THE WHOLE GROUP: IS SCENARIO THREE THE STANDARD?

The first results seem decisive. The 66 editors produced 728 papers in the three years before their appointment and 739 in the three years following. This would suggest Scenario Three: a world of editors who accept the added burden without serious fluctuation in their personal output of papers. But a closer look at individual records yielded quite a contrary result. Only four new editors maintained the same output, averaging nine papers over both test periods. The 62 remaining editors readily matched either Scenario One or Two profiles. Within each group there was a marked similarity of experience. Figures 1 and 2 tell the before-and-after tale of these groups. The average output of papers — and size of journal assortment — is listed for each category of periodical mentioned in the introduction.

32 SCENARIO ONE EDITORS			
Journal Categories	average no. papers/average size assortment		
Output in	Before Appt.	After Appt.	Net Change
The Journals They Edit	2.4/1.0	1.8/1.0	−0.6/ 0
Directly Competitive Journals	3.4/2.0	2.1/1.5	−1.3/−0.5
Prestigious Multiscience Journals	2.0/1.1	1.1/0.8	−0.9/−0.3
Neighboring Discipline & Subspecialty Journals	6.9/4.8	4.7/3.2	−2.2/−1.6
Composite	14.7/8.9	9.7/6.5	−5.0/−2.4

FIGURE 1. Average Article Output and Journal Assortment Data for matching three-year spans of 32 editors who experienced declines after being appointed editor.

30 SCENARIO TWO EDITORS			
Journal Categories	average no. papers/average size assortment		
Output in	Before Appt.	After Appt.	Net Change
The Journals They Edit	1.0/1.0	1.5/1.0	+0.5/ 0
Directly Competitive Journals	2.2/1.2	2.8/1.7	+0.6/+0.5
Prestigious Multiscience Journals	1.2/0.8	1.4/1.2	+0.2/+0.4
Neighboring Discipline & Subspecialty Journals	3.2/2.8	7.0/4.1	+3.8/+1.3
Composite	7.6/5.8	12.7/8.0	+5.1/+2.3

FIGURE 2. Average Article Output and Journal Assortment Data for matching three-year spans of 30 editors who experienced increases after being appointed editor.

SCENARIO ONE: THOSE WITH DECLINES

Thirty-two editors experienced diminished output, averaging about 31%. Three points are worth making:

1. Editors in this group spread their decline across most categories of journals. When cutting back several papers, the new editors tended to cut back a few papers in each category. In particular, they did not typically drop entire categories, retreating to the journal they edited.
2. A decline in output of papers in a given category of journals was not always matched by a meaningful decline in journal assortment. In Figure 1, for example, the reader notes that editors lowered their output in directly competitive journals from an average of 3.4 papers to 2.1, but note that the average assortment goes from two competitive journals to one and one-half. As a practical matter, few librarians take a subscription to half a journal. They must, of course, continue to take two.
3. The category containing neighboring discipline and subspecialty journals sees the sharpest dropoff both in output of papers — and assortment — always one, often two.

SCENARIO TWO: THOSE WITH INCREASES

Thirty editors became quite "hot" with an average 70% increase in output. Once again, three points are worth making:

1. The increase was spread across most categories of journals.
2. Changes in output in a given category of journal did not invariably mean an increase in assortment. Some new editors simply put more papers in their regular journals.
3. While neighboring discipline and subspecialty journals absorbed the largest share of "extra" papers, their assortment increased at only about one-third the rate of the growth of papers (46% vs. 120%).

The reader is left with a puzzle. What lessons do these tendencies teach librarians apart from noting that it seems equally likely that a new editor will have either a sharp drop or increase in papers after being appointed? Is there a common theme underlying these divergent outcomes?

IN GOOD TIMES OR BAD, SCIENTISTS MAINTAIN SPECIALTY CREDENTIALS

A key to understanding may lie in appreciating what these editors/authors are trying to accomplish in the first three journal categories that they may not be pursuing so ardently in category four. Let the reader review why editors contribute to the given categories.

Editors contribute to their own journal because their papers there qualify them as legitimate specialists. A geneticist is recognized as a geneticist in part because he or she repeatedly succeeds in publishing in *Genetics*. He or she receives no less credit or validation, as a rule, for sending papers off to reputable competitors such as *Molecular and General Genetics*.

The specialist credential value of submitting manuscripts to the prestigious multispecialty journals like *Science* or *Nature* is less apparent but quite real. Even though many other types of specialties are represented in each issue, publishing there confers a special status on both the specialist and the specialty. It is akin to having one's sport included in the Olympics, and being named to the national delegation. In other words, a specialist's papers in such a showcase imply that the specialty is worthy of the very large audience and that the field has the champions to make it through the typical 90% rejection rate trials of such journals.

Why, then, would specialists publish outside these three channels? The answer lies in the benignly opportunistic behavior of both research collaboration and scientific publishing. Publishing in neighboring discipline journals stems at least partly from the frequency of multispecialty collaborations. Biochemists can be useful to cell biologists. Epidemiologists cut deals with genetic toxicologists. Funding for much research revolves around missions that do not necessarily fall into any given specialty journal. A specialist might be able to get some of the team's papers into his personal specialty outlets, but this is not always tactful for team harmony, even in cases of unmixed disciplinary content. It may be better from a given specialist's point of view to preserve the collaboration — and the current funding—by sometimes assenting to publication in the reputable journals of another specialty. But in situations where new duties limit time for research and output, particularly when the specialist has not recently touched home base with a credential-reaffirming paper or two, these collaborations and their bastard outlets may have less appeal.

Publishers, particularly for-profit ones, also have a role in stimulating manuscripts in these situations. The bulk of the new journals that they introduce deal with new subspecialties or hybridized areas. Early issues often contain very frank appeals for papers, with offers of quick manuscript adjudication. Even established authors welcome relief from long delays as well as from page charges, now up to as much as $125.00 each, which are rarely charged by commercial publishers. A scientist who has already secured his professional standing with number of recent papers in the standard specialty assortment, may be willing to venture a few papers. In time, he or she reasons, these promising titles may themselves become standards. Conversely, when output is lean, no great loss of reputation is involved in setting them aside.

LIBRARY REACTION

The onset and extent of response should match the gradualism and prudence of the editor's own behavior. As the reader has seen, significant changes in output may have only modest significance for actual assortment. When urged to move abruptly with cancellations, consider the following quandary.

Suppose the reader were the librarian for two scientists who became editors. Both editors were happy with the assortment of journals each was provided. But experience showed that the first scientist's output went from fifteen papers to ten, making him the average Scenario One editor. Experience also showed that the second scientist's output remained at an even nine papers, making him one of the rare Scenario Three editors. Would the reader "punish" the undoubtedly declining Scenario One editor with one or two cancellations for remaining one paper "better" than the steady Scenario Three editor? Cancellations involving editors should proceed only under conditions of the most severe need or prolonged neglect of single-interest titles.

The situation is less difficult when dealing with Scenario Two editors, provided there is some funding. Given a choice of adding either established neighboring discipline journals or new subspecialty titles, the librarian might well prefer the latter initially. New subspecialty journals typically start with very limited circulation. Fewer lending institutions or commercial tearsheet services are likely to have them, as opposed to the established journals of other disciplines. While both types of journal deserve subscriptions if the use is serious, the established journal will likely be there until funding and justification are ready. This cannot be assumed with every new title if quick reader support is not forthcoming.

MORE WORK IS NEEDED

While the author is confident that the journal output fluctuations seen in this paper are materially related to the new duties and opportunities that come with being appointed an editor, an approach based on interviews or questionnaires might well confirm it. Similarly, it has been noticed that those scientists with the highest output before the appointment are the most vulnerable to a decline upon appointment, and conversely so of those with low initial outputs and a tendency towards post-appointment increases. Is there a maximum sustainable output operating here? There are, of course, more questions based on the size of the sample, on the age of editors and variations by discipline. This paper will be a success if it stimulates other researches along these lines and results in papers that help rationalize acquisitions in light of the career events and life changes of the clientele.

REFERENCES

1. Stankus, Tony. "Negotiating Journal Demands with Young Scientists Using Lists Derived from Thesis Advisor Records," *Collection Management* 5, 3/4(Fall/Winter, 1983), pp. 185-198.
2. Stankus, Tony. "New Specialized Journals, Mature Scientists, and Shifting Loyalties," *Library Acquisitions: Practice and Theory* 9(1985), pp. 99-104.

3. Stankus, Tony. "Journal Weeding in Relation to Declining Faculty Member Publishing," *Science & Technology Libraries* 6(Spring, 1986), pp. 43-53.

4. Bakker, P. and Rigter, H. "Editors of Medical Journals: Who and from Where?," *Scientometrics* 7, 1-2(1985), pp. 11-22.

5. Zsindley, S., Schubert, A., and Braun, T. "Editorial Gatekeeping Patterns in International Science Journals: A New Science Indicator," *Scientometrics* 4(1983), pp. 57-68.

6. Zsindley, S., Schubert, A., and Braun, T. "Citation Patterns of Editorial Gatekeepers in International Chemistry Journals," *Scientometrics* 4(1983), pp. 69-76.

7. Braun, T. and Bujdoso, E. "Gatekeeping Patterns in the Publication of Analytical Chemistry Research," *Talanta* 20(1983), pp. 161-167.

8. Brown, Norman B. and Phillips, Jane. "Price Indexes for 1984: U.S. Periodicals and Serials Services," *Library Journal* 59, 13(August, 1984), pp. 1422-1425.

9. Stankus, Tony. "Journals for Anatomists in Medical Versus Nonmedical Biological Research Institutions," *Science & Technology Libraries* 2, 2(Winter, 1981), pp. 61-85.

10. Stankus, Tony and Rosseel, Kevin. "The Americanization of Journal Loyalties of Foreign-Born, Foreign-Trained Scientists and Physicians Who Emigrate to the United States" in Stankus, Tony. *Scientific Journals: Issues in Library Selection and Management*. New York: Haworth (1987), pp. 71-83.

11. Stankus, Tony. "Collection Development: Journals for Biochemists," *Special Collections* 1, 2(1982), pp. 51-74.

The Academy Award Without Oscar: What Happens to Your Client's Journal Use After Election to the National Academy of Sciences and Guaranteed Acceptance into its *Proceedings*

SUMMARY. At the time of their election to the National Academy of Sciences, a substantial number of academicians appear to be undergoing a transformation of their publication pattern. Their original research papers appear less frequently in the literature, and are generally found within a contracting assortment of journals. While most academy members who had specially sponsored papers accepted into the *Proceedings* before election, increase their output within that journal after election, ready access to the journal is not the cause of the decrease in the overall assortment. Rather, at this stage of their career, many academicians are assuming a senior scientist's role. For some senior scientists this means that the composition of long, critical, overviews of their fields becomes more important than sustaining their customary high production of original research papers. Other senior scientists assist the careers of younger scientists by sponsoring their papers in the *Proceedings*. Variations in this career adjustment pattern are minor from class year to class year of newly elected academicians. By contrast, the pattern of biomedical academicians differs from that of math and physical sciences academicians in a number of ways significant for library collection management.

THE ACADEMY AND ITS JOURNAL

One of Abraham Lincoln's lesser known acts of 1862 had an importance for scientists then and science journal librarians now. In that year he endorsed the founding of a society of scholars to be called the National Academy of Sciences. The scholars were to be independent of the government, but would nonetheless take upon themselves from time to time the advising of the government on scientific matters. They would also meet occasionally for symposia, would underwrite expeditions, and would issue several types of publications. Existing members would vote for new members on the basis of the candidate's sustained record of scientific achievements.

Until the Nobel Prize came along, election to the National Academy was the pinnacle of scientific achievement for Americans. Even then, the Swedish Royal Academy tended to confirm the good voting judgment of their American counterparts by giving many U.S. academy members the Nobel Prize. Today about one of every twenty members of the National Academy is a Nobel Laureate, a ratio that is even more remarkable when one considers that the academy has many members whose fields are not eligible for the prize. While the publication patterns and library use of Nobel Prize winners in America might make for an interesting paper, there are only about forty institutions that would be currently involved. By contrast, the 1300 or so academicians are spread out over 400 libraries. A substantial number of librarians reading this chapter will, at one time or another, service the journal needs of an academician among their clientele.

An even larger number of librarians, well into the thousands, will handle the principal publication of the Academy at least twice a month. The *Proceedings of the National Academy of Sciences of the United States of America* (hereafter *PNAS* or the *Proceedings*), was established in 1918. It has developed a synergistic relationship with the Academy. It initially derived its prestige from its association with the Academy. Now access to its pages is one of the most coveted perquisites of membership. In general, only brief papers by members, or those brief papers by nonmembers that have been endorsed by a member, are allowed. Barring some eccentricity of content or style, each paper by a member is guaranteed acceptance under an informal honor system in which the academy member has a colleague of his choosing check the paper out before its submission.

The citation figures posted by *PNAS* are outstanding. *PNAS* typically scores in the top 1% in gross citations, citations per paper, and citations made to papers within a year of their appearance. Clearly, the academician and his journal represent an interesting case for those who seek to understand the interaction of career stages and journal usage. This paper seeks to explore what happens to the scientist and his own journal usage after election so that alert librarians might anticipate any shifts.

IDENTIFYING THE ACADEMICIANS AND THEIR OUTPUT

All U.S. based members elected in 1982, 1983, or 1984, and working in math or the physical and life sciences were tracked for journals publications. Periods examined included the three years prior to their election, and the three years afterwards. The year of election was held to be neutral and not included. Foreign associate members of the Academy were not included, nor were any social scientists. Data were sorted along two main themes: differences by year of election, which we term "class year," and differences between the math/physical sciences members and biomedical sciences members. Our sample gave us the following membership by years: 1982 = 51; 1983 = 54; 1984 = 54. There were seventy-four math and physical scientists, and eighty-five biomedical scientists.

DID THE NEW ACADEMICIANS INCREASE THEIR OUTPUT?

One of the first concerns of the librarian is to anticipate heavily increased demands after a major career event. Did election to the National Academy cause a blossoming forth? On the contrary, as Figures 1 and 2 illustrate, over half of the academicians actually showed a decline in number of papers after the election. A fair percentage, from a quarter to a third, stayed about the same. Sixteen percent showed a significant increase. The regularity of this pattern among the class years is striking. These results were similar between the biomedical and the math and physical sciences contingents, with a few nuances. First, life scientists showed more papers overall, and it seemed that their higher output was not sustainable, causing the greater number of members with a decline. Second, the higher rate of "essentially unchanged" among math and physical scientists is influenced by the flat output of mathematicians. (We counted shifts upward or downward only from those who had at least six papers in the period prior to election. This avoided desig-

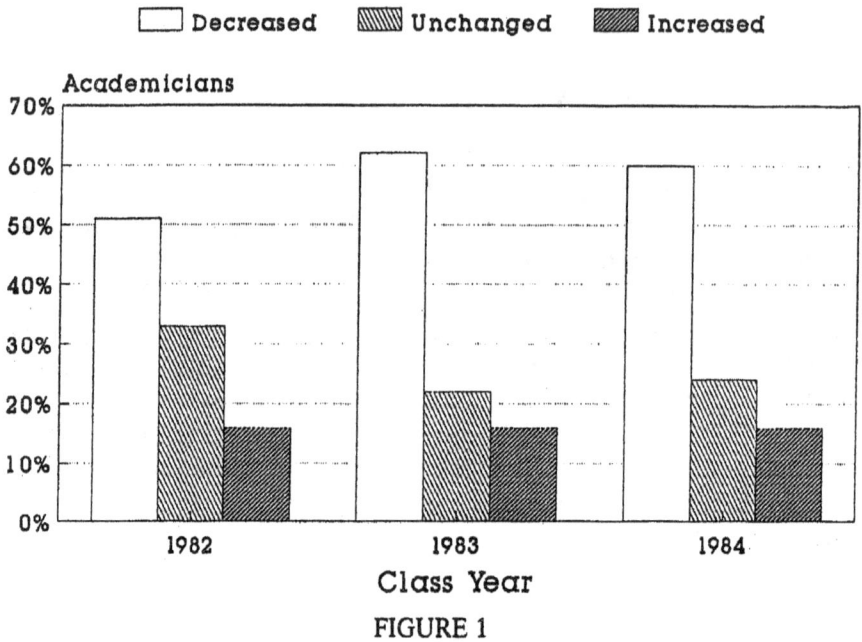

FIGURE 1

nating a scientist who produced only one or two more papers as having some significantly high percentage increase for only those few added papers.) Chemists and physicists were typically two to three times more active than mathematicians, but still showed an unmistakably downward trend.

DID THE NEW ACADEMICIANS EXPAND THEIR JOURNAL ASSORTMENT?

Are the newly elected academicians likely to venture into journals new to them? It might be argued that their newfound status would make them extremely attractive as contributors. This might well play havoc with the journal budget of the librarians who felt obliged to keep up in journal assortment. However, in light of our findings of decreased output, it is not too surprising to find that they were fairly conservative as a group. See Figures 3 and 4. By and

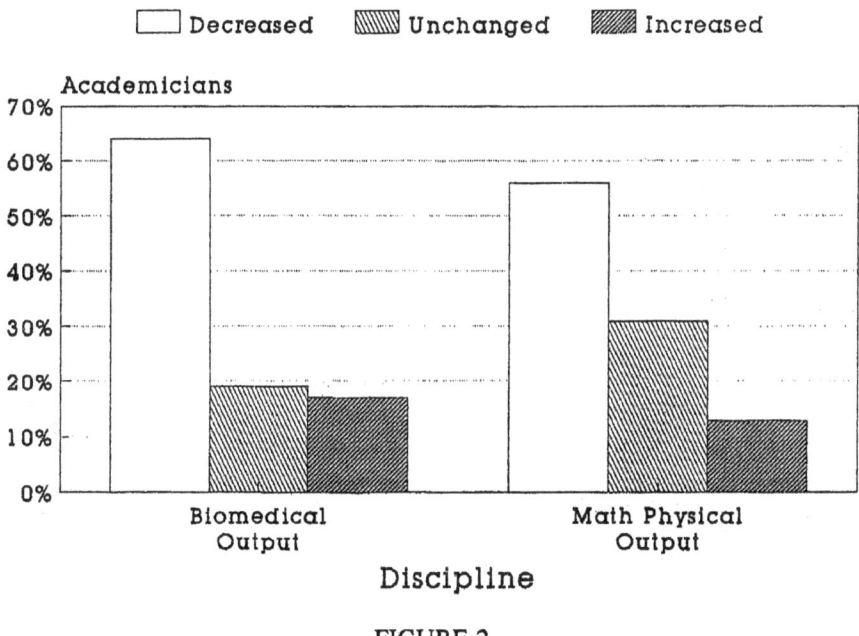

FIGURE 2

large, the number venturing into new journals is at least matched by those withdrawing from some of their old favorites. Once again, approximately a quarter to a third of both class years and disciplines stood pat. Once again, biomedical scientists typically had larger assortments with a median size of eleven journals, while math and physical scientists had smaller assortments of about eight journals. The number of journals to be added or dropped is likely to be modest in any case, two or three was a typical shift.

HOW MANY HAD "SPONSORED" PAPERS IN PNAS BEFORE THE ELECTION? AND DID AUTHORSHIP IN PNAS INCREASE AFTER THE ELECTION?

A librarian might well wonder if a client's paper in *PNAS* is predictive of a candidate's election to the Academy. About a quarter of

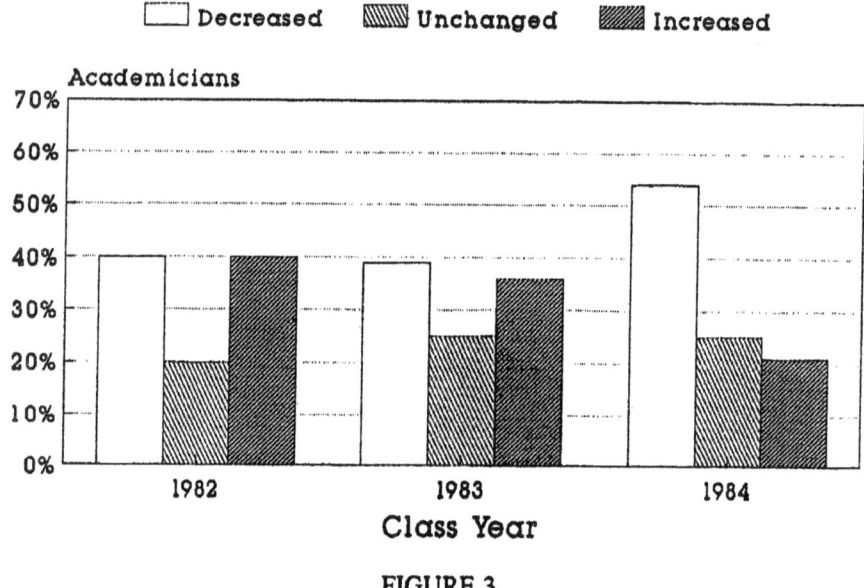

FIGURE 3

the future membership had convinced existing members to go through some fairly involved paperwork to endorse their manuscripts for *PNAS*. See Figures 5 and 6. The behavior by class years is especially uniform. However, Figure 6 shows a key difference between blocs of disciplines. Biomedical scientists, whom we had already discussed as having larger outputs and assortments, were far more likely to get a head start in *PNAS* than math and physical scientists. Both groups showed an increase in contributions after election, although the math and physical sciences group still features very low involvement.

WHAT OTHER JOURNALS DID PNAS DISPLACE?

PNAS features articles of five pages or less. While this might seem to be remarkable brevity to humanities and social studies authors, it is typical of the "letters" *genre* in many sciences. It might

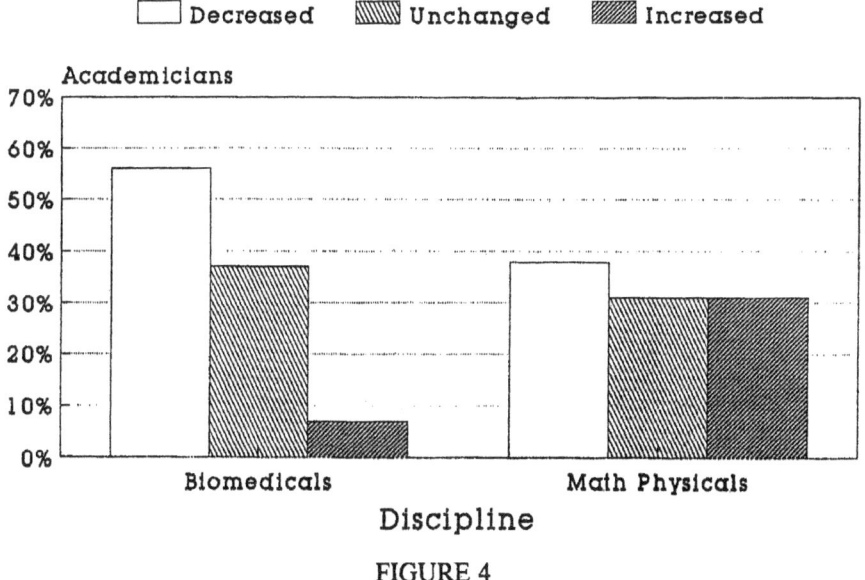

FIGURE 4

seem likely then, that letters journals would be the quickest to either drop out, or be at least severely diminished within the output of new academy members. Surprisingly, as Figures 7 and 8 show, this is not the case. While Figure 7 does show some differences in degree of deemphasis by class year, major specialty journals are in each year, and in each bloc of disciplines, the most vulnerable category of journal.

Why is this category most likely to decline? Perhaps it does not hold up its attractiveness or utility as well as the other categories. Letters journals maintain their advantages, not the least of which are acceptance of shorter papers and quick manuscript turnaround time. Multispecialty journals continue to provide extremely wide readership and high citation counts. Subspecialty journals target the audience most closely of all types. Major specialty journals can accept brief papers, and publish them quickly, be read by both broad and narrow audiences, and be highly cited as well, but not

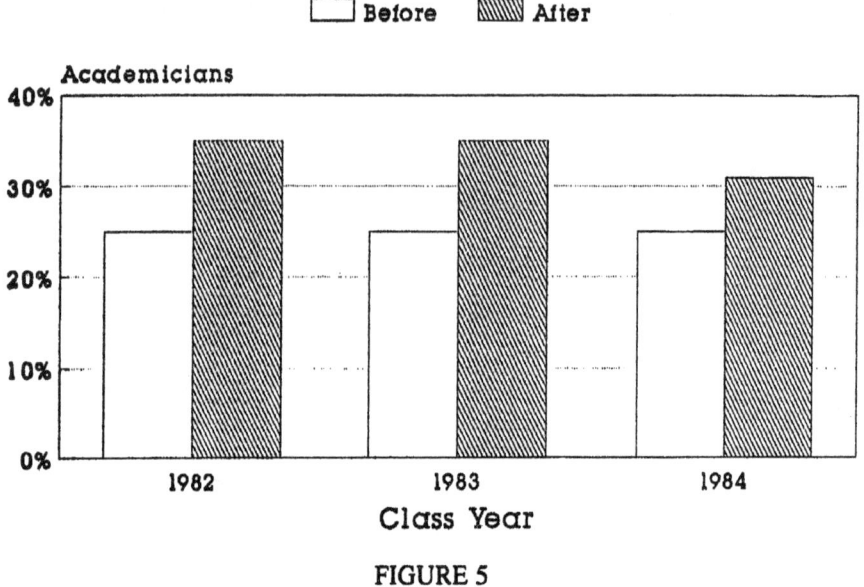

FIGURE 5

usually all of these things at once and equally well. Examination of papers in this study suggests that while academicians continue to publish some of their full-length studies in major specialty journals, they also tend to reduce or eliminate submissions of letters or short papers to them. Yet another reason for this decline of appearance in major specialty journals is the increased acceptance of some of the academician's papers in multispecialty journals such as *Science* and *Nature*. Getting into *Science* or *Nature* is a rare achievement, whose allure does not fade even for the exalted of the Academy.

Ironically, the dimished involvement with major specialty journals offers few savings for most libraries. They are scarcely cancellable in most instances since the bulk of most ordinary scientists on staff will very much continue to need them. Moreover, as some of the journals for original research disappear from the academician's

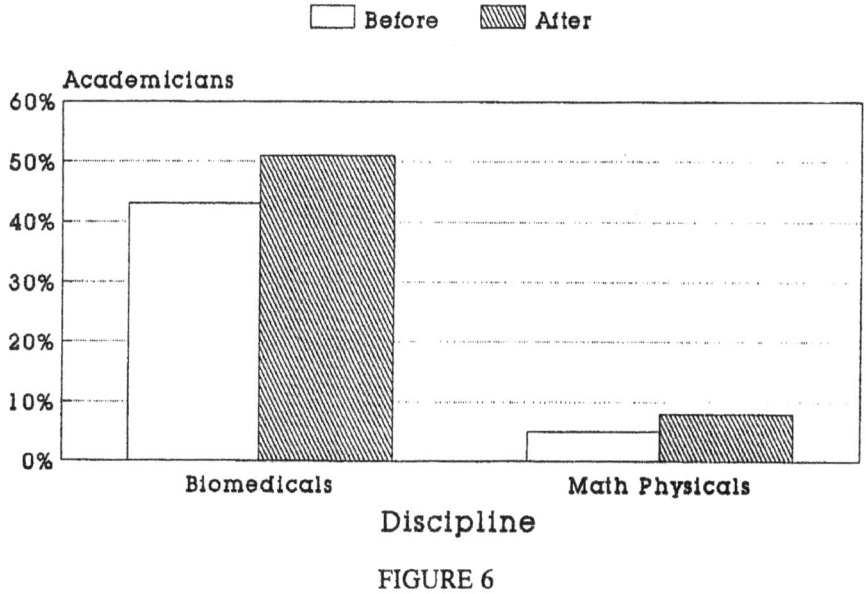

FIGURE 6

assortment of outlets, they are replaced by journals of a different function, as will shortly be seen.

IS ACADEMY ELECTION, THEN, A TIME OF DISENGAGEMENT FROM THE LITERATURE? WHAT A LOOK AT WRITERS OF REVIEW PAPERS SUGGESTS

It might seem that all the indicators point to a substantial reduction of involvement in the literature for many of the academicians. Certain conditions, such as the typical age of the member at election (in their fifties and sixties) suggest that this is possible. A number of the newly elected also get appointed to higher level administrative positions or to editorial boards, where duties take them away from

What Journal Types Does PNAS Displace?

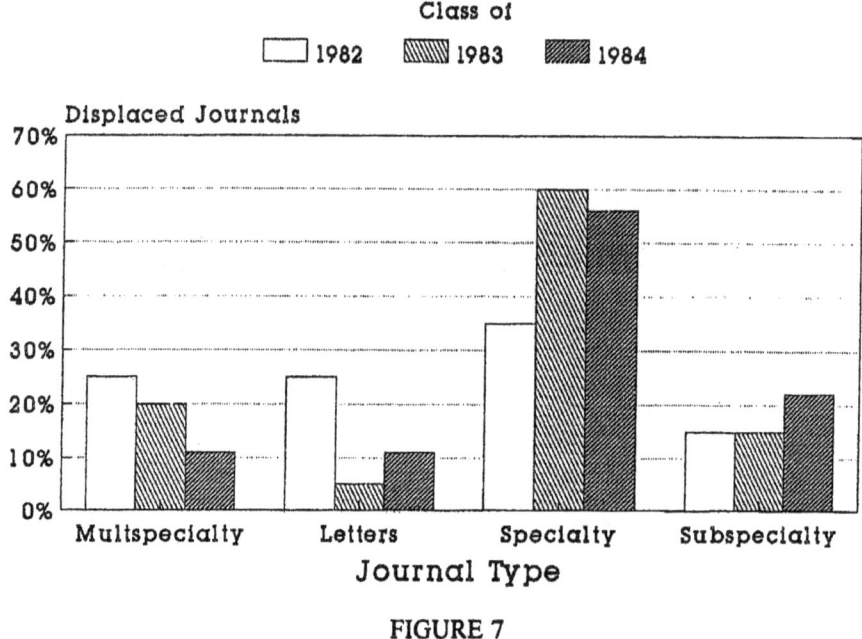

FIGURE 7

the lab. Still others receive endowed chairs that allow them tremendous freedom to teach or publish at whatever pace or with whatever frequency they choose. But at least one indicator of involvement with journals remains substantially above average: authorship of review papers.

The composition of review papers, and similar weighty assignments, such as the preparation of plenary talks for major scientific conventions, is extremely literature-intensive and time-consuming. It is very often a task that only senior scientists are ever asked to undertake since it does require considerable resources and perspective. No statistics could be readily found which report the ratio of review authors to all authors. But it is safe to suggest that the proportion of review papers to other forms of papers is very small. Moreover, most reviews are authored by authors working alone. Consequently, it is not unreasonable to suggest only a tiny number

What Journal Types Does PNAS Displace?

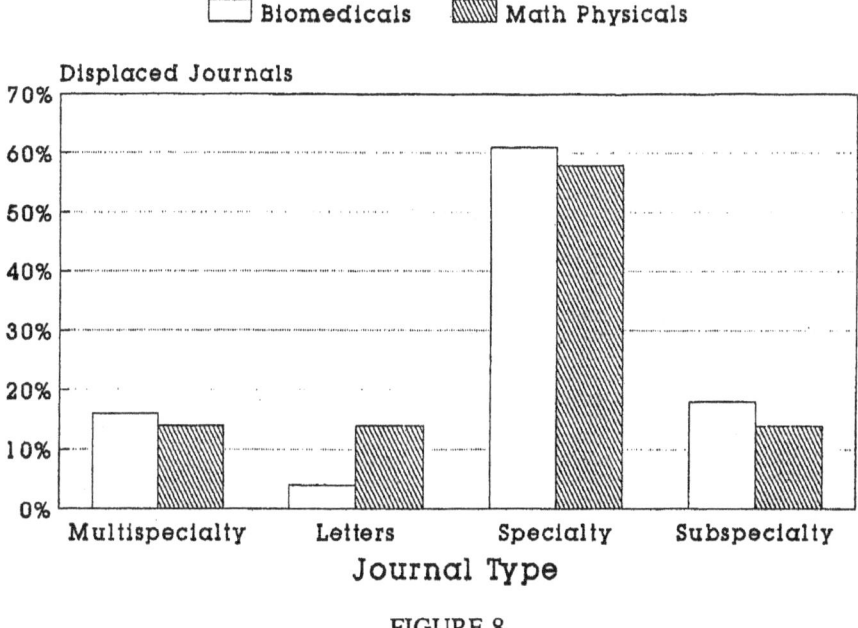

FIGURE 8

of authors, certainly less than 5% of all authors, are ever asked to write reviews.

Yet our research suggests that at least six times this proportion of academicians engage in this work. Figures 9 and 10 show that while the numbers of academicians involved in writing reviews declines after election, particularly for the class of 1984, no less than 30% of any class or disciplinary bloc are engaged in writing reviews. One aberration among class years deserves a comment. See Figure 9. Our research suggests that the class of 1984 simply had such an unsustainably high record of reviews before election (93 reviews compared to 41 and 42 for the other two years) that a letdown was inevitable. The actual output for the class of 1984 after election is only 12 papers less than that of the previous class after its election. There is however, a reliable and substantial difference in number of review authors by disciplinary bloc. From two-thirds to three-quar-

SCIENTIFIC JOURNALS

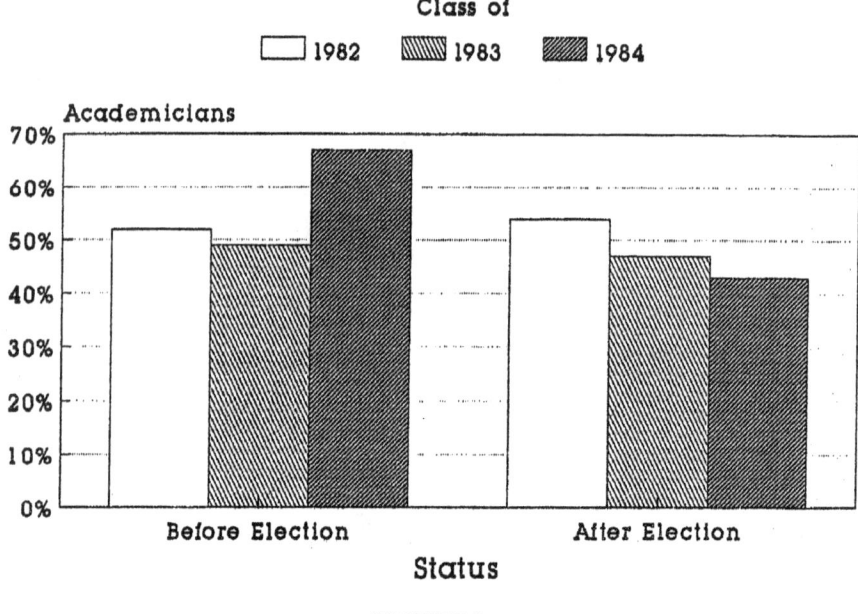

FIGURE 9

ters of biomedical academicians write reviews, while less than a third of math and physical academicians publish them.

In a great many cases, the time taken for such a project detracts from the time a scientist has for his own original research. This goes a long way to explaining the appearance of a decline in output. Some academy members with an apparent decline in number of papers may in fact be writing more, not less. The significance, and certainly the length, of some individual post-election works, such as reviews, will be much greater. Just as some types of journals in an academician's assortment served certain functions better than others, individual types of papers have their respective missions. The stream of letters-type papers discussed earlier sustains the academician's credentials as an original researcher, even as the review establishes his interpretative credentials and sets forth teaching and research agendas for many other scientists. Because of the huge

Review Authorship

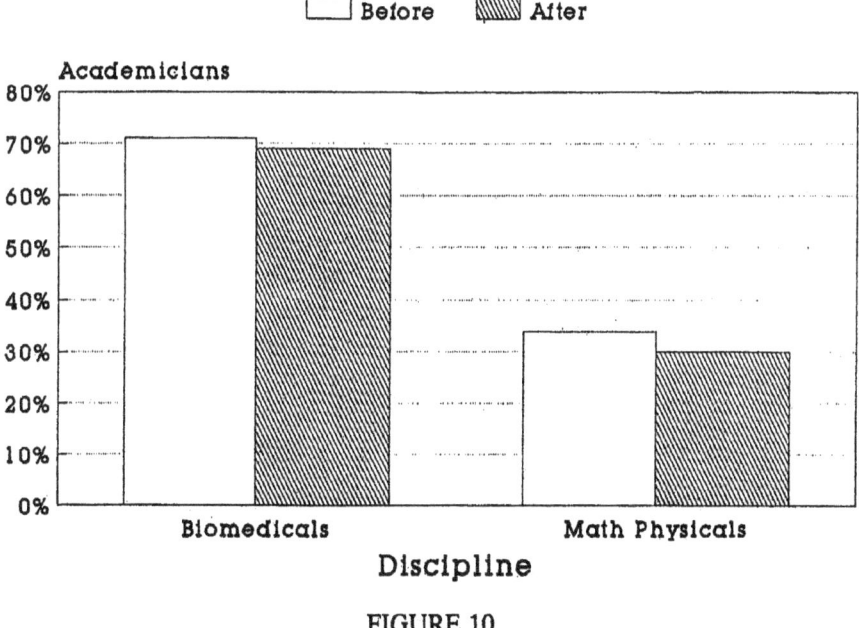

FIGURE 10

number of journal citations involved in conscientious review writing, the pressure on the journal collection may well be greater under this "less is more" situation.

IN WHAT TYPES OF JOURNAL DO THE REVIEWS APPEAR?

Given the seriousness of the academician's effort in review writing, the wise librarian will want to stock the serials that feature these reviews. While it is arguable that most authors who write a review for a given journal, will not soon write again in the same journal, they may well write other reviews in other journals on the themes of these earlier works. Moreover, the rest of the library's clientele, particularly younger scientists seeking to collaborate with these senior scholars, can gain quite an insight into the academicians and their fields through reviews. Four types of journal regularly feature reviews from academicians:

- The premiere outlet is probably the *Annual Reviews* . . . series from the not-for-profit Annual Reviews Incorporated foundation. Since the 1940s their editors, historically from Stanford and Berkeley, have issued invitations to the nation's foremost scientists to contribute critical surveys. This hardbound series began with a preponderance of series in broader areas of the biomedical sciences, although a number of physical sciences have been added over time. Impact factors for the *Annual Reviews* are generally the best for any category of reviews.
- For-profit publishers have sensed opportunities in the hardbound reviews genre. Their strategy has been to develop more specialized series in the biomedical sciences, and to add more physical sciences than the *Annual Reviews* series. The leader is probably Academic Press, whose biomedical *Advances in* . . . series is highly cited, although Wiley's physical sciences *Advances in Photochemistry* and *Advances in Chemical Physics* are also well regarded. Mathematics has had an unusual review history in that its *Advances in Mathematics* from Academic Press started out as a hardbound series stressing expository overviews. However, it quickly turned into a conventional softbound journal featuring lengthy, but not necessarily review-type, papers.
- Conventional softbound journals devoted strictly to reviews are common among most biomedical and physical sciences. (Math is an exception.) They typically appear on a quarterly basis, but some busy fields have monthlies. Historically most have been issued by not-for-profit societies. This has been particularly true for the basic physical sciences. Often a society sponsored review journal is part of a package deal that will include the complete array of journal types for a given field: the news journal, the journal for full length research papers, the journal for brief communications, and the journal for convention abstracts. Alternatively, the review journal serves as a unifying journal in a package deal that includes separate jour-

nals for the major specialties which when taken together make up a field. For-profit reviews are rarely marketed as parts of such packages. Indeed, for-profit firms have entered the softbound review journal field rather slowly. Perhaps the biggest surprise in the last decade has been the successful entry of CRC Press, historically known for its scientific handbooks. Despite competition from the most prestigious societies and the *Annual Reviews* . . ., a number of their titles have done quite well.

—Finally, reviews can appear in regular journals which stress original research, but have a review paper or two from time to time. *Science* and *Nature* are examples at the top of the range. The biomedical sciences tend to have more reviews in their general purpose journals than do physical scientists. This is particularly true in journals of clinical medicine. Within these journals, reviews are effectively long-term studies involving many patients at many facilities. The goal is to integrate and resolve as many conflicting preliminary reports as possible on the way to a consensus.

Figure 11 shows a fairly consistent pattern in placement of review papers by class year. When broken down by discipline, however, as in Figure 12, we see important, if predictable, differences. Biomedical academicians do seem to pursue the more abundant opportunities in for-profit hardbounds and within the general purpose journals, while the physical scientists adhere to society sponsored journals for reviews. In any case, review journals contain the major efforts of many academicians, and the library collections that academicians use should reflect this priority.

THE WHEEL COMES FULL CIRCLE, THE NEWLY ELECTED ACADEMICIANS BEGIN TO SPONSOR THE PAPERS OF YOUNGER SCIENTISTS IN THE PROCEEDINGS

Yet another emphasis common among some newly elected academicians is the sponsoring or "communicating" to the *Proceed-*

Where Do the Review Papers Appear?

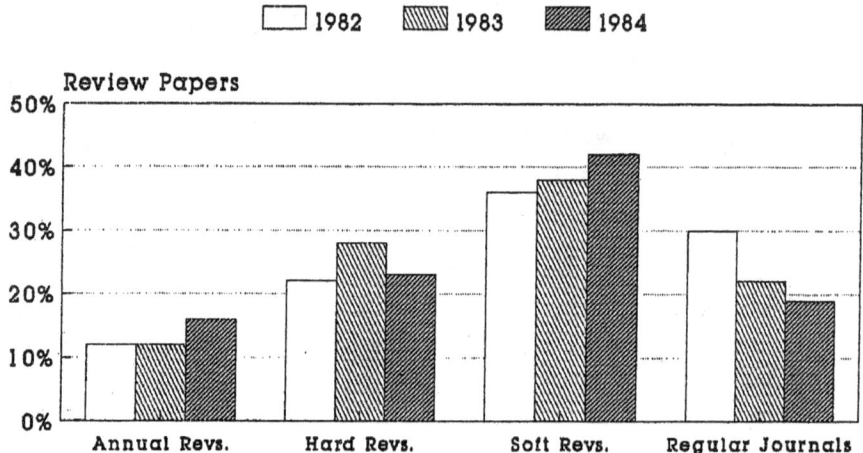

FIGURE 11

ings of the papers of scientists who are not yet members. As seen in Figures 5 and 6, about a quarter of the newly elected members had some of their own pre-election papers sponsored. And as seen in Figures 13 and 14, this activity starts up rather quickly among newly elected members. As Figure 13 shows, about half of each class year will sponsor some papers within their first three years of membership. Not surprisingly, biomedical scientists pursue this course more frequently. See Figure 14.

Sponsorship of these papers is very important to the careers of both these sponsored "young" scientists and to the sponsoring academician. For the sponsored scientist there are two opportunities to be noticed. On publication, the younger scientist gets his best work exposed to the voting members of the academy. But there is an opportunity even before publication. In recent years, the sponsor-

Where Do the Review Papers Appear?

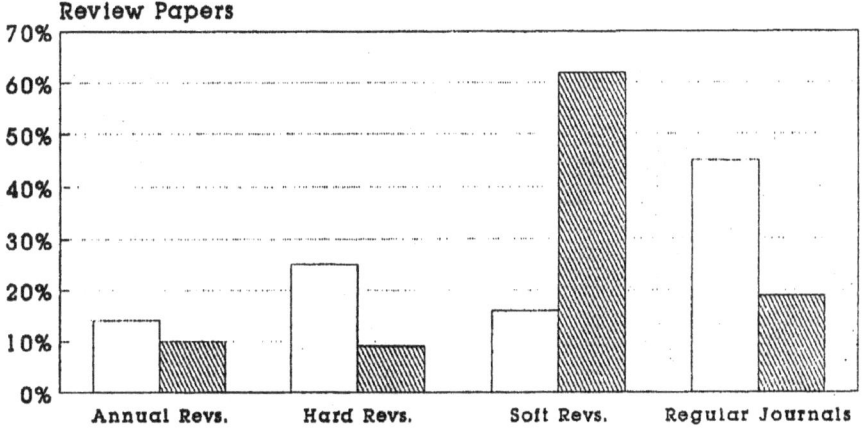

FIGURE 12

ship process has been tightened up so that at least two other qualified scientists, often academy members who do not work at the institution of the sponsoring academician, must also endorse the quality and urgency of publication of the paper. This further enhances the exposure of the young scientist, and may promote his eventual candidacy.

The academician who sponsors also has a stake in the process. One of the roles of a senior scientist is as a gatekeeper of the scientific quality of the people and papers in the leading journals, including the *Proceedings*. The ability to identify promising young scientists and worthwhile contributions is a mark of the acumen that is expected of an academician. In some ways it is a means to validate the academician's own career and choice of research themes. With sponsorship, the academician is in effect, saying, that the topics and

How Many Academicians Sponsor Papers of Other Scientists?

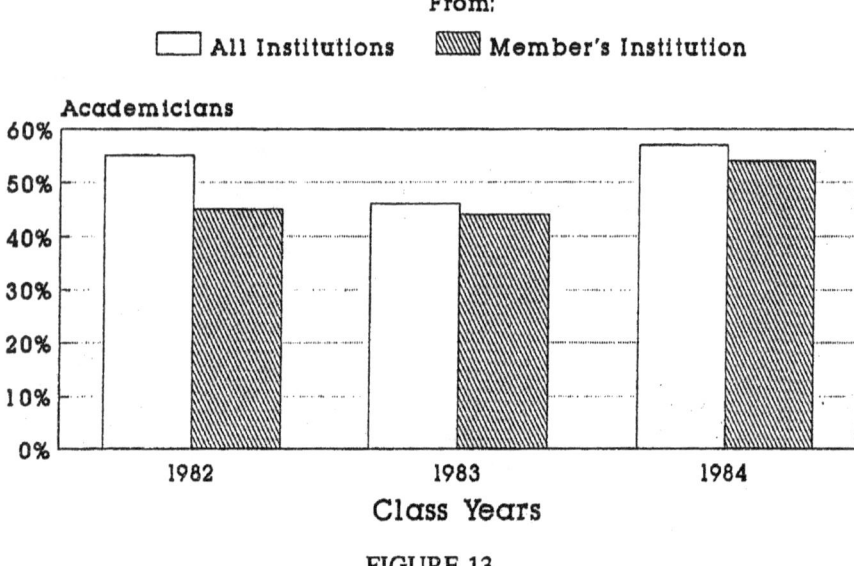

FIGURE 13

specialties that he himself pioneered are now being taken up by others. This is particularly likely since rules require that the sponsoring academician be an expert in the topic of the paper to be sponsored. Sponsorship can also be an inexpensive but very valuable reward for those who have shown interest or loyalty to the academician. A doctoral student, post-doc, or colleague whose paper appears in the *Proceedings* has a chit worth much more than the $500 in page charges, and is likely to repay this with added loyalty or interest. Finally, a record of having sponsored good people and good papers increases the academician's ability to cut quiet, informal quid pro quo deals on sponsorship with other academicians at other institutions. A reliable academician is more likely to be able to get the endorsements needed for his young people, because he is known to be quick and fair in dealing with their young people.

How Many Academicians Sponsor Papers of Other Scientists?

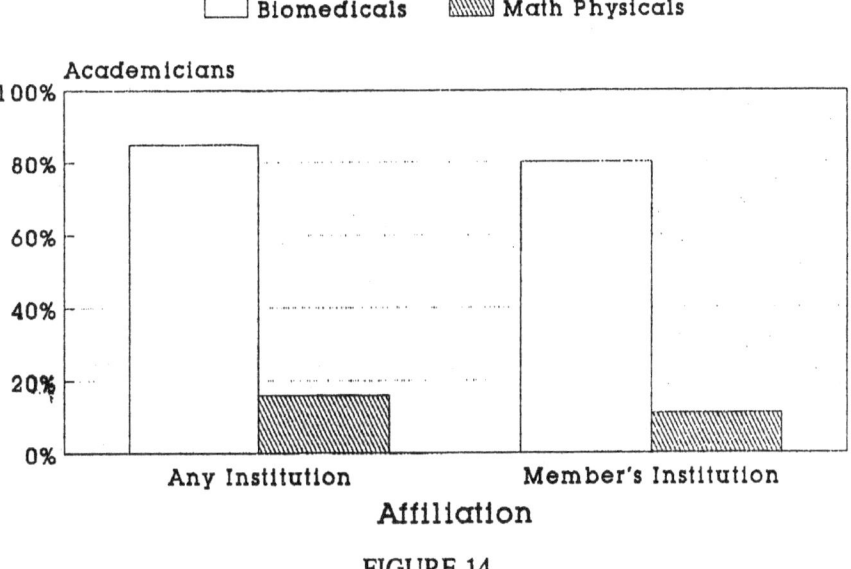

FIGURE 14

WILL THE DOMINANCE OF BIOMEDICAL PAPERS IN THE PROCEEDINGS CONTINUE?

One of the recurring themes in analyzing the *Proceedings* is the preponderance of biomedical papers. Several facts suggest that this emphasis will continue.

— First, more biomedical scientists are elected to the Academy than math and physical scientists. The difference is about 10-20% annually. Members vote by subject sections and any new sections are more likely to be made from the larger and faster growing life sciences contingent.
— The backlog of "pre-electee's" (nonmembers with papers sponsored by existing members) is in favor of the biomedicals

by an even greater margin (about 6:1). Not every person who had a paper will be elected, nor are all elected preceded by a paper, but the linkage is certainly suggestive among life scientists.
— The desirability of a biomedical scientist's papers appearing in the *Proceedings* is reinforced with each year's citation ratings and behavior. Virtually every biomedical research journal of note cites the *Proceedings* repeatedly and prominently, usually within the top ten journals. This is not generally true with math and the physical sciences. The best placing for frequency of *PNAS* being cited by elite physical sciences journals in the most recent *Journal Citation Reports* (1987) is among chemists: 18th in the *Journal of the American Chemical Society*. Good papers in math and the physical sciences occasionally appear there, just not often enough, to make the journal required reading in the physical sciences community.
— A major step at more prominently featuring math and physical sciences papers — distribution under their own separate covers between 1980-1984 — has already failed to substantially increase contributions from this clientele.

CONCLUSION

Election to the National Academy brings a slowdown in most of the more obvious measures of journal output. This apparent decline is most pronounced among the more prolific biomedical scientists. Among mathematicians and physical scientists, there are also a substantial number who show a low even output. Guaranteed acceptance into the *Proceedings* does not dislodge any category of journal that can be readily weeded for a subscription savings. While the dropoff in papers in the major scientific disciplinary journals is often quite marked, those journals are likely to be required for most other researchers in that field among the library's clientele. Any declines in journal assortment, even for titles of interest only for the academician, also tend to be less exploitable because the academician tends to stay involved in the field if not as an author of original research, then as an author of critical literature reviews. Indeed, adding more review journals is often advisable. Interestingly, the encouragement of having a newly elected member in the local community is likely to stimulate the journal involvement of the library's non-academician clients. A fair number of them, particularly in the biomedical sciences, will win the backing required from the new member to successfully submit their own work to the *Proceedings*. A few of these sponsored authors may themselves one day become new academicians, and begin the process again.

THEME TWO

What Do Shifts in World Science and World Publishing Mean for U.S. Librarians?

Is the U.S. losing its technological and economic grip? We dress for work in the morning in clothes with German synthetics. The cars we drive to work are Korean. The computer terminal at work is Japanese. The scotch after work is even from Scotland! This fear of gradually losing all-American control over our lives is extended to our journal collections. We tremble at every exchange rate fluctuation in Europe. We worry about how many more journals it will take to cover Asian developments.

The response of the library profession is of two parts: first we monitor prices, then we denigrate foreign publishers and their products. We act much like the renowned Herb White would like us to act: tough purchasing directors. There are several problems with this. Purchasing directors arguably know the price of everything, but not the real cost of doing without it. Do they know what cutting off legal access to the flow of information to your own institution's scientists does for your institution's domestic competitors? It enhances your competitor's ability to get information and then get the best people, the right equipment, and the contract or grant instead of you. White's notion that we should all go illegal on a national basis, pirate international information, and then let the foreigner sue us is foolish for two reasons. First, it presupposes gutsy collusion among hundreds of libraries, a very hard act in coordination and sustained resolve. Second, the dozen or so of the largest European publishers—a much more manageable coalition—would certainly react in a way that protected the most severely damaged among their fraternity from collapse. They would close ranks to choke off the flow of information. They have legal recourse. They have cash reserves.

If the purchasing manager's boycott or piracy schemes actually took hold in the country, our scientists would experience the onset of a bigger effect than the purchasing manager ever envisioned: you hurt the competitiveness of the country as a whole. What is being trifled with is not works of poetry or social commentary, scientific information is the chief fuel of a modern economy. Purchasing managers are short on insight: they bought us those Japanese computers and German chemicals because those products were smartly made but somehow figure the Europeans and Asians who made them aren't smart enough to seize whatever competitive advantage could come out of such chaos. A preferential or exclusive information access agreement is one option that would especially hurt. Of course it could be circumvented by roundabout means, but the delays would themselves be harmful. Scientific information is a perishable product.

Purchasing managers might hope that they can get American faculty authors and American scientific product consumers to fall in step out of patriotism. But the faculty and scientific product consumers have been driving Volvos and Audis for some time, both literally and journal-wise. If you throw the foreign papers out of American journals, you invite the unseating of tens of thousands of American papers from European outlets. Soon the costs of the savings made by the purchasing manager approach would be more intolerable than the costs of the appeasement approach we are currently enduring.

Are either appeasement or boycott/piracy the only alternatives? They are for those of the purchasing agent mentality. They have not the imagination to see that meat cleaver approaches will work neither on faculty nor on publishers. The purchasing manager approach makes the librarian the minion of the treasurer, the conserver of existing cash, not the ally of the grants winning faculty, the source of future cash. Even nationally it has become apparent that the money manager's approach to wealth production, junkbonds and asset stripping, goes only so far before a collapse. There must be a continuous flow of internationally competitive products to generate revenues both in the world of economics and scientific literature. Even the most fearsome treasurers will be dismissed if future funds have been choked off foolishly, and those who too readily agreed with their policies would soon follow.

The key people are the faculty, and the faculty will not respond to "Just Say No." The goal is not to tell the faculty that they can't have something they want, it's to make them not want it any more. Telling faculty that a journal is too expensive is just not enough to cause a shift in taste. Faculty that bring in hundreds of millions in the aggregate don't think a few thousand a year for this or that title is too outrageous. Here is the strategy for librarians who really want to gain control of their collections: be analysts of the literature beyond mere processing and pricing studies. Librarians serving American scientific authors are extremely fortunate in that influencing American manuscript placement does influence, albeit no longer absolutely controls, foreign publishers. (Purchasing managers think World War II ended yesterday.)

Because of the size of the American journals market, and because of a residual respect for American scientific prowess, the desirability of foreign journals to Americans is something that foreign publishers will pursue. The goal of the librarian interested in the long-term survival of his institution is to steer the faculty only to titles, domestic and foreign, that serve them very well and to cut those that don't. The role of the truly professional librarian is much more suitably and much more satisfyingly journal intelligence officer than allowance monitor. By earning the faculty's trust through extraordinary daily attention to their needs we gain the ability to subtly shift American papers around at a time when a foreign journal's having American papers is still valued by subscribers around the world as an endorsement of journal quality. It is important for librarians to be seen as having accumulated leverage with faculty because publishers are then likely to pay more attention to us than they would if we were mere purchasing agents. We will become people who have to be dealt with not because we are merely arrogant but because we are smart and because the key people, the faculty, listen to us.

Librarians as trusted manuscript investment advisors can eventually use their influence to point out realistic alternative to expensive journals in print—not, by the way, some paperless solution that may one day be adopted—but less expensive journals in print now, or soon manageable. But the recommendations must be carefully considered. The trust of the faculty is more important than an ill-considered quick fix. There need not always be solutions that sacrifice either faculty careers interests or budget balances. Careful analyses may show that supposed conflicts may not even be as bad as those of the purchasing agent approach would have you believe. There are just as certainly foreign publications that are worth more than what they cost as the opposite case. There are many borderline judgements to be made requiring a tolerance for ambiguity and subtlety lacking in the purchasing manager mentality. It is only when librarians get used to evaluating in shades of gray, rather than in screaming red ink, that they have a real hope of understanding and managing the foreign publication situation, and proposing any reasonable alternatives. That is the goal of the six papers that follow.

The Rise of Eurojournals: Their Success Can Be Ours

Tony Stankus
Kevin Rosseel

SUMMARY. The number of science journals that focus explicitly on European research is increasing. These Eurojournals are compared with individual national and international titles. Their success is gauged, and their remaining shortcomings discussed. As they earn the loyalty of the best European contributors, they provide Americans with an attractive alternative to a large assortment of foreign subscriptions.

A torrent of criticism concerning high and discriminatory pricing has recently cascaded upon European publishers,[1-8] threatening to drown out a very positive development in science publishing: the emergence of Eurojournals. If these journals succeed in their goal of consolidating the best European research, Americans may succeed in ameliorating one of their problems: the proliferation of journals for each country at a time when some U.S. libraries can afford only a few.

EUROJOURNAL CHARACTERISTICS

Eurojournals, which have been steadily increasing in number (see Figure 1), have been evolving certain common traits (see Figure 2).

Reprinted with the permission of the Office of Copyright and Permissions, American Library Association: Stankus, Tony and Rosseel, Kevin. "The Rise of Eurojournals, Their Success Can Be Ours," *Library Resources and Technical Services* 31(3):215-224; (July/September, 1987). Copyright, the American Library Association, 1987.

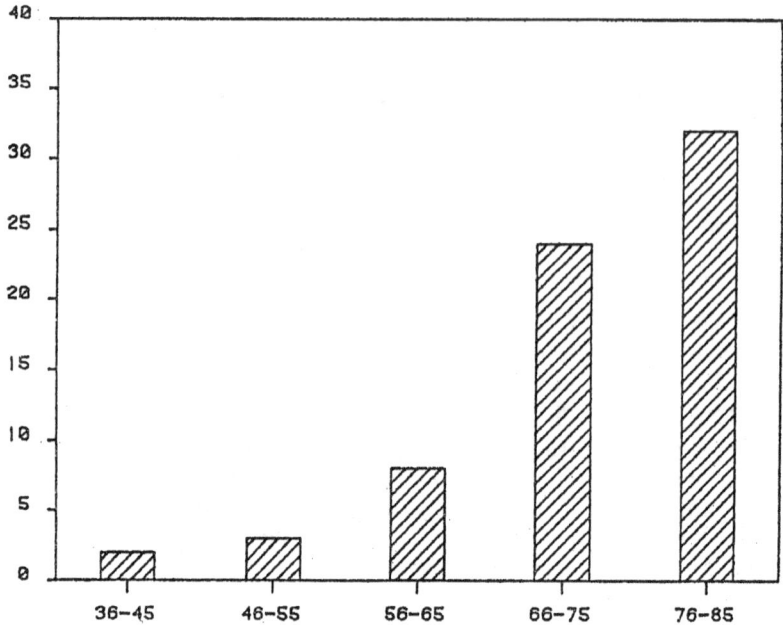

FIGURE 1. The Number of Scientific Eurojournals by Decade

— First and foremost, Eurojournals are intended to create a sense of identity and fraternity among European scientists. The strategy involves assembling quality papers by Europeans in a European outlet, along with conference proceedings, commentary, etc.
— Eurojournals often have predecessors in single-nation journals, some with histories going back eighty years. These Eurojournals have an advantage over entirely new journals, which must often wait for sufficient manuscripts to fill an issue, construct a reviewer network, build a certain academic respectability, and engender a faith in continuity necessary to maintain subscribers. For Eurojournals developed from single-nation journals, success is often a matter of progressively enlarging a good operation across frontiers.
— Some Eurojournals are endorsed by Pan-European scientific research societies. In some cases individual national societies

TITLE	PUBLISHER	AFFILIATION	PREDECESSORS
European Journal of Biochemistry 1967	Springer; West Germany	Federation of European Biochemical Societies	Biochemische Zeitschrift
European Neurology 1968	Karger; Switzerland	International Society of Neuroendocrinology	Psychiatria et Neurologia
Pfluegers Archiv; European Journal of Physiology 1968	Springer; West Germany		Pfluegers Archiv fuer die gesamte Physiologie des Menschen und der Tiere
Astronomy and Astrophysics 1969	Springer; West Germany	European Southern Observatory	Formed by the merger of five European national journals
European Journal of Clinical Investigation 1970	Blackwell; United Kingdom	European Society for Clinical Investigation	Archiv für klinische Medizin
European Journal of Medicinal Chemistry 1974		Societé Europeene de Chimie Therapeutique	Chimica Therapeutica
FEMS Letters 1977	Elsevier; Netherlands	Federation of European Microbiology Societies	
European Journal of Respiratory Diseases 1980	Munksgaard; Denmark		Formed by the merger of Acta Tuberculosea et Pneumologica Belgica and Scandinavian Journal of Respiratory Diseases
European Heart Journal 1980	Academic; United Kingdom	European Society of Cardiology	—
EMBO Journal 1982	IRL; United Kingdom	European Molecular Biology Organization	
Roux's Archives of Developmental Biology 1985	Springer; West Germany	European Developmental Biology Organization	Formerly Wilhelm Roux's Archiv fuer die Entwicklungs-Mechanick der Organismen
Europhysics Letters 1986	European Physical Society; French office	A consortium of 15 societies share some responsibilities	Formed by the merger of Lettere al Nuovo Cimento and Journal de Physique; Lettres

FIGURE 2. A Dozen Characteristic Eurojournals

have dropped their own titles and united with like-minded societies behind a Eurotitle.
— Some Eurojournals are based at designated European multinational research centers. These institutions, largely founded after World War II, have generally been outstanding both in research output and in promoting a sense of camaraderie.
— A source of strength for many Eurojournals is their affiliation with very strong publishing empires: Pergamon in England, Springer-Verlag in West Germany, Karger in Switzerland, Munksgaard in Denmark, Elsevier in the Netherlands, etc. This link provides quite an advantage in both advertising and distribution.
— Virtually all Eurojournals are based in Western Europe. This need not be the case in the future, particularly given the warm and open academic relations of countries such as Hungary and the immense research history of some East German institutions. A start-up by capitalists was probably for the best, however, given certain initially unpopular policy decisions and the levels of investment necessary for successful Eurojournals.
— The almost exclusive use of American English as the language of publication was the toughest of these policy decisions and had overtones of political and cultural imperialism. Editors also tended to lose their lofty independence in a number of matters, particularly in the ponderous pace at which issues were put together. Many journal editors were forced by their publishers to discard their time-honored, but stodgy, academic layouts and ancient typographies and even to accept advertising. The production of many of these journals became thoroughly Western: very slick, increasingly high-tech, and quite expensive, but generally more likely than their predecessors to be delivered on time. Readers today typically find heavily illustrated, U.S.-format pages with double columns. Multi-font computer typesetting is interspersed with computer graphics. More Western European journal publishers are putting into their scientific, engineering, and medical titles the same concern for quality that has long made their handling of visual arts materials so admired. As Eastern Europeans accept these con-

ditions and acquire advanced graphics capabilities, they will become more credible candidates for Europublishing.
- Most Eurojournals deal with the life sciences, perhaps reflecting recent explosions in bioscientific research. This may also reflect some negative experiences in bucking rather well established and highly conservative single-nation chemical, physical, mathematical, and geological societies.
- Finally, most, but not all, Eurojournals have the word *European* tucked somewhere in the title or subtitle.

DIFFERENCES BETWEEN EUROJOURNALS AND OTHER JOURNALS PUBLISHED IN EUROPE

Eurojournals are not synonymous with just any European journals, nor is the somewhat informal Eurojournal movement synonymous with certain formal publishing developments there.

- Eurojournals are not the same as those single-nation journals that accept many papers from both other European and non-European countries. Examination of the latter's editorial boards, level of local professional society controls, placement services, product advertisements, etc., still reveals an essentially national flavor, even if contributions have become more international.
- The Eurojournal movement is akin to the Europhysics journal movement—indeed, two Europhysics journals qualified for our purposes as Eurojournals—but there are important differences. The Europhysics journal designation is given to a rather large assortment of well-established and often mutually competitive journals. One of the purposes of this commendable arrangement by the European physics community is to limit further duplication. But the essentially unorganized Eurojournal movement is probably more successful. Few, if any, Eurojournals compete with one another. Each seems to have held onto the stake it has claimed.
- Finally, Eurojournals are generally smaller in variety of author nationality than most international journals, both of U.S. and European origins. While Eurojournals will accept some U.S.,

Japanese, and Third World papers, there are noticeably fewer than in most international journals. Indeed, most Eurojournals have a higher proportion of purely European papers than most single-nation journals that have an international circulation. See Figure 3 for a comparison based on the categories of designated Eurojournals, U.S. journals, and a Common Market category. This last group was composed of equal parts single-nation journals with a tradition of international authorship and designated international journals — both types based in Europe. Thirty matched journals with more than three thousand papers were sampled.

TWO MEASURES OF EUROJOURNAL SUCCESS

How are Eurojournals doing? We have devised two performance measures. First we took a look at their market share of manuscripts in the life sciences — the most prevalent disciplines for Eurojournals.

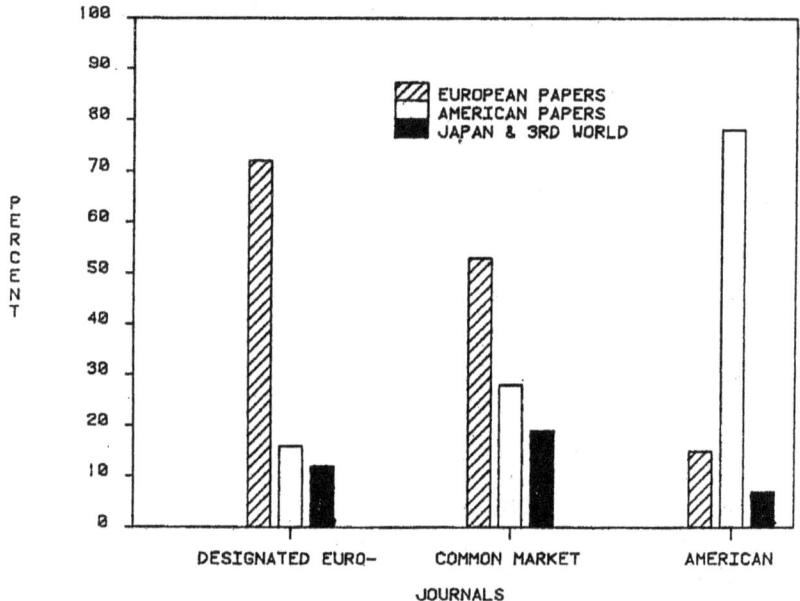

FIGURE 3. The Composition of 30 Journals Compared

Using the corporate index of the *Science Citation Index*, we classified the output of articles from five of the most influential European universities and research centers for the period 1982-85.[9] We used the same journal categories as in Figure 3. The countries selected for study—West Germany, England, France, the Netherlands, and Switzerland—are not only important as homes for these institutions, but are also cases of very competitive publishing environments. These countries have publishing empires within their borders, and their authors traditionally have a cosmopolitan outlook in the dissemination of their papers into the Common Market.

With Eurojournals constituting less than 2% of all journals available as vehicles for their research, how often did prestigious research centers submit papers to them? See Figure 4. After examining exactly 14,578 articles, we got some answers. Eurojournals hold a disproportionately high share (from 6 percent to 10 percent) of these prime markets. These figures are remarkably consistent from year to year. In all the nationalities except English, there was actually a gradual two-point gain in market share. (The British gained only one point.)

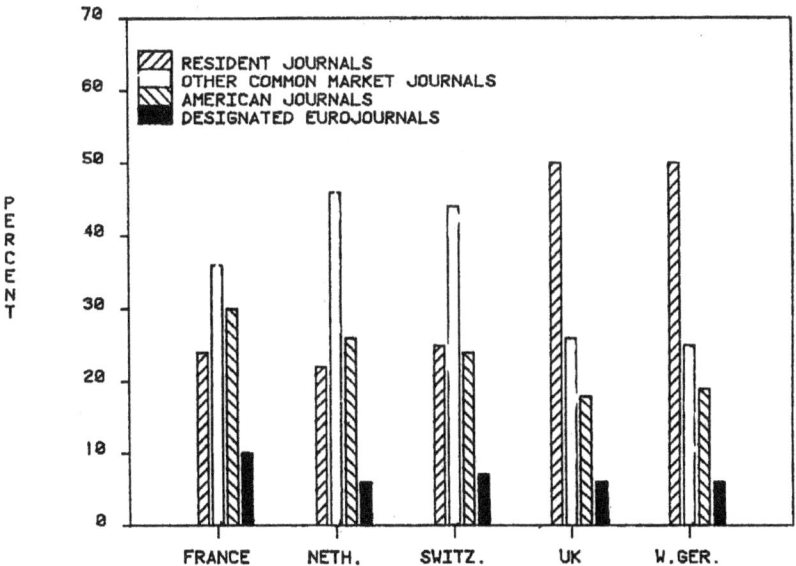

FIGURE 4. Manuscript Market Share by Journal Type

Grabbing a good share of the papers—even those of leading institutions—may not demonstrate conclusively whether the journals are of high quality. Our second test involved "impact factor" measurement. This gives us a figure roughly equivalent to "average citations per article per year." When comparing Eurojournals with national titles in the same subject field, impact factors can be another useful yardstick of quality. Fifteen sets of matching journals from the five previously mentioned countries were studied, plus journals from the U.S., as a test group against our Eurojournals. Eurojournals placed third out of seven, rather closely followed by West German journals, but exceeded among the European titles only by the British. See Figure 5. It is clear that, at the very least for smaller European scientific powers, Eurojournals are not only a popular choice but also a higher-quality one.

Despite these generally excellent showings, some nagging questions remain. What would it take to improve the standing of Eurojournals? What is holding them back from always being the best in

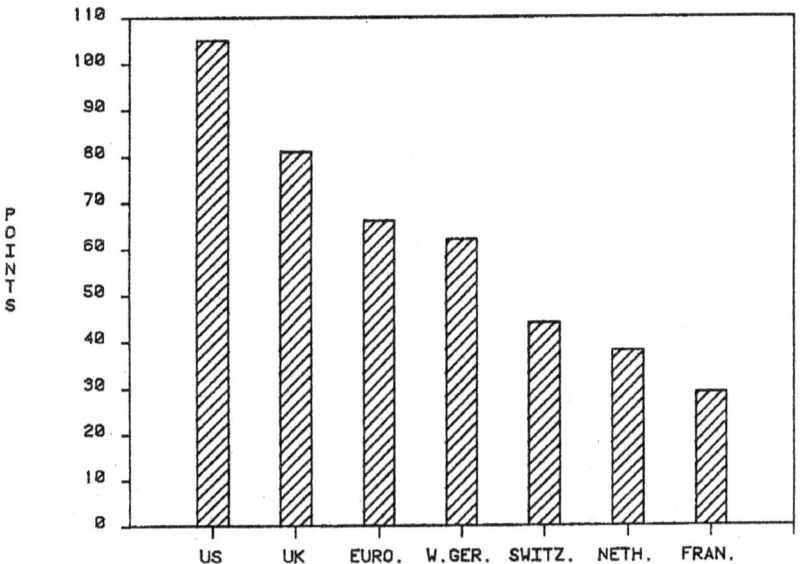

FIGURE 5. Point Tables over 15 Sets of Impact Factors: 7 Points for Highest Score; 7 Matched Journals per Set

Europe and even seriously challenging the Americans in impact factors?

FAILINGS AND OPPORTUNITIES

Is there a failure of the British to see themselves as Europeans? The excellent overall performance of British journals was quite consistent in each contest. Rarely did any British journal rank below third in any matchup. Some of the credit must go to the unique qualities of British research and publications, and some is attributable to the fact that British journals share many of the characteristics and functions that make Eurojournals attractive outlets. Both types of journals use English, have strong publishers with wide distribution, feature modern design, etc. Yet with few exceptions (specifically *Nature*, *Lancet*, and the *Journal of Molecular Biology*) they, too, have little chance of catching up with U.S. titles. Moreover, the notion of having all continental Europe come to Britain for a better outlet is probably less practical than wholeheartedly integrating those high-quality British papers into continental European journals.

Is there overextended generosity – and a failure of critical judgment – involved in accepting so many non-European papers? One of the most striking impressions formed during the course of this research was the enormous number of Third World papers in European journals of any sort. While some of these papers are excellent by any standard, many show the effects of poor funding and reduced contact with the most current trends in developed countries that one finds in the less-affluent scientific centers. Americans could certainly take on more Third World papers as part of their duty to promote science in underdeveloped countries. It is also high time for those ubiquitous and economically capable Japanese contributors to European journals to aggressively promote Pan-Asian or Pacific basin English-language journals. With the marketing and production skills for which they are justly esteemed, the Japanese could develop journals worthy of their own excellent research. These journals could also serve as an effective magnet for a reasonable share of the best work of their talented Third World neighbors.

It is easy – and regrettably appears racist – to single out Third

World or Japanese papers as ones whose individual impact factors are likely to weaken those of the journal overall. Previous work suggests that at least some U.S. papers could also stand closer scrutiny.[10] The cited study asks why Americans, whose journals—as demonstrated in Figure 5—almost always have the highest impact factors, still send so many of their papers to European outlets. While the increasing attractiveness of some of these journals is a consideration, and while no definitive interpretation could be reported, some surprising results were demonstrated. U.S. papers on average do not raise the impact factors of European journals that publish them—in fact, they lower them. Generally, European impact factors are already lower than those of U.S. journals. After a moment's reflection, one discovers a common denominator in some U.S. manuscripts exported to European journals: impact factors of only half the value of U.S. papers intended for publication in U.S. journals. See Figure 6. Embarrassingly, a lingering number of U.S. scientists will still use European journals as a dumping ground for

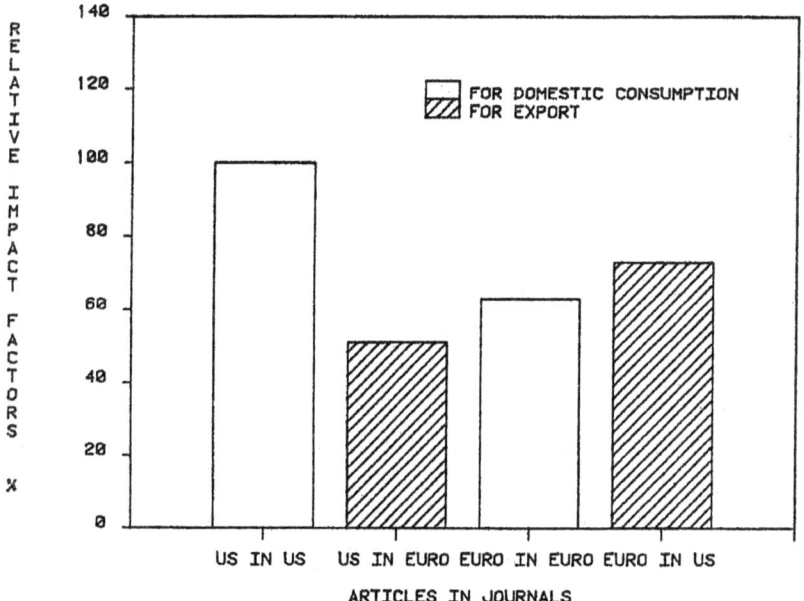

FIGURE 6. An Imbalance in the Transatlantic Impact-Factor Trade

research of less-than-stellar quality, a tradition that must be discouraged by Eurojournal editors who seek to command the respect of themselves and others. We acknowledge the criticism that it would take a doctoral dissertation's worth of verification to demonstrate this condescending misbehavior. As for the criticisms that (1) Eurojournal issues would become too slim; or (2) they would become chronically delayed waiting for enough papers to fill the void in issues bereft of non-European papers; or (3) Americans won't subscribe to journals in which they can't readily publish, we offer answers in the last two discussion items.

Is there still a lack of confidence on Eurojournals on the part of some Europeans? We have extended this work to look at the other side of the coin: the impact factors of purely European papers appearing in U.S. journals that have Eurojournal competition.[11] While the 110 European papers studied fell short of those of their U.S. hosts, their impact factors were higher than if they had published in the matching Eurojournals. Ironically, this gives us a definition of "best European papers" that still holds lingering validity for some Europeans: those manuscripts sent off to U.S. journals. Once again, see Figure 6. Eurojournal editors must work harder to win over these defectors.

Is there a lack of leadership in the European publishing community? While some firms have done well in realizing the profits presented by Eurojournals, it is time for thoughtful, concerted action. Perhaps there should be a division of publisher responsibilities according to discipline: Springer for biochemistry, Munksgaard for clinical medicine, etc. A general goal would be the buy-out or merger of European-based single-nation or international Eurojournals. While all this sounds unfair in terms of promoting monopolies or cartels, it may be the only fair way for one continent — Europe — to compete in impact factors and prestige with what amounts to another continent — the U.S. These consolidations would offer advantages for both European authors and U.S. subscribers. Both groups would have fewer, but more respected, journals to deal with. There would be less bewilderment concerning choice for either manuscripts or subscriptions. With all this consolidation one gets more substantial and timely issues that are not dependent on waiting for lesser contributions from authors outside Europe to fill a number.

One also sustains truth in advertising: European journals that are overwhelmingly European.

Consolidations would not come cheaply, and some U.S. libraries would choose to opt out of Eurojournals altogether. But those who cannot afford a serious commitment to science have been canceling already, one scattered title at a time, and their absence from subscription roles is inevitable. Such subscriptions to Eurojournals as remained would be indicative of genuine interest and would be dependable. Emphatically, they will not be taken for the demeaning and ultimately unreliable reason that some U.S. librarians will maintain them as occasional outlets for the lesser papers of their U.S. faculty clients. Rather, the best U.S. scientists will be smart enough to know that they need access to the best in European research, and the best U.S. librarians will be smart enough to provide it.

REFERENCE NOTES

1. Hamaker, Charles and Astle, Deana. "Recent Pricing Patterns in British Journal Publishing," *Library Acquisitions: Practice and Theory* 8:225-32 (1984).
2. Rushin, Siegfried. "Why Are Foreign Subscription Rates Higher for American Libraries Than They Are for Subscribers Elsewhere?" *The Serials Librarian* 9:7-18 (Spring 1985).
3. Joyce, Patrick and Merz, Thomas E. "Price Discrimination in Academic Journals," *Library Quarterly* 55:274 (1985).
4. Tuttle, Marcia. "The Pricing of British Journals for the North American Market," *Library Resources & Technical Services* 30:72-78 (Jan./Mar. 1986).
5. Astle, Deana and Hamaker, Charles. "Pricing by Geography: British Journal Pricing 1986, Including Developments in Other Countries," *Library Acquisitions: Practice & Theory* 10:165-81 (1986).
6. Houbeck, Robert L. Jr., "British Journal Pricing: *Enigma Variations*, or What *Will* the U.S. Market Bear?" *Library Acquisitions: Practice and Theory* 10:183-97 (1986).
7. Dorn, Knut and Maddox, Jane. "The Acquisition of European Journals," *Library Acquisitions: Practice and Theory* 10:199-202 (1986).
8. White, Herbert S. "Differential Pricing," *Library Journal* 111:170-71 (Sept. 1, 1986).
9. Cambridge University, the Pasteur Institute, the universities of Leiden, Heidelberg, and Bern, and any clearly affiliated hospitals or special institutes.
10. Stankus, Tony. "American Authors in Foreign Science Journals: Reviewing the Range of Initial Attitudes and Adjusting Library Investment to Client Experience," *Scientific Journals: Issues in Library Selection and Management*

(New York: The Haworth Press, 1987), pp. 57-69. This study included an analysis of the impact factors of 317 U.S. papers appearing in eight British and West German journals similar to Eurojournals. Americans scored 19 percentage points lower than their host journals. Given that their host journals averaged only 63 percent of the impact factor of matching U.S. journals, this yielded a citation rate for exported U.S. papers only about half that of their peers for home consumption.

11. A preliminary study of 110 European papers appearing in U.S. journals showed them scoring about 27 percent less impact factor than their host journals overall. This was still 10 percent better than the rate for the comparable Eurojournals. The fact that neither exported U.S. nor European papers did well suggests that papers, like some wines, do not travel well.

How Vulnerable Is the European For-Profit Sector Within U.S. Science Journal Collections? Comparing Its Staying Power with that of the American For-Profit Sector in an Incremental Cancellations Trial, with Special Attention to the Subspecialty Journals of Both Sectors

SUMMARY. The journals of the European for-profit publishing community are thoroughly entrenched in the information exchange and rewards systems of U.S. scientists. American researchers also feel particularly well served by the proliferation of subspecialty journals. Financially distressed librarians are not likely to gain the science faculty as allies in an overt program of boycotting either of these categories of journals. Nor will they be able to argue successfully from bibliometric data that a good number of them are of low quality or unneeded. One alternative, American for-profit titles, both subspecialty and more general, have a price advantage for librarians, and score higher than their European competitors in subject areas where they compete directly. But the scope of the American for-profit sector is quite small compared to that of the Europeans, and would not readily allow the Americans to quickly supersede them. There are so many more European titles in place already that even after waves of systematic cancellations, a strong European for-profit presence is likely to continue to dominate the for-profit segment of most U.S. scientific collections. A financial plan is presented which allows for more direct financial contributions to the serials budget from faculty grant monies. This is suggested in return for an end to threats to the European and subspecialty segments of the collection made by an increasingly militant library community.

HEIGHTENING TENSIONS OVER TWO ISSUES

The uproar from American serials librarians over the costs of science journals, particularly those issued by commercial houses, has continued unabated since 1986.[1-3] Two grievances have received greater attention recently. First, that European publishers pass through all of the increases in dollar prices, caused by the decline of the dollar against European currencies. This forces libraries to bear the entire loss. Second, that the same publishers are establishing too many expensive subspecialty journals. Hamaker[4] alleges that European for-profit publishers of scientific, medical, and technical journals are operating on a basis of "the least reading for the smallest number at the highest price."

The most common response has been to suggest that librarians cancel as many as possible of the titles from publishers that they consider to be particularly grasping.[5] Another approach suggested by Dougherty and Johnson[6] has been to consider whether or not American university presses might enter the fray more actively as low-cost competitors to foreign commercial giants. A related possibility might be for American collections to favor American for-profit publishers, sparing themselves at the very least the exchange rate woes of the falling dollar. This last strategy had better be examined quickly. Hamaker suggests that American publishers are becoming envious of the high rates that their European counterparts are able to charge and seem ready to follow suit.

COVERTLY TARGETING OFFENDING PUBLISHERS BUT PROCEEDING OVERTLY ON CANCELLATIONS BASED ON DEGREE OF NECESSITY

While librarians might well wish to cancel journals on the basis of costs alone, with the most expensive or those most offensively escalating in price targeted first, it is more likely that some notion of relative necessity would have to enter. It is extremely unlikely that grants-winning scientists would ever go along with the cancellation, for example, of the most-cited journal in their fields just to satisfy the need for fiscal revenge of their librarians. An intermediate situation, based on cancelling journals that are not frequently cited by the leading journal, is, however, conceivable. While not too obviously singling out publishers that librarians dislike, this quantitative approach might give the librarians a less vindictive-appearing justification for getting rid of the journals they regard so suspiciously.

For purposes of this study, we envisioned a large research university collection in the sciences, engineering, and medicine. The inventory of journals for original research that welcomed papers written in English, and were published by Elsevier, Pergamon, and Springer, represented the European for-profit segment. The journal inventory, subject to the same qualifications, and published by Academic, Plenum and Wiley, represented the American for-profit component. For reasons of simplification, we considered all journals sponsored by American houses to be American, even though some have a European connection, and all European sponsored journals to be European even though some have an American connection. Because of complicating factors in terms of their being cited, we excluded review journals, newsletters, exclusively foreign-language journals, and translated journals.

For this study we assumed:

- that there was local demand for each title from all six publishers under study. In other words, the school would be taking geology titles, because it had a geology department. This avoided the argument that maybe some of the titles were simply out of the scope of the university from the start.
- that the needs of the local clientele for each journal in a field were very much like the needs of similar researchers around the world in that field. Local faculty did not have an especially strong desire to publish in the fifth most cited journal instead of the most-cited.
- that as a corollary, the leading journal in a field, which we took to be the journal with the highest impact factor, defined the field and its citing pattern defined the relative need for researchers in that field for other journals in that field.

We were cognizant of the criticisms of Scanlan,[7] and were careful to assign ratings involving only journals of very similar subject matter and scope. Using 1987 *Journal Citation Reports* data, we assigned the following values to journals from the inventories of our six publishers:

- itself the most cited journal of its type in a given subject field
- second most cited journal of its type in a given subject field
- third most cited journal of its type in a given subject field
- placing fourth or worse among journals of its type in a given subject field

The idea of using these different priorities reflects the reality of most cancellation programs: they are gradual and tie in with getting rid of the less-needed items before proceeding to the most-needed items. We sought to determine whether it would be American or European inventories which were most affected with each need-based cutback. Secondarily, we sought to determine whether the much despised subspecialty journals would be particularly likely to fall more quickly in incremental cutbacks.

Figure 1 displays a stark reality. The inventory of scientific titles from the major European for-profit publishers is much larger than that of the American for-profit sector. This seemingly skewed representation, is however, genuinely reflective of the actual collection situation in a variety of larger universities. It is the major reason that librarians at those universities feel so entrapped by what happens to prices based on European currencies. Figures 2 and 3 indicate what happened after we cut any journals from the six publishers that finished in fourth place or worse. Figure 2 also demonstrated a paradox: even though a lower percentage of American for-profit titles was cut at this point, fewer American titles remained because of the initial disparity in size of inventory. It is only after cutting third place finishers, as had been done for Figures 4 and 5, that there was even a slight equality. At this point Academic and Springer were tied for remaining titles. Only after the second place finishers were also cut, as is shown in Figures 6 and 7, did we see the remaining inventory of an American for-profit publisher, Academic, exceed that of any European for-profit publisher, Springer. The final standings shown in Figure 7 calls us back to the lesson of Figure 1. Even though American for-profits held onto a

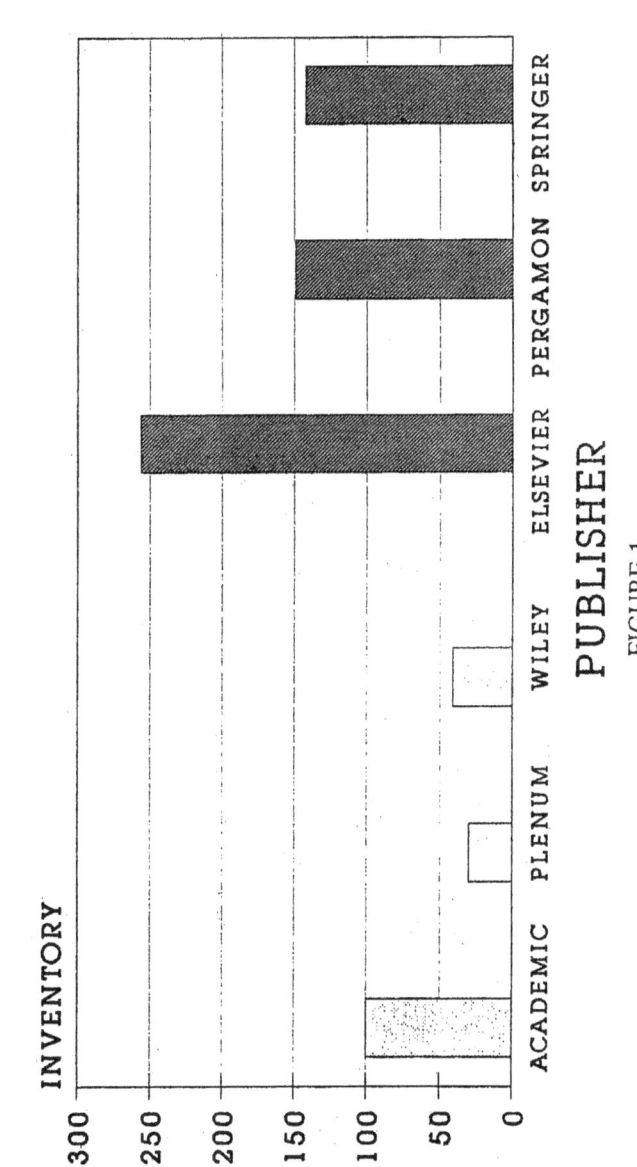

FIGURE 1

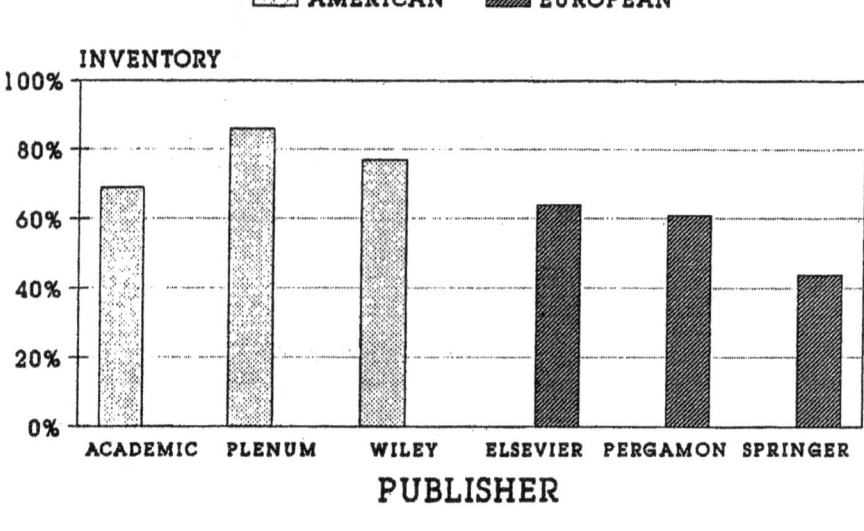

FIGURE 2

larger percentage of their initial inventory at each cut, American libraries still end up with more European for-profit titles than American ones. This is small solace to those with a special antipathy for the European for-profits. Perhaps they will feel better when the special situation of the the subspecialty journals is examined and that portion of their complaint has a chance to be verified.

THE CONTROVERSY OVER THE SUBSPECIALTY JOURNAL

By a subspecialty journal it is meant one with a narrower scope than that of virtually all academic undergraduate majors, and indeed finer in focus than that of many master's degrees. A journal that focuses on organic chemistry is too broad by this definition. A journal of physical organic chemistry, or organic mass spectroscopy

Inventory Remaining After Cutting Fourth Place Finishers

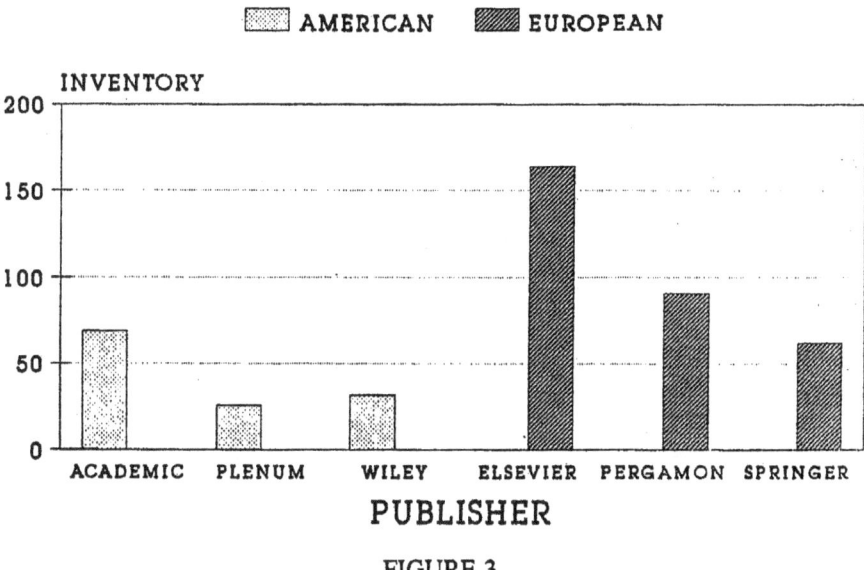

FIGURE 3

would be sufficiently specialized to be regarded as representing a subspecialty. Figure 8 gives some pertinent examples drawn from this study.

Serials librarians have tended to levy several charges against these subspecialty journals:

- First, that these journals typically cost annually several hundred dollars for only a few hundred pages in many cases. Unlike not-for-profit science journals, the bulk of them are not subsidized by page charges drawn from the grant money of contributing scientists. The library alone bears their high cost.
- Second, that these journals are consulted within the library by at most a handful of readers per title. More often the library pays for the holding of a title that is often of use to only one professor. Is that the role for a university library? If individual

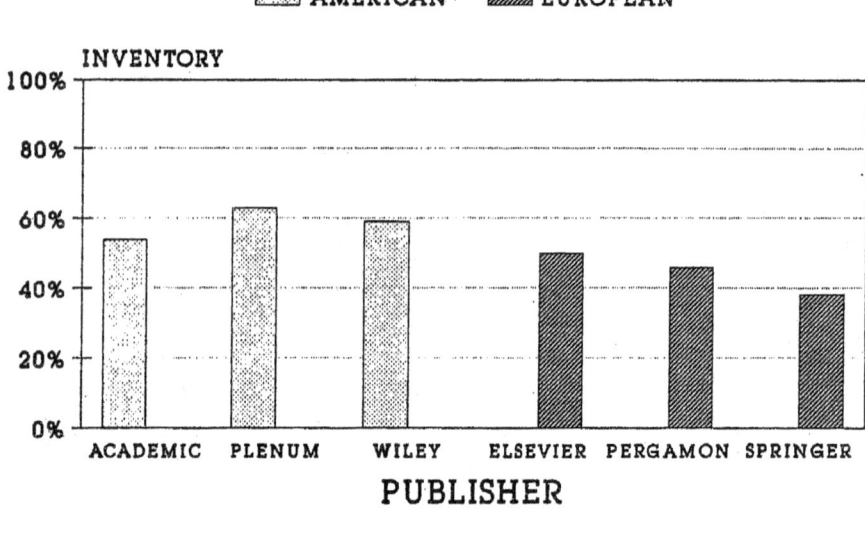

FIGURE 4

professors think so highly of these titles, why do so few take personal subscriptions?
— Third, that these titles are at face value ridiculously overspecialized, dealing in what librarians sometimes regard as truly bizarre subjects.
— Fourth, that the numbers of these journals multiply like cancer cells. Could any field really need so many new journals?
— Fifth, that excess money or profit is being made off the whole process, a notion that librarians find distasteful. Hamaker reports with obvious disgust that some editors report receiving $20,000 for their work. He finds it particularly disagreeable that publishers basically get their material to publish free, and then send it back to the university in journal format for quite a fee.
— Sixth, that librarians, who are professionals in their own right, have "library-scientifically" determined that the cost and

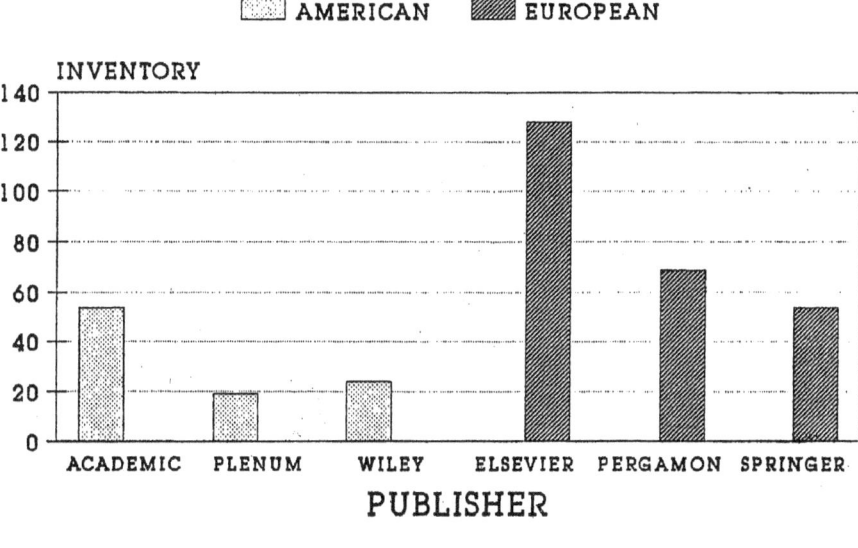

FIGURE 5

number of journals is forcing a serious imbalance in the budgeting and storage ratio of journals to books, to the detriment of books.
— Seventh, that ultimately, subspecialty journals exist because scientists cannot get their weaker papers into journals of broader scope. Rather than admit the substandard nature of a work and not publish it, dossier-inflating scientists will send it off to a subspecialty journal which probably will publish anything within its tiny scope.

Scientists reply that subspecialty journals have many advantages:

— First, they are economical in that they levy no page charges at a time when university press or scholarly society journals might charge $100 per page. A single ten-page article that appears in a for-profit journal instead of a page-charging society outlet has probably already earned its keep.

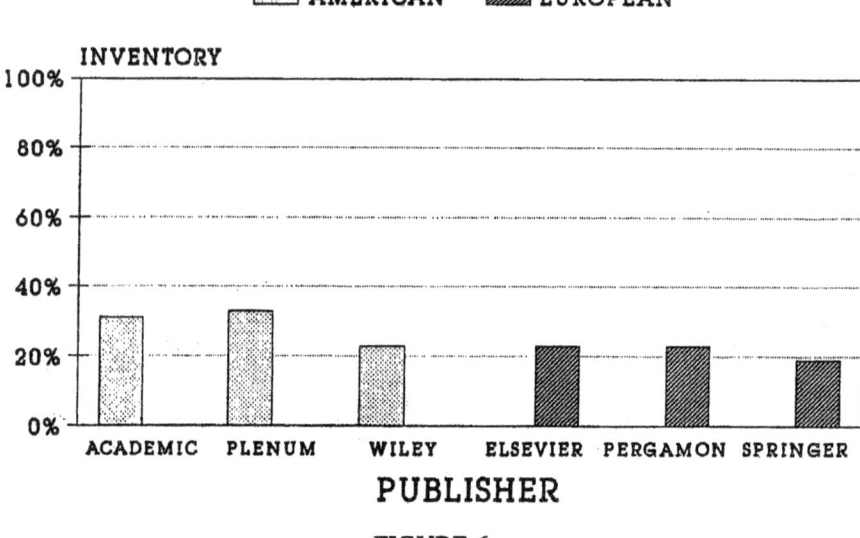

FIGURE 6

— Second, they are very efficient in that they save the reader's time poring over materials that are not directly relevant to one's research needs. The notion that all scientists in a subspecialty already know one another and send reprints and communicate electronically ignores the notion of exclusion through competitive factors and the need to tool up quickly when one is not already well-versed in a field.

— Third, that such journals are a necessary part of the growth of knowledge. A small field must be cultivated before it makes headway. There is scarcely a field of serious importance today: computer science, noninvasive cardiology, genetic engineering, that wasn't considered an obscure subpecialty at one time.

— Fourth, that to the truly informed, the rate of growth of scientific knowledge really is explosive and that new journals are often required or appropriate. The proliferation of departments

Inventory Remaining After Cutting Second Place Finishers

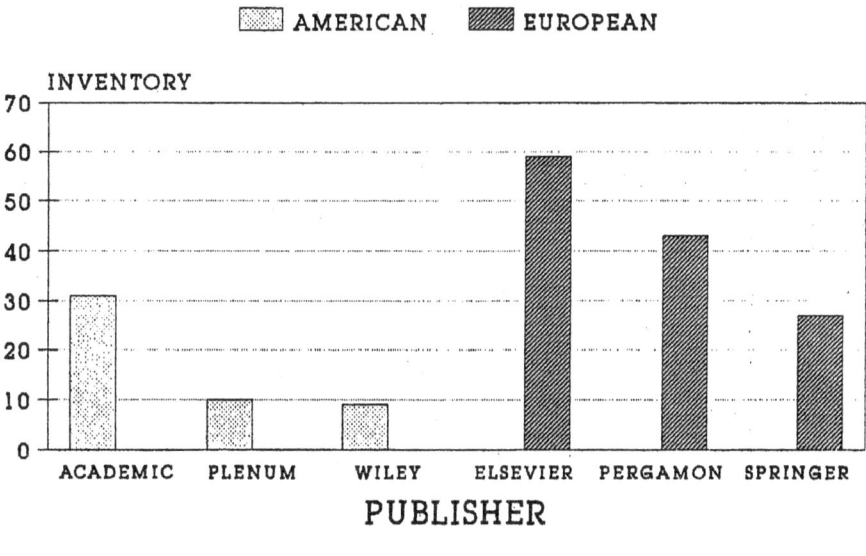

FIGURE 7

and journals that serve them is man's recognition of his finite ability to master all knowledge well.

— Fifth, that librarians' notions of the cost of things in the real world is woefully puerile. At a time when the scientists bring into the typical land-grant university well over $50,000,000 annually in funding, a journal that costs a few thousand dollars is nothing but a sufficient payback to the scientists for all the funding they bring in. Humanists and social scientists are rarely subject to the "overhead" deduction that the treasurer's office exacts from virtually every grant the scientist brings in because the grants are both typically much smaller and much rarer. By contrast, with scientific grants, it is not unusual for a university to take as much as 70% off the top for the general maintenance and support of the university's facilities, including the library. As for personal salary considerations, in light of this ability to generate income, a scientist in today's market

Examples of Distinctions Made Between Major Specialty vs. Subspecialty Journals

Publisher	Major Specialty	Subspecialty
ACADEMIC	Advances in Mathematics	Journal of Number Theory
PLENUM	Int. Journal of Theoretical Physics	General Relativity and Gravitation
WILEY	Geological Journal	Earthquake Engineer. & Struct Dynamics
ELSEVIER	Inorganica Chimica Acta	Journal of Fluoride Chemistry
PERGAMON	Int. Journal of Biochemistry	Insect Biochemistry
SPRINGER	Marine Biology	Coral Reefs

FIGURE 8

would think that $20,000 for editing a major journal like *Biochimica et Biophysica Acta* part-time, is about adequate.
— Sixth, that the little data that librarians do manage to generate suggests that journals really are supremely important in the sciences, and science books conversely much less so. If librarians really were professionals acting on verifiable facts, should they not follow the facts? The idea that librarianship is a "hard" factual, data-and-analysis driven profession has not yet occurred to many scientists, because of this sort of nonconformity. Scientists will believe in the seriousness of librarianship when grad students drop out of library school as being too tough and turn to nuclear physics as easier.
— Seventh, that scientific authors are vitally concerned about the quality and visibility of the journals within which they publish. Their dossiers are examined constantly for a continuing flow of well-placed papers. Many a librarian holds onto his job forever even if he or she never publishes, whereas the scientist's career will often be ruined without a continuing pattern of prestige publications to ensure success in grant-winning.

Whatever viewpoint is adopted concerning these journals, one surprising fact came to light when the relative proportion of major specialty journals to subspecialty journals was examined. Contrary to the impression in recent librarians' literature, American for-profit publishers are proportionally more dependent on subspecialty titles than are European firms! See Figure 9. The mistaken impression is due to the overwhelming inventory of European titles: even with a lower proportional representation of subspecialty titles, European subspecialty titles outnumber those of the Americans in most large collections.

What of the notion of relative need? Were subspecialty titles more readily eliminated in the system of cuts elaborated earlier, or not? This cannot be demonstrated either way with the quartile graphs used earlier. This is owing to the fact that in a number of the quartile cuts either no major specialty or subspecialty titles would be cut for certain publishers. This gave us individual quarterly comparisons of major *vs.* subspecialty journals which would have zeros in the ratios, yielding a meaningless number.

Instead, a top half (less-likely-to-be-cut) *vs.* bottom half (more-

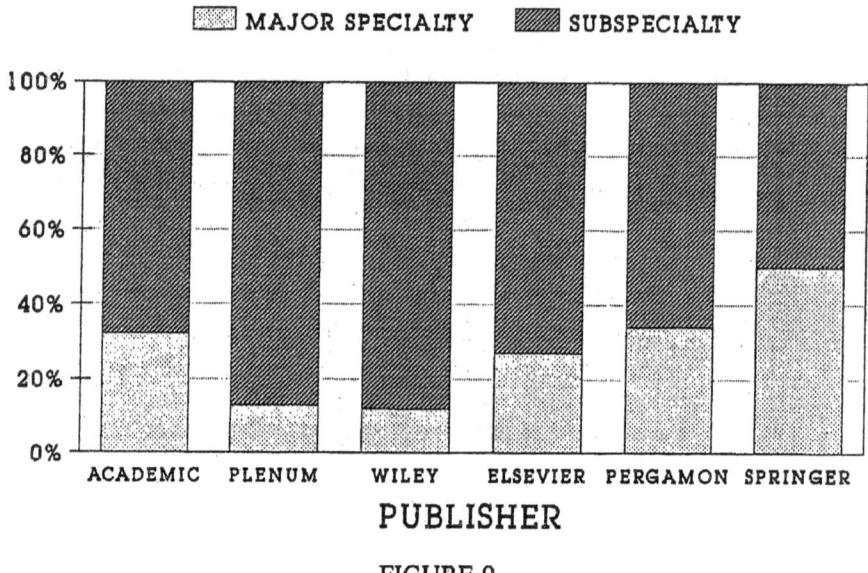

FIGURE 9

likely-to-be-cut) calculation was used. Those results can be readily expressed with a single graph. See Figure 10. It represents the titles in the top half directly, and by inference, what happened in the bottom half as well. It shows whether it was the major specialty journals, or the subspecialty journals, that were most likely to survive a cut of the bottom half. The numbers the reader sees are percentage points *over* 50%. So that if there were a 10% score posted for the major specialty journals in Figure 10, it would mean that 60% of the major specialty journals were in the top half. One would expect that with some publishers the major specialty journals would score better; with others, the subspecialty. But as the reader can see from Figure 10, the subspecialty journals of all six publishers always dominated the top half. Major specialty journals were concentrated in the at-risk lower half. In the case of none of the publishers did at least half of the major specialty journals reside in the top half.

Greater Than Expected Contributions to Top Half Finishers

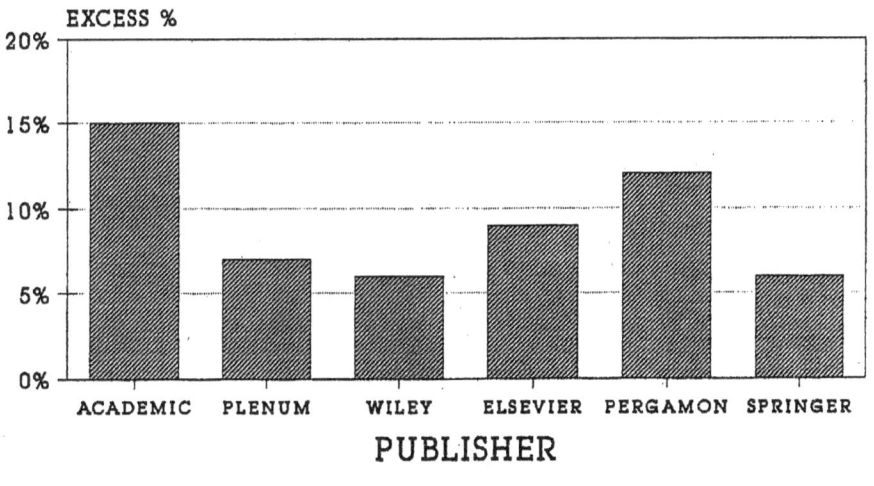

FIGURE 10

What are the underlying sources of this superior performance from subspecialty titles? A look at some of the original arguments for and against subspecialty journals answers provides clues. The arguments against them are not, in all cases, entirely invalid. They simply were not enough to override the results.

GENERALIZING THE FINDINGS

First, it is clear that while many scientists agree that appearing in one of the few unambiguously outstanding general science (e.g., *Science* or *Nature*) or major specialty journals (e.g., *Journal of the American Chemical Society*) is a wonderful achievement, they also feel free to send quite good papers to subspecialty journals. Those papers do get noticed, and citations to them have contributed to the strong performance of subspecialty journals in this trial. In fact, some small subspecialty journals have more gross citations — unexpected given their small number of papers — than larger major journals in the same general field but of less distinction.

Second, it is clear that one of the reasons that these subspecialty journals do so well is lack of timely competition in their particular niche. Our study suggested that there are rewards for those publishers, whether American or European for-profits, who aggressively discover and occupy niches first. The *Journal of Organometallic Chemistry*, one of the most expensive subspecialty journals from Elsevier at over $3,000 annually, had the organometallic niche much to itself for several years. When *Polyhedron*, a Pergamon for-profit entry and the not-for-profit *Organometallics* came out in 1982, covering much of the same territory, at a fraction of the cost, the Elsevier title lost only about 15% of its subscriptions. This was not due so much to the lack of librarians' awareness of its cost disadvantage as to the loyalty of a generation of organometallics chemists who continued to insist on its retention despite those costs.

Third, a major reason for the poorer showing of major specialty journals is that too many do compete with one another. There are relatively few recognized major specialties and still very many publishers, particularly national societies. What sets apart the many similar journals that result from this? Often it is competition based not so much on quality *per se* as on the dominant nationality among contributors. While most national journals are explicitly open to contributions from any country, Americans have long displayed a rather narrow preference at the general science or major specialty level. Americans tend to read, and contribute to, major specialty journals dominated primarily by American articles, and secondarily by papers from Western Europeans and Japanese who have the manuscript marketing sense to publish in English. This narrowness is reinforced by the fact that in a great many fields American scientists and institutions are still the leaders, and it is their interest that non-American authors seek to attract.

Over time, highly motivated foreign papers, attuned to American audiences, tend to gravitate towards the handful of major journals favored by Americans. This migration is perpetuated by the many foreign scientists studying at American institutions. As the developing young scientist becomes accustomed to the literature of his field, it is obvious to him or her after examining a few top general or major specialty titles, that the proportion of American and other English language papers tends to quickly decline. This is almost what scientists would call a "threshold" phenomenon. Early in its history, a journal either attracts and sustains sufficient American papers, or it will have almost none. Where American or other English language papers from major scientific powers are missing, foreign language papers and papers from lesser scientific powers rush in. The young foreign scientist sees little or no advantage in having his early manuscripts appear in these fourth or fifth best major specialty journals. No Americans will go looking for them. Rather, the young scientist will go to an Americanized subspecialty journal instead. The hiding grounds for the poorer papers from Americans is not among American or European for-profit subspecialty journals, but rather among the fourth and fifth place more general or major specialty journals.

Most European for-profit publishers have appreciated the subspecialty advantage and the need for their journals to think, act and look like American journals. It is instructive to note that the majority of European for-profit subspecialty titles are slickly Americanized in language and format from the start. This places them in contrast with several of Springer's older titles. These titles are part of the reason for Springer's more modest performance in these retention trials. It is partly because Springer has historically maintained a great many titles with admirable, but no longer compelling, connections to old German, Austrian, and Swiss institutions that some of its inventory is less cited and less contributed to than it might be among American scientists. Moreover, a great many older Springer titles are also of a more general or major specialty nature, and compete with one another. The ancient and honorable *Mathematische Annalen* competes with the ancient and honorable *Mathematische Zeitschrift*. Both compete with another Springer title with a shorter history but a much more Americanized feel: *Inventiones Mathematicae*. In an incremental cancellation program in a given discipline, like mathematics, not all of these more general journals can be sure of being of first, second, third or even fourth priority, and thus being spared. Indeed, in a draconian cancellation program *Inventiones* might be the only survivor among this group.

Springer is, of course, entirely capable of fielding very highly competitive subspecialty titles, for example, *Communications on Mathematical Physics*, a title unlikely to be cut at any institution with an interest in this area, despite its expensiveness. And Springer is a leader in a development involving major specialty journals that has tremendous promise and meaning for both librarians and scientists: the Eurojournals consolidation movement. For example, its journal *Astronomy and Astrophysics* represents the consolidation of five individual major specialty journals from as many European countries, and carries the involvement and endorsement of scientists throughout the Continent. It is either in second or third place as a source of information or as an outlet for papers in many American centers of astronomy and astrophysics. This is a standing much higher than that achieved by any of its individual national precursors. Once again, it is not a likely target for cancellation despite its high cost.

The fourth major finding is that it is extremely unlikely that even America's higher quality, for-profit press, at the scale at which it currently operates, could quickly take over the lion's share of any of the inventory or publishing duties of the European for-profit sector. Indeed the reverse is currently more likely, and almost happened when Robert Maxwell of Pergamon Press made a move on William Jovanovich of Harcourt, Brace, and Jovanovich, parent of the Academic Press in 1987. Likewise McGraw-Hill has been vulnerable. SDC's ORBIT and BRS have already been gobbled up.

Ironically about the only way the American for-profit firms can strengthen their basis in publishing is to issue additional successful subspecialty titles, indeed many more than they currently do. Librarians would be galled by this development, but it may be better for them in the long run in light of what appears to be a long-term federal policy of a weak dollar to encourage exports and foreign investments in the U.S., and to discourage imports and unemployment.

Curiously, this policy might also work to continue the Americanization of the actual journal production of the European for-profit firms. With each passing year, Elsevier, Pergamon, and Springer have added American-based titles, or transferred the editorial handling and sometimes the actual printing of some established titles from Europe to America. American labor relations, including wage rates and acceptance of print technologies by production workers, and relative in frequency of strikes, are at least as favorable, and often more agreeable, to European publishers than their own situations. Raw materials availability, and often raw materials pricing, is clearly more favorable. Moreover, a great many titles from European publishers have the majority of their subscribers in America. It is cheaper to ship the minority of subscriptions from America to Europe than the majority to America from Europe. American libraries might have some exchange rate relief if more American-produced titles were priced strictly on the dollar.

It would be unwise, however, to encourage Academic, Plenum, and Wiley, to drop their small offices in England, a cost-saving frequently suggested by librarians to publishers at joint meetings. While the cost of maintaining these bureaus is steep, given their small size, it is more than paid for by the high quality of the titles British affiliations add to the inventory of these firms (Academic's *Journal of Molecular Biology* is a case in point). Moreover, that small European presence *via* London may be sufficient to allow these American publishers to operate on a nontariff basis as tariff barriers in the European Economic Community drop and tariffs against non-Europeans are raised.

TIME FOR A COMPROMISE?

It is clear from this study that the European for-profit titles and subspecialty journals from either Europe or America, have become thoroughly embedded in the structure of scientific literature in America and elsewhere. European for-profit titles are not so dramatically poorer in quality that they are more likely to fall out of place owing to some intrinsic weakness than would any American titles. In light of the political power of science faculty over librarians in terms of bringing in university income, it is unlikely that the librarians would be allowed to pull all of the European components out of the structure just because of their own antipathy. For one thing, it is clear that the American for-profit sector, while providing high quality components for the existing structure, could hardly plug all the holes in time to prevent a collapse of outlets for American research and the concomitant collapse of grant income this would bring.

What is needed is the mortar of more money to sustain as much of the structure as possible. Curiously, there may be a supply in science faculty grant monies. Librarians may be able to employ it, in return for less carping about, and less discretionary control over the specific for-profit titles, American or European, major specialty or subspecialty, that are maintained in the library. In this scheme, that portion of the "overhead" deduction that the treasurer claims is automatically passed on to the general support of the university library would be eliminated.

Initially, the library would be required to carry only the less expensive society and university press titles in the sciences that all departments are generally allowed, whether they ever brought in grant dollars or not. The library would initially be free of the journals they claim are bankrupting them. Scientists could publish in the less expensive journals, paying only their customary page charges to the journal publishers. With none of their grant money now going to the library, their grant accounts would be free of the overhead deduction that the scientist feels is paying for the financially nonproductive nonscience collections.

Now, after a time, when the accounting was all cleared up, scientists could also publish in the more expensive for-profit titles as well, but would have to turn over a fee to the library in lieu of page charges. That fee would directly support the journals in which the scientist chose to publish and no other.

This does not require the faculty member to effectively subsidize the not-for-profit journal twice (page charges and overhead charges), nor require the library to subsidize the for-profit journal alone. The result might be a library full of science journals, but such a result is already on the way. To the criticism of librarians or humanities faculty that this would somehow unbalance the library comes the ready response that, to a large extent, the scientists pay for any imbalance they create. Nothing in this scheme prevents humanities, social science, or library science professionals from contributing whatever grant money they bring in to their collection's expansion in for-profit titles. This scheme, much like the ongoing lack of a workable scheme in many universities, would also result in a collection that is heavily European for-profit and heavily subspecialty. But this *is* the price that must be paid as long as the library and nonscience segments cannot come up with anything like comparable funding, or point out publishing alternatives that will gain wide and quiet acceptance in the scientific community.

Of course the new arrangement would also force the librarian and scientist to get together on the accounting. Then they will probably discover that the treasurer has not been treating either of them well. That realization, not arguing with each other or even with many of these publishers, is the beginning of a real solution.

But in the short run, reevaluate the major specialty foreign journals. The subspecialty journals, foreign and domestic, that you know to be targeted to active subspecialists in your clientele, are doubtlessly more expensive per page, but probably have an offsetting value for them over journals less exclusively devoted to their interests. If those major journals do not concentrate on either the papers of Americans or those of a bloc of other scientifically competitive countries, number them among the more vunerable when budget pressures cannot be withstood.

REFERENCE NOTES

1. Stankus, Tony. "The Year's Work in Serials: 1986," *Library Resources and Technical Services* 31, no.4(October/December, 1987): 306-320. See the section entitled "Differential Pricing."

2. Stankus, Tony. "The Year's Work in Serials: 1987," *Library Resources and Technical Services* 32, no.3(July, 1988): 217-232. See the section entitled "Cost Analysis and Collection Contraction."

3. Stankus, Tony. See recent versions of the annual overview: "The Year's Work in Serials" within *Library Resources and Technical Services*.

4. Hamaker, Charles. "The Least Reading for the Smallest Number at the Highest Price," *American Libraries* 19, no.9(October 1988): 764-768.

5. White, Herbert S. "Differential Pricing," *Library Journal* 111, no. 14(October,1986):170-171.

6. Dougherty, Richard M., and Johnson, Brenda L. "Periodical Price Escalation: a Library Response," *Library Journal* 113, no.9(May 15, 1988):27-29.

7. Scanlan, Brian D. "Coverage by *Current Contents* and the Validity of Impact Factors: ISI from the Journal Publisher's Perspective," *The Serials Librarian* 13, no.2/3:57-66.

Is the Best Japanese Science in Western Journals?

Tony Stankus
Kevin Rosseel
William C. Littlefield

SUMMARY. Any notion of cancelling very expensive American and European science journals in order to subscribe to Japanese titles is shown to be questionable. Analysis of the published output of several firms and universities, sampling from dozens of journals, and examination of thousands of articles and citations suggest that with a few exceptions, the Japanese themselves place primary emphasis on appearing in these same, very expensive, highly cited American and European titles. While the Japanese do have journals well worth acquiring, their acquisition must be funded by other means.

A COLLISION OF TWO POWERFUL MOVEMENTS

Two developments preoccupy the science serials librarian today: the rise of Japan as a power in science and the crushing prices of scientific serials particularly for-profit American and European titles.

Both in scientific and library contexts, Japan has been making news. Japan has now surpassed all of the world save the United States in spending for scientific research.[1] It probably is already the world's leader in corporately sponsored research, constructing industrially endowed laboratories at a feverish rate. Recent estimates have placed the Japanese as third in the world in output of chemistry, physics, and cancer research papers, fifth in general life sciences, and seventh in mathematics.[3-5] The library and information

---

This article is reprinted from *The Serials Librarian*, Vol. 14(1/2) 1988.

communities have increasingly acknowledged these new realities. *Japanese Technical Abstracts* is now online as JAPAN TECHNOLOGY ONLINE as a result of an agreement between University Microfilms International, the Japanese Technical Information Service, and DIALOG.[6] STN, the scientifically and technically oriented database network, has set up a Tokyo service center in cooperation with the Japan Information Center for Science and Technology.[7] *Nature*, arguably the world's most prestigious multiscience research journal is adding a third printing and editorial center in Tokyo to match those in London and Washington.[8] In August, 1986, the U.S. Congress passed the Japanese Technical Literature Act as a means of improving American competitiveness through better availability and analysis of Japanese information in this country. Clearly, alert librarians feel under pressure to expand their access to Japanese scientific literature, particularly in serial holdings.

But these same librarians may not feel free to act because of journal budget pressures. An absolute torrent of criticism has cascaded on European and American for-profit publishers of science journals. In the 1986 "Year's Work in Serials"[10] no fewer than 15 articles mentioned deal with various aspects of the crisis: differential prices for American libraries vs. non-American libraries or individual subscribers; exchange rate fluctuations; the cutting out of jobbers or agencies sympathetic to libraries; the sacrificing of book buying to pay for subscriptions; political infighting during reduction of subscription lists, etc. The common denominator is a call to cancel publications that libraries no longer can afford or whose publishers seem underhanded or arrogant in their dealings with libraries.[11] One of the few defenses of the Europeans comes from Stankus who suggests that while the costs for their titles are very heavy, the importance of those journals for American scientists is commensurate with that cost.[12-14] Yet another, even broader attack on expensive scholarly serials has since appeared in *American Libraries*. This comes from the influential and respected Lubans,[15] who suggests that the current system of expensive scholarly journals has become hopelessly unwieldy, and is virtually impossible to monitor well in terms of quality of papers contributed or retrieved for referral. He sees some slight hope in electronic publishing on a pay-only-as-you-print basis, but strongly recommends cancellations as the only feasible way of funding new journals now. Stankus once again replies, suggesting hardnosed negotiations for a share of the research funding overhead charges assessed scientists by top administrators as one way to proceed, while a get-tough policy of inculcating literature skills in students is presented as another. According to Stankus, the bargaining leverage and literature monitoring tools are there as never before, but librarians feel more awkward in arguing with administrators than with faculty and feel a lack of authority in forcing students to work.[16] Nonetheless, an overwhelming consensus holds it necessary to cancel as a way of funding new titles, or, in terms of the current context, cancel some expensive American and European journals and replace these with Japanese. This paper examines, by way of testing such a strategy, the journals the Japanese seem to regard as valuable vehicles for their own manuscripts.

A LOOK AT JAPANESE PUBLISHING OUTPUT

With the goal of detecting a geographical emphasis in manuscript placement from members of the Japanese scientific community, the basic science output of nine Japanese institutions was examined through the use of the Corporate Index of *Science Citation Index* for the years 1983-1985. Three firms noted for high technology products and research, NEC, Hitachi, and Fujitsu, were selected for review, as were appropriate hi-tech departments at three distinguished universities: Tokyo, Osaka, and Nagoya. A search of the recent patent literature suggested the inclusion of three firms involved in biotechnology: Dainippon Pharmaceuticals, Ajinomoto, and Tanabe. The same universities were followed for their biotechnology related departments. This search produced 3,632 papers. While there were a number of variations[17] among corporate vs. academic and hi-tech vs. biotech component groups, the following fact was most striking. When each group was given equal weight in the calculations it became apparent that the Japanese export about 60% of their papers! As Figure 1 indicates, about 25% of Japanese papers appear in European-based journals, and about 35% in American titles. This would at first seem unlikely. Perhaps, as Garfield pointed out in an earlier study of Japanese scientific literature, ISI

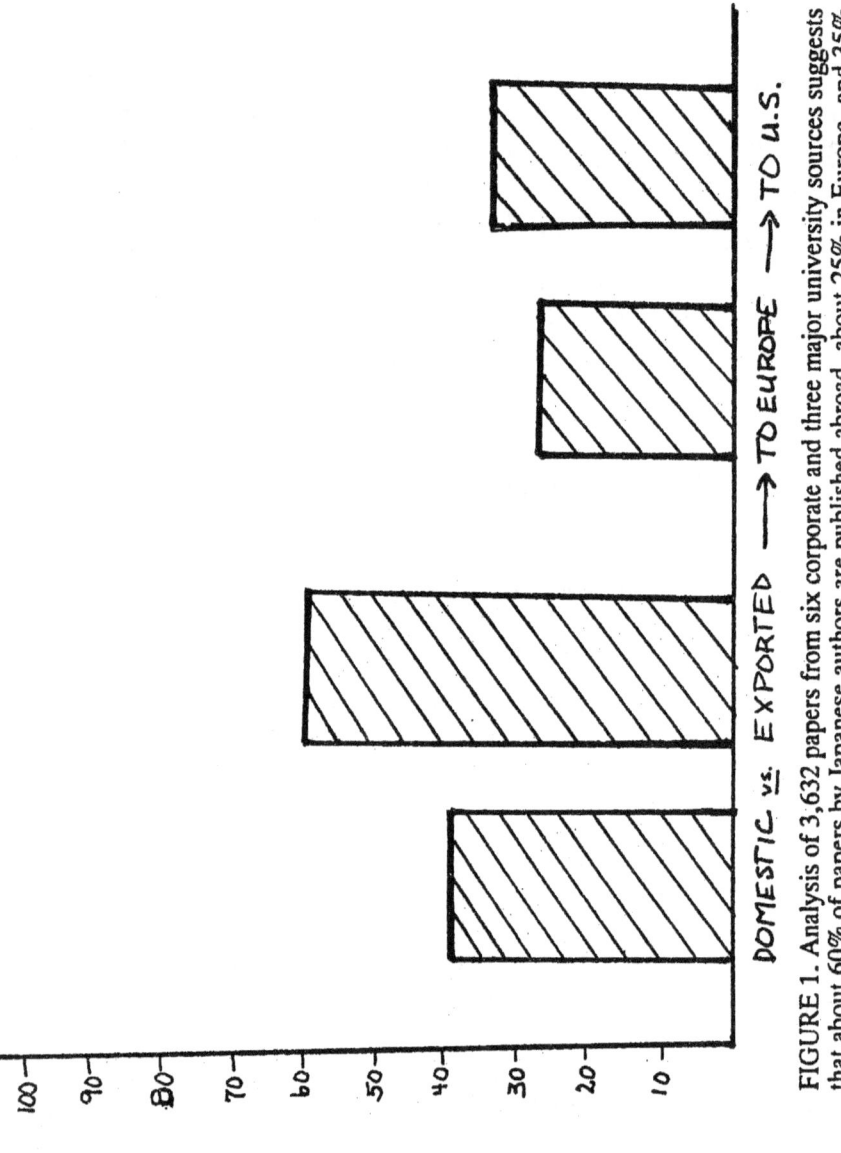

FIGURE 1. Analysis of 3,632 papers from six corporate and three major university sources suggests that about 60% of papers by Japanese authors are published abroad, about 25% in Europe, and 35% in the U.S.

compilers are merely emphasizing English-language references in *SCI* coverage to the detriment of Japanese references.[18] Some confirmatory evidence was needed.

In the first series of tests, it was reasoned that a large sampling of leading occidental journals would partly confirm or reject the initial finding of a substantial Japanese commitment to non-Japanese titles. Four thousand papers in forty journals were examined. Once again, by deliberate design, physical sciences (hi-tech) were exactly balanced with life sciences (biotech), and this time European journals were exactly balanced with American titles.[19] Once again, results are striking. As Figure 2 shows, the Japanese represent the third most common contributors to European journals. They are behind the British and Americans, and essentially tied with the West Germans, but ahead of all other Europeans and the Canadians. Figure 3 makes clear that they are the third most common contributors to U.S. journals. They are behind the Americans and Canadians, but maintain an edge over all other European countries and Israel.

The possibility remains that while the Japanese are clearly making a commitment of quantity to journals foreign to them, perhaps they are saving their best papers for their own journals. It was decided to test this on the basis of comparative performance in worldwide citations made to Japanese papers in Japanese journals as opposed to citations to Japanese papers in occidental journals. Using papers produced in 1982, 1983, and 1984, impact factors were determined for Japanese papers in six Japanese journals, Japanese papers in six European journals, and Japanese papers in six American journals, with each set matched for subject.[20] Exactly the methods for impact factor calculation for 1984 and 1985 were used that ISI uses; and since Japanese journals are largely all-Japanese, ISI figures were used for Japanese performance in their own journals.[21] Altogether citations to 7,835 papers were involved.[22] Once again equal parts of life sciences (the biotechnically important fields of biochemistry, genetics, and microbiology) and physical sciences (the hi-tech fields of applied physics, solid-state physics, and the major letters journals in theoretical physics) were included. Once again, as shown in Figure 4, the various component results were given equal weight for a striking demonstration: on average the best

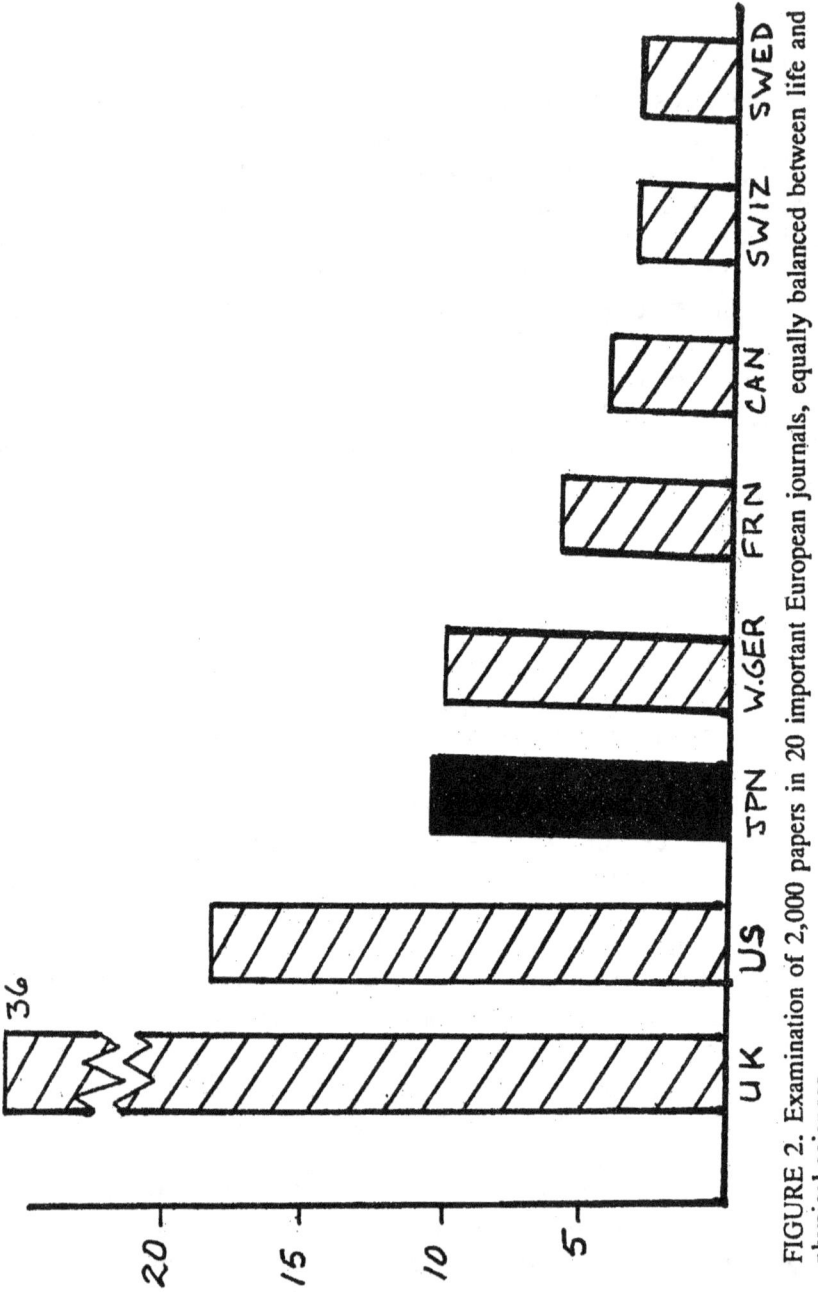

FIGURE 2. Examination of 2,000 papers in 20 important European journals, equally balanced between life and physical sciences.

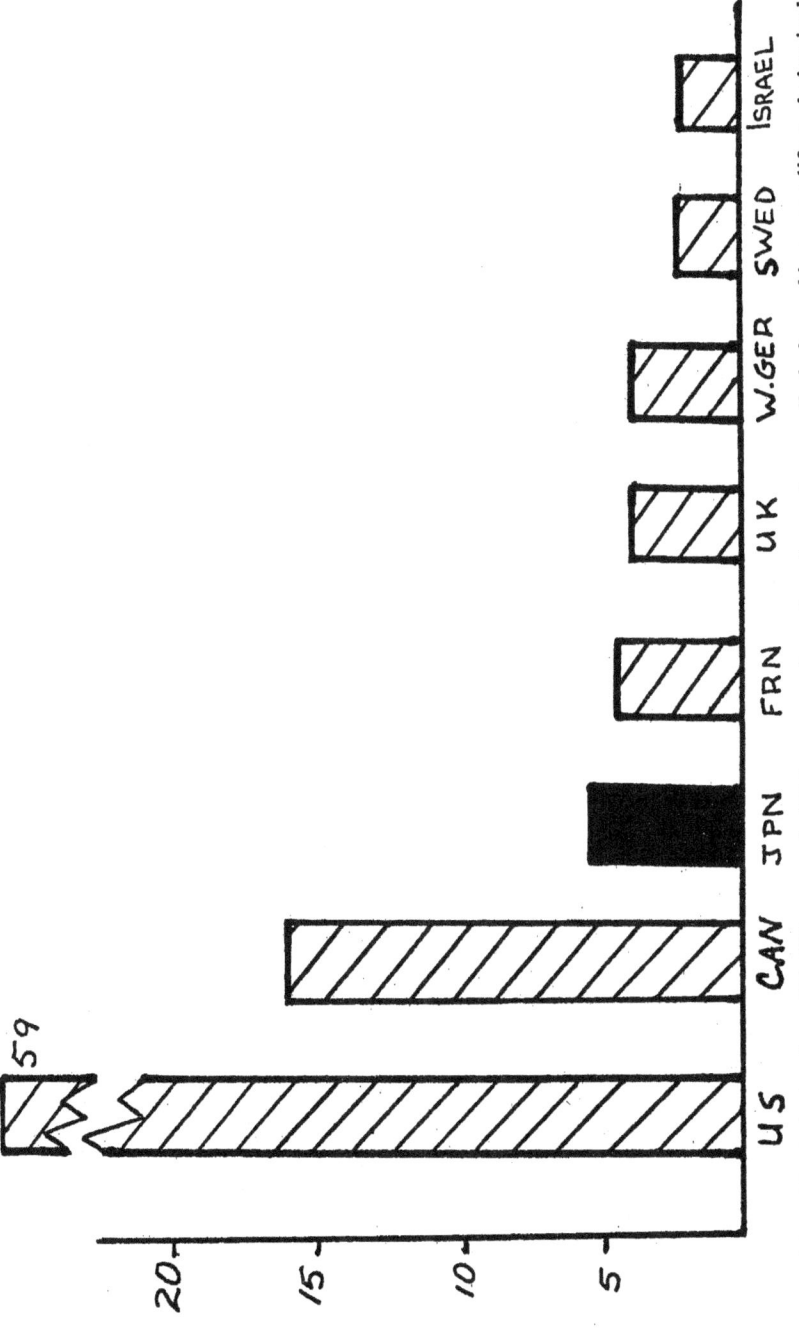

FIGURE 3. Examination of 2,000 papers in 20 important American journals, equally balanced between life and physical sciences, indicates that the Japanese are the third most frequent contributors.

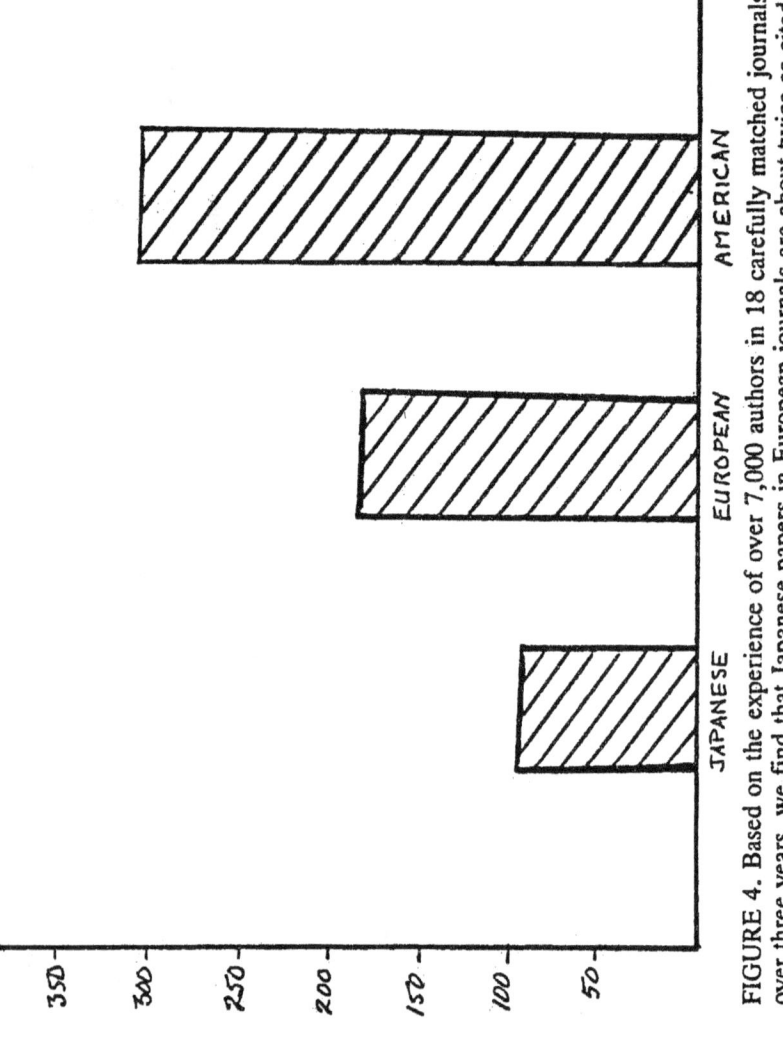

FIGURE 4. Based on the experience of over 7,000 authors in 18 carefully matched journals over three years, we find that Japanese papers in European journals are about twice as cited, and Japanese papers in American journals over three times as cited, as Japanese papers in Japanese journals.

Japanese papers appear in American journals, then in European journals, then finally in their own.[23] This time, however, two of the eighteen journals exhibited some anomalies in both 1984 and 1985 impact factors.

Japanese papers in the European genetics entry, *Molecular and General Genetics*, actually outperformed Japanese papers in both American and Japanese entries. Japanese papers in the Japanese journal *Journal of the Physical Society of Japan* (a nominally general journal in fact heavily devoted to solid-state physics) clearly outperformed the European entry *Physica Status Solidi*, but not the American title, *Physical Review B*. At first it was felt that these results were accidents of test construction. But on reflection, some underlying imperatives of Japanese research communication may have been uncovered.

JAPANESE IMPERATIVE 1:
GO FOR THE TOP, USUALLY IT'S AMERICAN

The winning journals in five of the six comparison sets share at least one characteristic: they are American. But there is a second more fundamental characteristic that all six winners share, they are arguably the most cited in their discipline. It appears that characteristics of geography and quality are routinely, but not absolutely, mutual. The Japanese may well be showing some sophistication here in a hunt for the optimum chance of being seen and cited. The European-based *Molecular and General Genetics* has, over time, done something few Americans suspected could happen. It has surpassed the American entry largely through a process of out-Americanizing it.[24] The slick production quality, modern molecular approaches, and timeliness of this journal belie its origin as the 1908 *Zeitschrift fuer Verebungslehre*. Its American competitor *Genetics*, has had the same look (for at least 30 years the typography and layout has remained virtually unchanged) and a far more traditional approach to the subject. Interestingly, *Genetics* finally in 1987 expanded to a modern, full-page format, largely under the influence of an aggressive new editor. It will be interesting to see if it can regain the characteristic place for Americans (first), and if over time

Japanese authors will come to prefer it, and once again perform best within it.

JAPANESE IMPERATIVE 2:
IF EUROPEAN, WEST EUROPEAN

The choice of a European solid-state journal for comparison testing was not clear-cut. A wide variety of individual national journals had sections for solid state physics, but none had an overwhelming lead in Japanese papers. *Physica Status Solidi*, an East German title, came closest to fulfilling the needs of the study, but clearly not the needs of Japanese seeking optimum citations. Japanese authors may have taken the same manuscript marketing approach to this less competitive market as they do selling advanced consumer electronics in the Soviet Bloc: while it doesn't have to be as good to be as accepted, there is also less profit in citations or cash to be gained.

JAPANESE IMPERATIVE 3:
YOU DON'T HAVE TO RUN THE STORE
IN ORDER TO PROFIT FROM THE
DISTRIBUTION OF YOUR MERCHANDISE

There are two models of Japanese point-of-sales marketing strategy before the American public today: cars and stereos. It is increasingly clear that the marketing of Japanese scientific papers is following the stereo marketing example. The car pattern is based on advertising the "Japanese-ness" of the product at a captive dealership. This way advantage can be taken of the public perception that Japanese cars are of superior quality, and no unfair comparisons need be made by a dealer who may also be selling Plymouths or Chevys. But Japanese stereo makers are not worried about having non-Japanese distributors. Typically one goes to Bill's Stereo or Jill's Video to buy a Panasonic, Sony, Akai, etc., not to a captive dealership. The same holds true in the case of Japanese scientists as makers of manuscripts. As journals are in fact distributors of manuscripts, Japanese authors have evidently come to feel confident that their best papers will receive fair handling in American and European journals even when those papers compete with the best American and European manuscripts. The Japanese realize that the world's scientific public (as opposed to the American library community) is not seriously disaffected with most American and Western European journals. They know that readers in all the world's competitive scientific communities already look to occidental journals for papers of high quality. The Japanese are not in any big rush to go through the expensive process of merging domestically competing Japanese titles in order to build Japanese-based international competitors,[25] when it is clear that Japanese papers are already earning good "citation-profits" abroad. In short, the Japanese have access to a fair, well-regarded distribution system without any serious investment on their part.

PRACTICAL RECOMMENDATIONS

While more research is likely necessary both to prove decisively the main assertions of this paper and to identify important exceptions, working librarians need guidelines now. Some recommendations are:

- Retain as many highly cited American and Western European titles as possible, even if this allows for only a few of the better Japanese journals initially.
- Add Japanese titles at the expense of Soviet Bloc or Third World titles when the Japanese journals have better impact factors. The Japanese will have some journals that do better in a number of scientific fields.
- Base campaigns for the funding of more Japanese titles on statistics such as those provided here. At the same time, run a search of your scientists' citations to Japanese journals, and vice versa. This might well provide a local argument that reinforces emerging national information imperatives.

REFERENCE NOTES

1. Swinbanks, D. "Japan Overtakes Soviet Union in Research Spending League," *Nature* 325 (January 15, 1987):188.
2. Anderson, A. "Japanese Research: Companies Go for Basics," *Nature* 311 (October 4, 1984):404.
3. Braun, T., Glanzel, W., and Schubert, A. "One More Version of the Facts and Figures on Publication Output and Relative Citation Impact in the Life

Sciences and Chemistry, 1978-1980," *Scientometrics* 11, nos. 3-4 (March, 1987):127-140.

4. Braun, T., Glanzel, W., and Schubert, A. "One More Version of the Facts and Figures on Publication Output and Relative Citation Impacts in Physics and Mathematics, 1978-1980," *Scientometrics* 12, nos. 1-2 (July, 1987):3-16.

5. Lawani, S.M. "Some Bibliometric Correlates of Quality in Scientific Research," *Scientometrics* 9, nos. 1-2 (January, 1986):3-26.

6. Company Advertising Release. "How to Get the Most Up-to-Date Information on Japanese Research in Seconds. JAPAN TECHNOLOGY Online: Now on DIALOG," UMI Japanese Technical Information Service, University Microfilms International (1986).

7. Editorial. "JICST Becomes STN-Tokyo Service Center," *STN News, North American Edition*, 2, no. 2 (July, 1986):1.

8. Editorial. "Nature's New Venture in Japan," *Nature* 328 (July 9, 1987):97.

9. *Japanese Technical Literature Act of 1986.* Public Law 99-382 [S.1073]; August 14, 1986.

10. Stankus, T. "The Year's Work in Serials: 1986," *Library Resources and Technical Services* 31, no.4 (October/December, 1987), pp. 306-320.

11. White, H.S. "Differential Pricing," *Library Journal* 111 (September 1, 1987):170-171.

12. Stankus, T. "White's Lesson to Librarians," *Library Journal* 111 (December 1, 1986):6.

13. Stankus, T. and Rosseel, K. "The Rise of Eurojournals: Their Success Can Be Ours," *Library Resources and Technical Services* 31, no.3 (July/September, 1987):215-224.

14. Stankus, T. "American Authors in Foreign Science Journals: Reviewing the Range of Initial Attitudes and Adjusting Library Investment to Client Experience," [a chapter in] Stankus, T. *Scientific Journals: Issues in Library Selection and Management.* New York: The Haworth Press, 1987, pp. 57-69.

15. Lubans, J. "Scholars and Serials: Will Electronic Journals Save Us from the Heartbreak of Scholarly Drivel, the Embarrassment of Book Budget Bankruptcy, the Halitosis of Salami Publications, and the Morbid Obesity of Our Collections?," *American Libraries* 18 (March, 1987):180-182.

16. Stankus, T. "Guest Editorial: Scholarly Serials and Serials Librarians," *The Serials Librarian* 13, no. 4 (Winter, 1987):1-4.

17. Corporate papers (1,945 of the grand total) score about four percentage points higher in American journal placement, much as hi-tech papers (2,162) do. It is considered that a link exists between these two preferences. Japanese hi-tech research and development have already proven financially rewarding, and are heavily underwritten. This helps cover the typically $100 per page charges that many American scientific society publications now levy. Academic (1,687) and biotech (1,470) papers are, on the whole, less well-funded. Academics typically turn more often (eight points) to European outlets. Biotech firms (438) appear to be a special case. Of all component groups, they are the only ones with a majority of papers in Japanese journals (by six points). This may be attributed to their basis

in very traditional Japanese industries such as brewing and fermented food processing. One gets a feel for this link in Jarvis, W. "A Brief Fermentation Guide to Biochemical Engineering, Industrial Microbiology, and Fermentation Literature," *Science & Technology Libraries* 5, no. 1 (Fall, 1984):113-122. Academic biotech departments are much more cosmopolitan, and export 63 percent of their papers, largely to Europe.

18. Garfield, E. "Journal Citation Studies. 24. Japanese Journals—What They Cite and What Cites Them," *Essays of an Information Scientist* 2 (1974-76):430-435.

19. American Physical Sciences = *Journal of Chemical Physics, Journal of Organic Chemistry, Journal of Mathematical Physics, Organometallics, ACM Transactions of Mathematical Software, Physical Review C—Nuclear, Reviews of Modern Physics, Journal of Computer and Systems Sciences, SIAM Journal on Mathematical Analysis, Review of Scientific Instruments*. European Physical Sciences = *Chemical Physics Letters, Tetrahedron Letters, Communications in Mathematical Physics, Journal of Organometallic Chemistry, Software Practice and Experience, Nuclear Instruments and Methods in Physics Research, Europhysics Letters, Mathematical Systems Theory, Numerische Mathematik, Journal of Physics E—Scientific Instruments*. American Life Sciences = *Biochemistry, Cell, Journal of Cell Biology, Molecular and Cellular Biology, American Journal of Physiology-C-Cellular Physiology, Developmental Biology, Environmental Mutagenesis, Medical Physics, Journal of Experimental Zoology, Physiological Zoology*. European Life Sciences = *Biochemical Journal, Journal of Molecular Biology, Experimental Cell Research, EMBO Journal, Journal of Physiology, Roux's Archives of Developmental Biology, Mutation Research, Physics in Medicine and Biology, Comparative Biochemistry and Physiology, Journal of Comparative Physiology*.

20. Journals involved are listed in triplets in the following sequence: U.S. title, European title, Japanese title. They are: *Journal of Applied Physics, Journal of Physics D-Applied Physics, Japanese Journal of Applied Physics; Physical Review Letters, Physics Letters B, Progress of Theoretical Physics; Physical Review B-Condensed Matter, Physical Status Solidi B-Applied, Journal of the Physical Society of Japan; Journal of Biological Chemistry, Biochimica et Biophysica Acta, Journal of Biochemistry-Tokyo; Journal of Bacteriology, Journal of General Microbiology, Journal of General and Applied Microbiology; Genetics, Molecular and General Genetics, Japanese Journal of Genetics*.

21. The ISI method of calculating impact factors takes citations found anywhere during a single year to papers published in the journal under consideration during the two previous years. It then divides the total number of those citations by the number of papers appearing during those two previous years.

22. ISI covered 6,935 papers. In this study 900 were tracked down, with 300 drawn from 1982, 1983, and 1984 respectively. While each year's sample of papers by Japanese authors in non-Japanese journals was matched for equal parts American and European journals, and life and physical sciences, the final calculations were based on a strict journal vs. journal vs. journal basis.

23. Averaging 1984 and 1985 impact factors together, and then expressing the

Japanese performance in their own journals as 100%, the following by subject journal triplets appear: Applied Physics = Japan 100%, Europe 232%, U.S. 310%; Theoretical Physics = Japan 100%, Europe 127%, U.S. 182%; Solid State Physics = Japan 100%, Europe 56%, U.S. 204%; Biochemistry = Japan 100%, Europe 90%, U.S. 440%; Microbiology = Japan 100%, Europe 126%, U.S. 450%; Genetics = Japan 100%, Europe 531%, U.S. 373%. Average Japanese performance in Japanese journals = 100%; in European journals = 194%; in American journals = 326%.

24. Stankus, T., Schlessinger, R., and Schlessinger, B.S. "English Language Trends in German Basic Science Journals," *Science & Technology Libraries* 1, no. 3 (Spring, 1981):55-66.

25. Nakayama, S. [Dusenbury, J., translator] *Academic and Scientific Traditions in China, Japan, and the West*. Tokyo: University of Tokyo Press, 1984, p. 109.

Asia's Other Sci-Tech Dragons: The International Publishing Patterns of Hong Kong, the People's Republic of China, Singapore, South Korea, and Taiwan

SUMMARY. The increasing importance of five, non-Japanese Asian powers in economically vital sci-tech fields is documented. The hitech and biotech output of these countries is analyzed for 1985-1987. Substantial differences in the nationality of journals chosen by authors from the individual countries are noted. Publications from professional societies and from competing for-profit houses hold sway over one another in ways that are characteristic of the given Asian country under study. The variations are predictable, and reflect individual national histories. On a broader geopolitical scale, it is clear that soon-to-merge Hong Kong and the People's Republic of China differ greatly on authorship in cosmopolitan outlets. Further, there is very little chance that a Japanese-led Asian Co-Prosperity Sphere journals movement akin to the Eurojournals movement is likely to soon develop. It is nonetheless possible to plan one collection strategy in hitech areas and another in biotech areas in a way that takes into account the more important idiosyncracies of individual Asian nations. Fortunately for hard-pressed library budgets, many of the most suitable titles are already likely to be in Western collections.

THERE'S MORE TO SCIENTIFIC ASIA THAN JUST JAPAN

One of the more remarkable findings in a remarkable bestseller by Brandin and Harrison[1] is that a number of Asian countries apart from Japan are becoming serious economic competitors of the United States in the fields that make up information technology. Current competitors include South Korea, Singapore, Hong Kong, and Taiwan. The People's Republic of China and a number of other countries will be joining the fray in the fairly near future. While reassuring the reader that the U.S. maintains a decent lead in basic research, the authors note that the current competitors — or "dragons" as they are respectfully nicknamed in the literature — share several characteristics that demand their being taken seriously:

Annual growth rates of nearly 10% in Gross National Product at a time when Western countries rarely attain 5%.

Long term strategic agreements between business and the national government to develop and sustain technical industries that are highly competitive in Western markets in both price and quality. This includes concurrence on subsidies, heavy reinvestment of profits, low taxes, high tariffs, and the cultivation of a pro-business labor policy.

An increasingly well-educated, highly-motivated, and generally company-oriented scientific and technical workforce. While many of the scientists and engineers will have received bachelor's degrees in their own highly competitive schools, a great many seek advanced training in American graduate schools.

A policy of monitoring scientific developments in the lab and in the literature as generated both in their own research centers and in those of the Western world. The goal is to incorporate as quickly as possible reported technical improvements into their own products.

A willingness to strike alliances with Western scientific institutions and firms. This gains access to new markets and new technology as well as an advantage over other Asian competitors without such an alliance.

Such a combination of features has already served to stimulate a tremendous pouring of scientific papers from these dragons into the international technical publishing community. Comparing 1983 and 1987 outputs, as displayed in the Corporate Index of *Science Citation Index*, we find that the U.S., West Germany, France and Sweden generally showed a 3%-5% average annual growth rate in papers. By contrast the dragons have a range of 33%-45%.[2] See Figure 1.

The American library and information science community can play an important role in any national response to the challenges

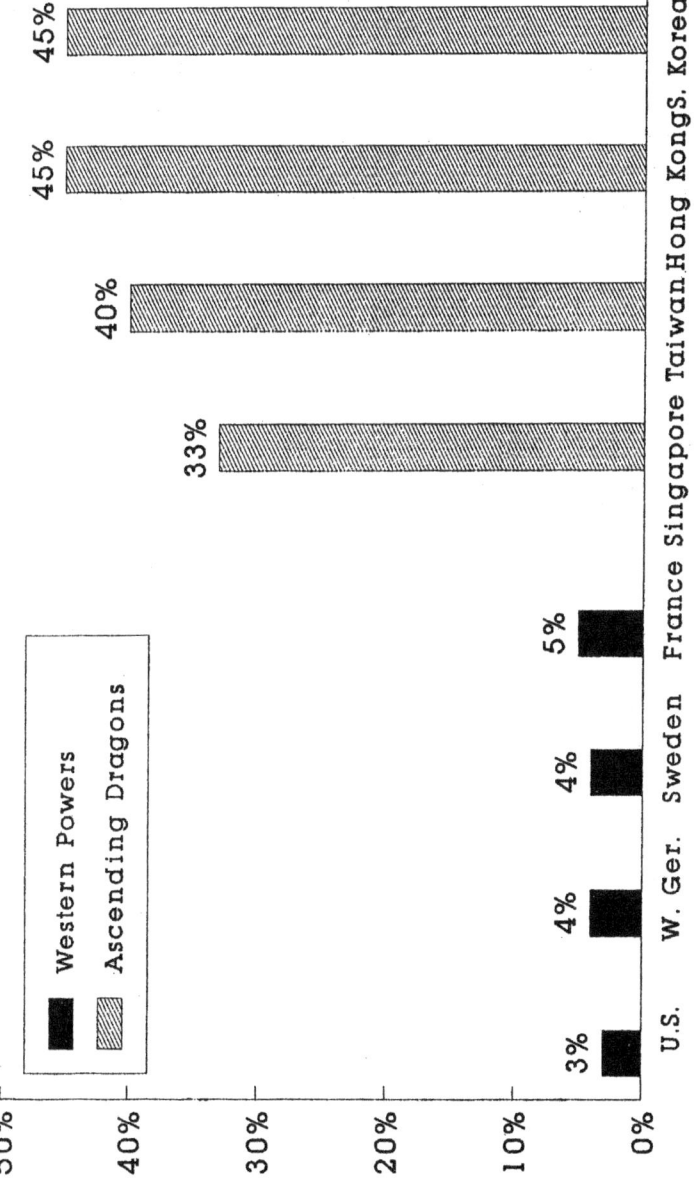

FIGURE 1. Annual growth rates in scientific paper output in long developed countries increase at the low single digit level. The output of the dragons, by contrast, grows explosively.

represented by these dragons. The following are appropriate actions:

Monitoring dragon literature to detect patent infringement or theft of intellectual property. While some critics too readily dismiss Asian successes as due to the imitation or stealing of American ideas, there has been some basis for their complaints.

Forecasting competitor moves. The first step in competition is knowledge of the competitor. American firms and academic institutions have a genuine need to know what is going on in order to plan any countermoves.

Identifying areas of possible business or scientific collaboration. The competitive nature of Asians vs. Asians, particularly when the competitors are of such high quality, makes recruitment of partners advantageous to both Americans and the selected dragon partner.

Bolstering sagging graduate enrollments in the United States. Americans may finally be waking up to the steady decline in the numbers of graduate students in the sciences and engineering, and the sad state of the facilities within which they study. But until this situation is actually reversed, a good supply of aggressive Asian graduate students from abroad may serve to stiffen the in-class competition for those Americans currently still there. Many a graduate school professor and many an ongoing grant is currently sustained by the presence and efforts of young dragons in training. This is particularly true since the number of graduate students from India have been declining recently. Moreover, the appeal of America as a permanent home for foreign-born talent should be maintained in this time of American scientific manpower shortages. Well-stocked university libraries are one item under our control.

Laying the framework for fruitful, formal participation in faculty exchange programs. American faculty deserve an up-to-date profile of their prospective sabbatical site. Conversely, exchange scholars from abroad should find their accustomed journal outlets available in the collection.

A number of other developments prompt our interest in Asian activities:

— Hong Kong, for example, is slated to begin merging back into Mainland China during the 1990s. What is the compatibility of current publishing practices within the PRC as compared with those of scientists in the soon-to-be returned territory?
— Recent studies of Japanese practices disclose a surprising emphasis on Western journals as preferred outlets for scientific and engineering papers.[2] Is this situation also true for the other dragons?
— Other current work has demonstrated a move towards pan-national merging of scientific journals among individual European countries resulting in consolidated Eurojournals.[3] Could Japan serve as a center for a Pan-Asian publications empire?

UNCOVERING NATIONAL PATTERNS

Using the Geographic Section of the Corporate Index of *Science Citation Index*, the entire biotech and hitech output of Hong Kong, Singapore, South Korea, and Taiwan was examined for the years 1985-1987. From the very large output of the Peoples Republic of China, the works of the influential Academy of Sciences in both Beijing and Shanghai, were extracted and analyzed. By amassing papers in computing, electronics, electrical engineering, automation, control, robotics, materials science and scientific instrumentation, a total of 2512 entries were gathered together to serve as our hitech database.[4] By consolidating papers in biochemistry, genetics, cellular biology, and non-clinical microbiology and virology, a biotech profile containing 646 references took shape.[5] Journals were sorted into the categories of not-for-profit professional societies and universities as opposed to for-profit publishers, and divided into geopolitical blocs. The latter included the U.S., the U.K., Continental Europe, and Japan. The division between U.K. and Continental European journals proved necessary, since work on Eurojournals showed that, apart from the efforts of for-profit Pergamon Press, there was little evidence of whole-hearted British involvement in the Eurojournals movement. By contrast no distinction was necessary between Eastern Bloc and Western European countries.

So few papers were placed in the journals of Socialist countries that exceptions did not skew general findings.

RESULTS AND DISCUSSION COUNTRY-BY-COUNTRY

South Korea

Hitech output in South Korea was dominated by an enormous reliance (62%) on U.S society outlets, most typically the publications of the IEEE (Institute of Electrical and Electronics Engineers, not to be confused with its important British competitor, the IEE, the Institute of Electrical Engineers) and the American Institute of Physics. British (7%) and Continental European (1%) society outlets fared rather modestly, as did those of the Japanese (4%). The showing of this last group is somewhat surprising in that the Japanese have a number of joint ventures with the Koreans and the countries are in close geographic proximity. While no national for-profit publishing group had dominance it is interesting that both the British (largely Pergamon, Taylor & Francis, and Chapman Hall) and Continental European (largely Elsevier and Springer) for-profit sectors, at 11% and 13% respectively, clearly beat major American counterparts (Academic, Plenum, and Wiley, chiefly) at 2%. (See Figure 2.)

South Korean biotech, by contrast, is dominated by for-profit sector publications (80% of the total). Once again, British (32%) and Continental (30%) for-profits easily hold sway over U.S. competitors (18%). By way of compensation, U.S. society publications lead the modest pack of not-for-profits at 10%. Once again, surprisingly, neighboring Japan scores only 4%.

Taiwan

Hitech in Taiwan features a strong showing by U.S. societies with 46% of the total papers. But even more remarkably, U.K. and Continental European for-profits grab more than a third of the remaining papers, with 21% and 17% respectively. Once again, U.S. for-profits and U.K., Continental European, and Japanese society presses do rather poorly. Japanese outlets account for about 1% of Taiwanese hitech literature.

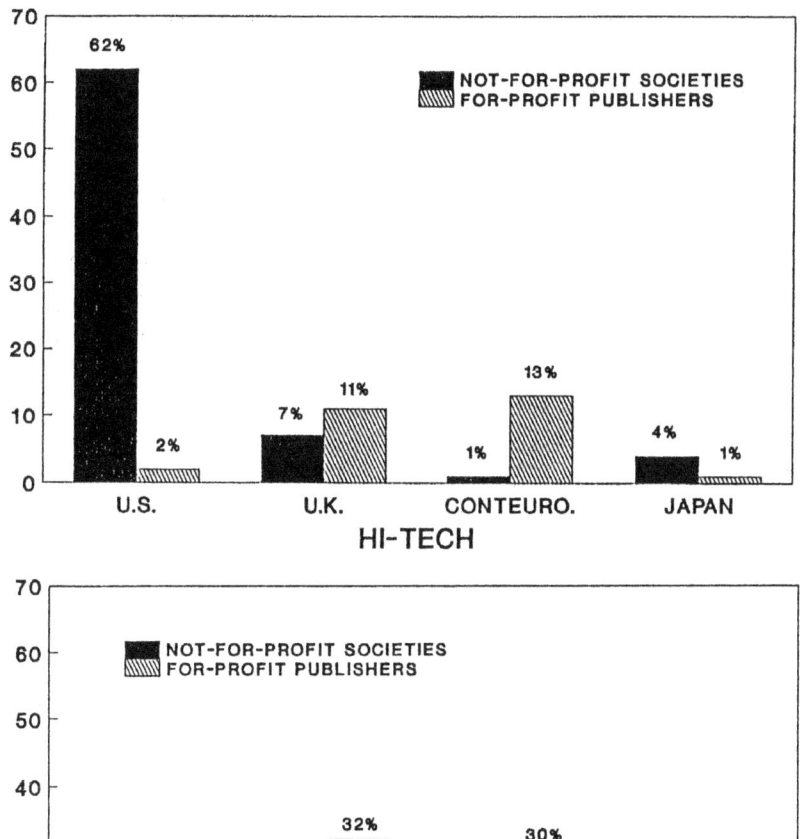

FIGURE 2. South Korean hi-tech is dominated by U.S. not-for-profit societies. Biotech is overwhelmingly for-profit, with U.K. and continental European leadership.

Taiwanese biotech is dominated by the for-profit sector, but interestingly in this case, U.S. for-profits tie with Continental European outlets at 25%, the British posting a respectable 17%. Among society presses, the Americans again lead at 14%, with the others trailing along at ranges of 5%-8%. (See Figure 3.)

Singapore

Hitech in Singapore shares the Asian propensity for heavy publication in U.S. society journals. What makes Singapore different from Taiwan and South Korea is that British society journals make a very strong showing at 21% of the output. Continental European society outlets account for moderate 8% of output, a figure higher than Taiwan and South Korea but not as striking as the British result. Japanese society outlets account for only 2% of the output. (See Figure 4.)

The hitech for-profit sector is led by the British at 12%, followed by the Continental Europeans at 10%. Once again, American for-profits do relatively poorly at 6%.

Singaporean biotech is unambiguously led by Continental for-profits at 36%. U.S. and British for-profits tie at 15% each. Society publications are once again a situation for a dead heat, both British and American outlets score 15% of output, with the Continental Europeans and the Japanese scoring very modestly at 2%.

Hong Kong

Hong Kong shows strong similarities to Singapore in hitech publishing. U.S. societies lead by a substantial margin, while British societies are themselves significant leaders over any Continental European outlets. The Japanese option is rarely chosen (2%). (See Figure 5.)

Further, British (16%) and Continental (15%) for-profit outlets substantially dominate American counterparts at 1%.

Biotech is clearly a matter of for-profit dominance, with the Continental Europeans (33%) and British (27%) clearly ahead of the Americans (15%). Unlike Singapore, however, the U.S. society press (8%) does not match its British peer at 15%. Both lead over

TAIWAN

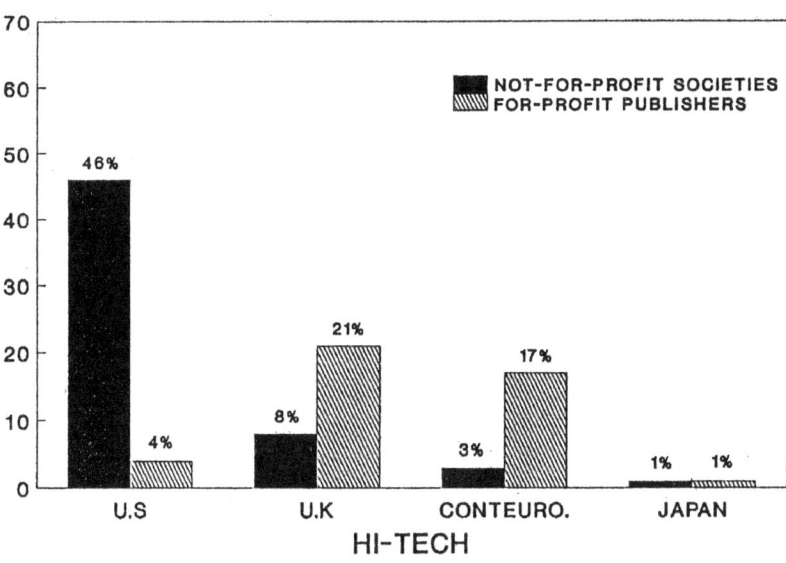

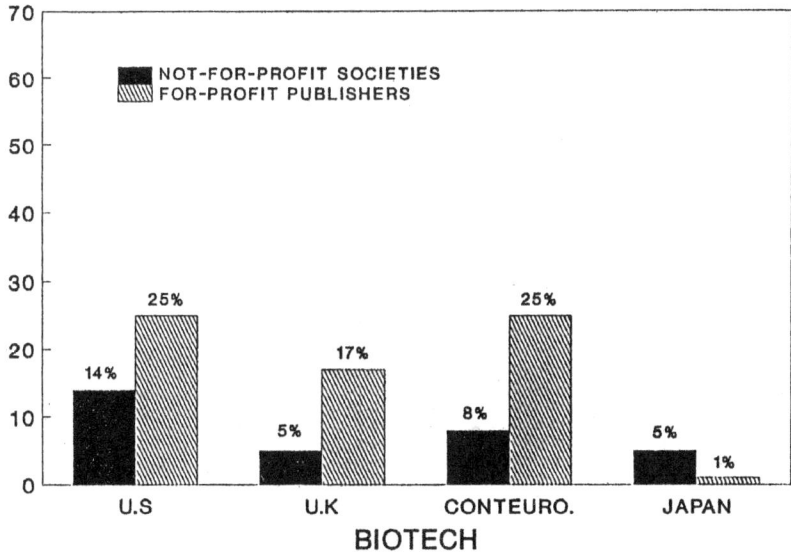

FIGURE 3. Taiwanese hi-tech is dominated by U.S. not-for-profit societies, although U.K. and continental European for-profits are significant. Biotech is heavily for-profit, with U.S. and continental European leadership.

SINGAPORE

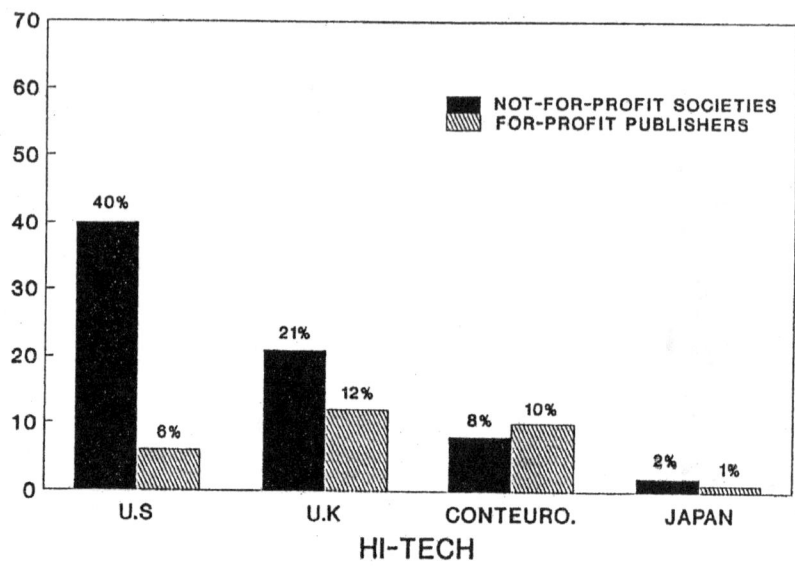

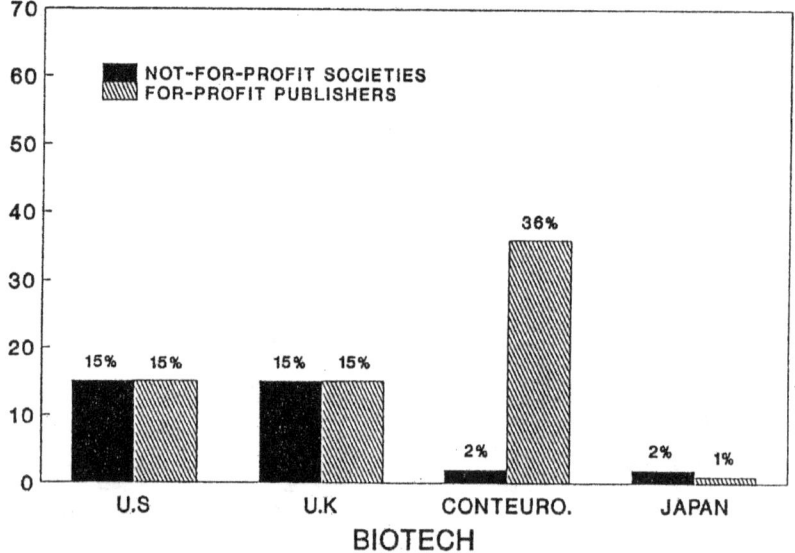

FIGURE 4. Hi-tech in Singapore sees U.S. not-for-profit leadership, but the involvement of British societies is quite important. Biotech is clearly dominated by continental European for-profit houses.

HONG KONG

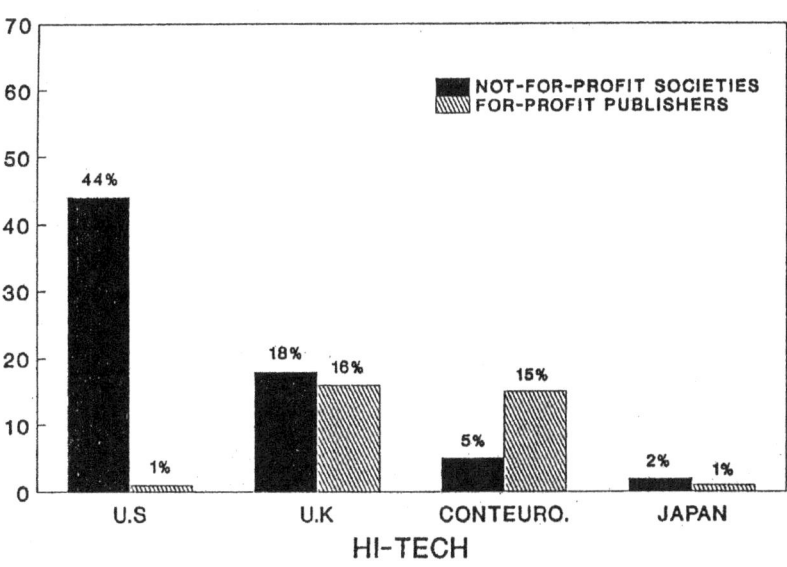

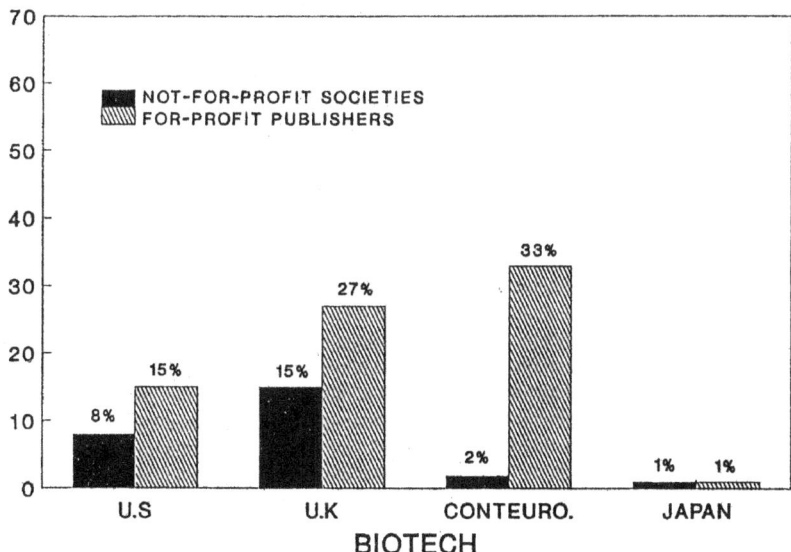

FIGURE 5. Hi-tech in Hong Kong is led by U.S. societies, but the involvement of British societies and for-profits is notable. Biotech is led by the Continental and U.K. for-profits.

both Continental European and Japanese societies at 1% or 2% each.

The People's Republic of China

The PRC has a pattern strikingly different from most other Asian hitech powers. While the U.S. at 34% clearly leads all other blocs of national societies, no other comes even close, with 5% each for the U.K. and Continental Europe. Japan continues its unremarkable performance at 1%. Even more unusually, Continental European for-profits are the overall hitech champions at 35% of total manuscript share. The British come in second at 16%. The Americans once again do poorly at 4%. (See Figure 6.)

Biotech is somewhat reminiscent of Taiwan. The Continental European for-profits are as always the leaders (44%), but American for-profit's score a healthy 25%. British for-profits manage a modest 6%, twice as much as their society journals. The Japanese attract a dismal 1%.

A further complication is the problem of indigenous publication. The four other Asian powers publish the overwhelming bulk of their most significant papers in internationally prominent journals. While the graphs for the PRC have been adjusted to match those of their capitalist neighbors, the mainland Chinese publish at least 40% of their hitech papers in Chinese, with only their abstracts in English.

A GENERALIZED HITECH COLLECTION STRATEGY

A number of tendencies recur in the pattern of Asian hitech manuscript placements. Figure 7 suggests graphically the strategy to be followed in terms of share of titles in the collection. In the discussions to follow we group the various geopolitical and profit/nonprofit journals into two large priorities: "core" followed by "marginal."

American society publications are an absolute must. Virtually all the publications of the IEEE and the more applied titles of the American Institute of Physics and its affiliate societies attract papers from every target country. Recommended journals include

PEOPLE'S REPUBLIC OF CHINA

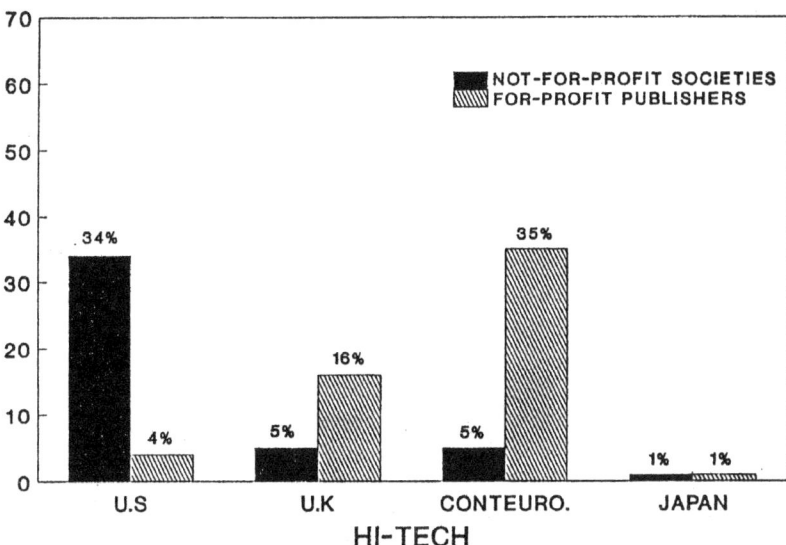

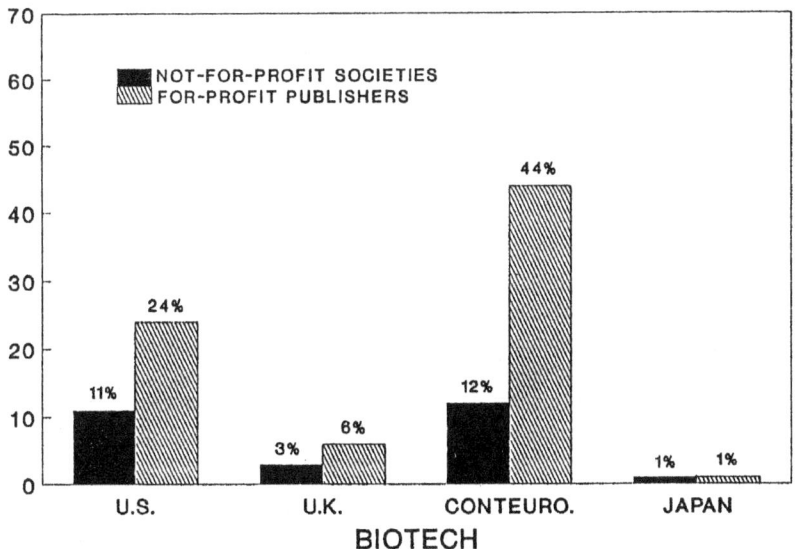

FIGURE 6. The PRC's hi-tech is most remarkable for the strong showing of continental European for-profits alongside the customary U.S. societies. The biotech picture is more typical of other Asians. Continental and U.S. for-profits do best.

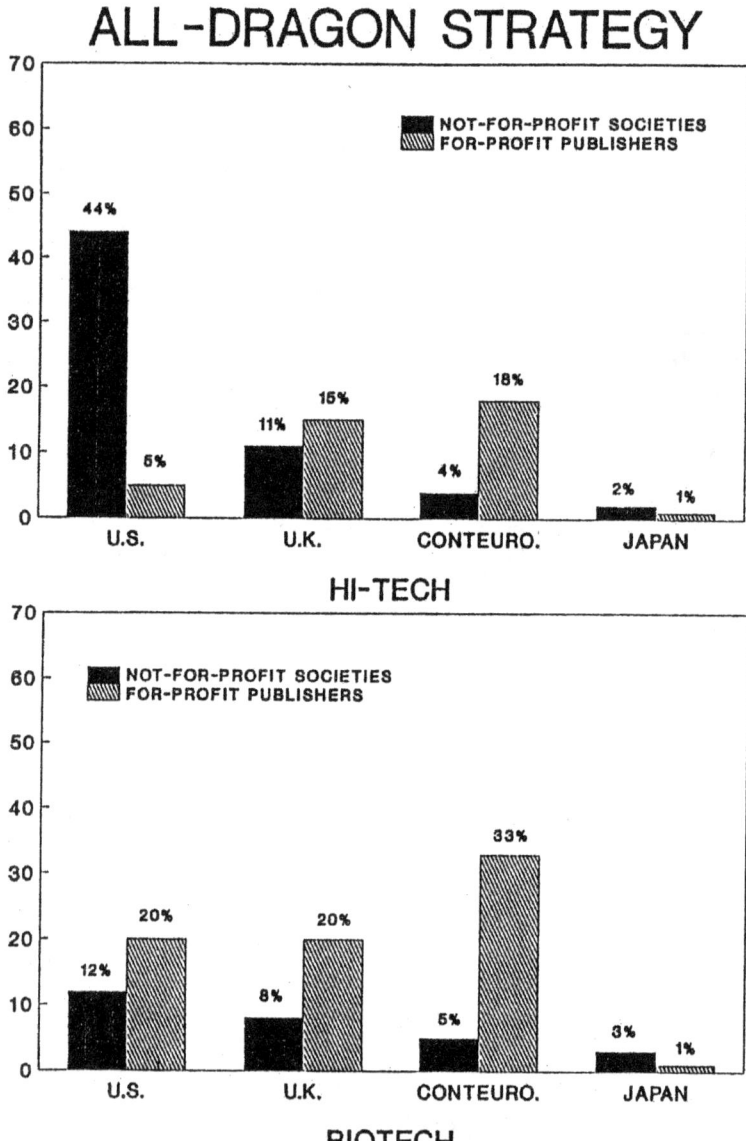

FIGURE 7. The best strategy for overall dragon coverage identifies the common leader among the various publishing sectors and buys heavily. Sectors of intermediate standing are treated more or less evenly on a funds available basis. In hi-tech, that clearly means that U.S. society titles have highest priority, followed at a distance by British society and both British and continental European for-profit titles. In biotech, the identity of the leader is also clear but not so dominant. Continental European for-profits do not stand entirely alone. U.S. and U.K. for-profits play a significant role.

stalwarts such as the *IEEE Transactions on Electronic Devices* and the *Journal of Applied Physics*.

There is a collision of three publishing blocs for next priority. With British society publications, you get the second most numerous outlets of Singapore and Hong Kong high technologists. With British for-profits, you have a similar situation for Taiwan and the PRC. With Continental European for-profits you get the first choice of the PRC and the second of South Korea. The results of this study and intrinsic qualities of some of the individual titles of the leading contenders suggest a compromise. Buy in groups of three. Effectively, for coverage that is both even-handed and maximized, the librarian should proceed positively on three representative titles at a time, choosing those that top out in citation data within each group first. For example, *Electronics Letters*, a publication of the British society, IEE, garnered the most Asian papers, and has an impact factor of 1.351. *Solid State Electronics*, a product from British for-profit Pergamon Press, comes in second in papers from the area and third in impact factor with .756. Third in papers and second in citation data (.96) is the highly specialized, but high Asian interest level *Sensors and Actuators*, from the Continental European giant, Elsevier, a for-profit. Additional layers along these lines can be constructed using IEE titles for the British society sector, British for-profits from Taylor & Francis such as the *International Journal of Electronics* or the *International Journal of Control*, with Continental European for-profits represented by Elsevier titles such as *Artificial Intelligence* or a Springer entry such as *Acta Informatica*. The beauty of this compromise is that with each added triplet, the coverage extends not just more deeply into the preferences of one Asian country but to three to five of them simultaneously.

The blocs of journals above are recommended as top priorities. A major relief for the American librarian comes from the fact that Asian favorites are already likely to be in the collection. The next categories of journals are recommended subject to the library striving for academic completeness. Collections in industry may not need all of them. While many of the titles mentioned below have collection value for other reasons, the yield of Asian papers per title added, goes down with each effort to include another of them.

American for-profit journals seem surprisingly marginal. A few titles were common in almost every country's output, most notably Academic's *Computer Vision, Graphics, and Image Processing*, and Technical's *Solid State Technology*. Wiley's *Software Practice and Experience* also showed relatively well. All three are more applied titles, and this fits the Asian pattern.

Also surprisingly, Japanese journals did not fare very well. Despite the high international standing and good impact factors of titles such as *Progress of Theoretical Physics*, *Proceedings of the Japan Academy*, and others, few collaborations with non-Japanese dragons appeared. In light of our general finding of an applied, practical bias in dragon research, it was not surprising that the most frequent source of those collaborations that were noted was the *Japanese Journal of Applied Physics*. Two factors probably underlie the Japanese disjunction with their Asian neighbors. The first is historical. Japan has militarily occupied virtually all of its Asian neighbors for extended times within the last century. While the Japanese often claimed that they did so to exclude non-Asian exploitation (of which there was a great deal), their rule was generally unwelcome. It was characterized by its own form of Japanese racist pride and suppression of local cultural and educational movements. Even today with its military spending long reduced to a tiny fraction of its GNP, and massive increases in beneficent foreign aid, Japan remains hostile to non-Japanese immigration into its lands. The second factor requires no historical insight. It is the fear of the other Asian dragons that Japan, Inc. will swallow them up. While eager to form partnerships with a variety of Asian and non-Asian countries, they do not wish to form collaborations that will aid their own economic demise.

The official journals of individual national Continental European societies, however, do not seem to have been the chosen place for contacting potential allies. The non-Japanese dragons do not seem to have developed an identity or sense of place that is comfortable in French, Swedish, or Italian journals. This is particularly so when there is a significant amount of non-English language content or cultural matters in those journals. Dragon scientists and engineers are, if possible, even more linguistically limited in European languages and uninterested in European institutions than Americans. The success of the Continental European for-profits in attracting dragon papers may come from the Asian perception of them not as European forums, but as another English-language forum which they can share with the Americans.

The indigenous journals of the non-Japanese dragons are rarely important, at least as evidenced by this study and citation data. While each country studied does have its own subject journals, some of which are covered by *SCI*, most Asian scientists seem to publish more papers in the foreign subject journals that compete with them. The PRC may well be an exception and a few words about its pattern, particularly as contrasted with Hong Kong, are appropriate. As with Japan, historical and current reasons may underlie our findings. Like many former colonial powers, the British had a particularly poor history of relations with China in the past two centuries. They literally promoted the drug trade in China in the 19th century and have continued to hold onto territories which the Chinese have regarded as their own up through much of the 20th century. True, the British contributed to the education of upper class mainland Chinese in England. They also set up a fine educational system to support the development of local civil, mercantile, and professional services in port cities like Hong Kong and Chinese ethnic centers like Singapore. However, they did little educationally or culturally for the overwhelming bulk of Chinese apart from missionary efforts. Those efforts often included a racist denigration of Chinese traditions and religious practices. Perhaps because the scale of the overall colonial operation was much more manageable and humane, the British tradition is not so despised in Hong Kong and Singapore. Singaporeans and Hong Kong scientists continue to have rather good relations with the British. They maintain many contacts with British scientific institutions and societies, and feel comfortable in British journals. But on the mainland, there is a lingering resentment among some in the educational and policy-making spheres.[6] Many mainland Chinese feel most unwelcome in British society journals, and are quite insistent on China's need to maintain its own Chinese-language journals.

Current events may change this. Hong Kong is reverting to the PRC. The British for-profits ironically led by that most successful of capitalists, Robert Maxwell, have maintained offices in Beijing for over 20 years. His success in recruiting papers from Chinese scientists may result partly from two factors characteristic of many Pergamon titles: although using British English, they lack obvious ties with the various royal societies and imperial traditions — and — they have worldwide authorship similar to that of any good competitor from Amsterdam or Heidelberg.

The political leadership of the PRC must realize that publishing a piece of science in English in a Western journal is essentially an apolitical event that involves no notion of submission to linguistic or cultural imperialism. Technical serials have nothing to do with certifying the ideological correctness of either papers or authors. The masses really do not go out to a journal of solid state physics and somehow come out with a notion that a given professor's observations on electron flow have meaning for politics. Western-style publication in English has to do with optimizing the chances for a piece of Chinese science to be seen and appreciated by scientists of every stripe. That is the job of a journal in today's world.

Coming from the opposite side, Hong Kong scientists must work to understand the mainland devotion to *Acta Academia Sinica*, and similarly locally venerated outlets. They must encourage modernization without insult. In their contacts with their new colleagues, Hong Kong scientists must urge the consolidation of hundreds of extant fragmented Chinese publications. Major goals must include the use of English as language of initial publication, the incorporation of apolitical editorial practices, and production speedup.

The leverage of Hong Kong authors in urging those changes may well lie in their superior level of access to Western journals. Influence over mainland journals can be brokered at manuscript submission time when a new Mainland colleague is eager for his or her first international publication. Moreover, the PRC perception of what constitutes timeliness has to be sped up. Hong Kong authors can demonstrate just how quick the international competitive pace has become. Lags in original journal issue production and waits for a translation undermine the desirability of PRC manuscripts. Moreover, many translation journals are essentially digests of selected articles, not cover-to-cover translations. Publishing in Chinese adds a measure of uncertainty to ever being translated in these cases. This can be eliminated by using English from the start.

A GENERALIZED BIOTECH COLLECTION STRATEGY

Geopolitical preferences in biotech manuscript placement offer some reversals when compared to hitech, but a number of historically and culturally influenced behaviors remain the same. Yet another reversal is that dragon authors appear to stress the more basic parent disciplines of biotechnology. This is at least partly due to the relative youth of the field and the fairly small number of journals covered by *SCI* that explicitly focus on the field. Despite these circumstances, a common, encompassing strategy remains possible, serving the bulk of the needs of coverage from the bulk of the countries. Journals explicitly mentioned in the first three groups are recommended strongly for most collections.

Continental European for-profits are the leading source of dragon biotech papers in four of the five countries. This includes Elsevier's *Biochimica et Biophysica Acta* and *Mutation Research*, and to a lesser degree, that publisher's *Gene* and Springer's *Molecular and General Genetics*. Once again, three reasons seen in the hitech situation, seem to underlie this preference. These include fairly good impact factors, the genuine lack of a distinctly European flavor or pronounced ties to any given national society, and their popularity as forum for American and other English language papers. They are quite acceptable even to the PRC. Despite their expense they are an absolute must for serious coverage.

British for-profits are first in South Korea and second in Hong Kong and Singapore. Once again, Pergamon titles are prominent, particularly *Comparative Biochemistry and Physiology* and the *International Journal of Biochemistry*. The very most outstanding papers appear in Macmillan's *Nature*, which seems to be preferred over *Science*, the *Proceedings of the National Academy*, or *Cell*, America's elite bioscience trio. American for-profit's share first place in Taiwan and second place in Singapore, and hold an uncontested second in the PRC. This is a significantly better showing for them than was seen in hitech. What is the reason? American for-profit publishers in the life and biomedical sciences have not been forced to compete with a mega-society like the IEEE. The IEEE almost single-handedly dominates the local American market with an internally well developed, highly responsive network of tailored subspecialty journals. The organizational and publishing structure of the life sciences is more fragmented. There is nothing like the IEEE publications empire in the American society sector. Two examples should suffice. Leadership in the key discipline of biochemistry is historically split between university (*Biochemistry*, American Chemical Society) and medical school (*Journal of Biological Chemistry*, American Society for Biochemistry and Molecular Biology) biochemists. Cell biology is split at least four ways among those loyal to a journal historically produced by a foundation (*Journal of Cellular Physiology, Wistar Institute*) *two originally from university presses* (*Journal of Cell Biology* from Rockefeller; *Cell* from MIT, but now on its own) and a fourth from a society devoted to all phases of physiology (*American Journal of Physiology: Cell Physiology*). This gives dragon authors no clear cut first choice of an American society title that will automatically carry the same universal distinction of IEEE titles. American for-profit publishers, sensing this opportunity, have simply fielded proportionally more titles in biotech than in hitech from which Asian authors might choose.

While a number of journals recently established and explicitly devoted to biotechnology were noted, most particularly Wiley's *Biotechnology and Bioengineering*, most of the papers found in this study were in the more basic sciences underlying biotechnology. While Plenum, Liss, and Liebert all have titles that attracted dragon papers, three titles from Academic clearly stood out. These included the well-established *Archives of Biochemistry and Biophysics*, and its companion for the rapid publication of brief papers *Biochemical and Biophysical Research Communications*. The surprise finding was the quick emergence of *Biochemistry International*, a title that competes head-on with Pergamon's well-established *International Journal* . . . noted above. This match between transatlantic rivals suggests another paired-off title addition policy: one British for-profit added with each American for-profit added.

American and British society journals are probably more important than the number of dragon papers actually detected (3rd through 5th place) would suggest. It may well be that next to *Nature*, the outlet preferred for the very best biochemistry papers would be either the American *Journal of Biological Chemistry* or

Biochemistry or the British *Biochemical Journal*. All three journals do have consistently better impact factors than the American and British for-profits in which many more dragon papers were found. Two findings are clear. The premier choice of dragon microbiologists appears to be the American Society for Microbiology's *Applied and Environmental Microbiology* and its somewhat more fundamental *Journal of Bacteriology*. The second finding is that the British *Journal of General Microbiology*, a publication of the Society for General Microbiology in London, follows closely, particularly in Hong Kong and Singapore. Once again, a paired British: American strategy is suggested when buying.

At this juncture, we have completed the clearly essential subscriptions. Unfortunately for American serials librarians, the heavy Asian emphasis on Continental for-profits has been expensive. Many of these titles have been dropping out of smaller American collections owing to their high price. It is clear that Americans served by those cancelling libraries will be missing many papers from these rising countries. The bulk of remaining titles are very likely to be in many American collections. Just as the geopolitical membership of the upper group within biotech was similar to hi-tech, but had a somewhat reversed order, so with the membership and relative fortunes of the remaining geopolitical groups. Their titles are recommended only for collections striving for completeness.

Japanese journals contributing to biotechnology compared favorably with those of individual European societies. Part of the reason for somewhat more mutual interest and lack of mistrust may lie in the lack of gigantic, highly developed, highly competitive biotech firms in Asian countries. While the effects of the unfortunate cultural history between Japan and its neighbors remain, ongoing economic fears within each country for their biotech industry — as opposed to electronics industries — have yet to develop. Moreover the Japanese have long been respected for their serious interest in various forms of industrial microbiology, especially in fermented foods. Basic titles such as the *Journal of Biochemistry-Tokyo*, and more technical titles such as *Agricultural and Biological Chemistry*, the *Journal of General and Applied Microbiology* and the *Journal of Fermentation Technology* attracted dragon papers and are first choices for extra money purchases. While a 5% marketshare of papers is by no means a harbinger of a Japanese-led pan-Asian biotechnology journals movement, some collaboration is likely to increase.

Generally, European society journals did poorly. As in hitech, these titles often have a high intrinsic interest for Western readers for reasons of quality and their own tradition, but appear to be unlikely to attract many dragon papers. There is not the depth of feeling that Hong Kong and Singaporean scientists have for British institutions and outlets. Moreover, as dragon scientists may have perceived, the continental for-profits have been quicker to go to English language publication and become a part of American reading.

Indigenous titles are important only in the PRC. Once again, the most marked difference between scientists in the PRC and those of Hong Kong lies in their receptivity to foreign titles as the principal means of communication of research. Our research suggests that at least 50% of PRC biotech papers are published in Chinese language outlets, and that in particular, only 9% of PRC papers, as opposed to a group average of 28%, appear in British journals of any stripe. Once again, historical reasons may well play a part, and once again, Maxwell's Pergamon titles (at 6%) do about twice as well as society-connected serials. A long-term resolution along lines suggested in the hitech strategy discussion may be possible.

SUMMARY

Through their choices of manuscript outlets, Asian hitech and biotech dragons are moving into the mainstream of scientific literature. These dragons tend to agree on the number one publishing sector in either field, a situation making its selection easy. In the intermediate priority range, there is some variation. Selection then becomes a matter of buying in multiples: a balanced diet from each of the major journal groups at each sitting. Most of the important journals involved are already likely to be in American collections. Surprisingly given geography, but not so startling given history and current economic fears, most Japanese outlets have clearly been bypassed by many other Asians in favor of Western manuscript markets. Japanese titles in industrial microbiology and fermentation constitute a slight exception. The mainland Chinese have a substantial way to go to catch up with their Hong Kong partners in terms of placing manuscripts in journals widely read outside the PRC.

REFERENCE NOTES

1. Brandin, David H., and Harrison, Michael A. *The Technology War: A Case for Competitiveness*. New York: Wiley, 1987. See p.190-196, "Asian Projects."
2. Stankus, Tony, Rosseel, Kevin, and Littlefield, William C. "Is the Best Japanese Science in Western Journals," *The Serials Librarian* 14, nos.1/2 (1988):95-107.
3. Stankus, Tony. "The Rise of Eurojournals: Their Success Can Be Ours," *Library Resources and Technical Services* 31, no.3(1987):215-224.
4. Hitech subtotals: South Korea=592; Taiwan=1053; Singapore=201; Hong Kong=194; PRC=472.
5. Biotech subtotals: South Korea=134; Taiwan=179; Singapore=81; Hong Kong=150; PRC=102.
6. Reed, Steven R. "As Xenophobes Posture, the Scientists Invent," *The Scientist* 2, no.10(May 30, 1988):1,8-9.

Greater Familiarity Will Not Breed Contempt: Canadian Scientific Journals as Economically and Professionally Attractive Outlets for U.S. Researchers and the Libraries that Serve Them

SUMMARY. A variety of data suggest that Canadian journals are a highly practical alternative for manuscript submission for U.S. authors instead of expensive European for-profit titles. The Canadian titles are just as attractive visually, publish many U.S. papers, and have a wider and more secure subscription base in U.S. academic and research libraries as a result of highly favorable subscription rates. While Canadian journals do not achieve impact factors as high as those of multinational Eurojournals, they tend to surpass the ratings of a number of individual national society journals and those of for-profit titles based in Europe that are outside the Eurojournal mantle.

HOW WELL DO SCIENTIFIC AMERICANS KNOW SCIENTIFIC CANADIANS?

Canadian scientists and Canadian scientific journals in laboratory-based sciences are somewhat familiar to the American scientific community, but are still the victims of some misunderstanding. The familiarity is understandable:

- Canadians constitute one of America's largest source of legal immigrants, this includes a substantial number of scientific, technical, and clinical personnel.[1]
- Canadians are the second most frequent non-U.S. contributors

to American scientific journals, and sixth most frequent to internationally prominent European journals.[2]
— Canadians are frequently members of U.S.-based research and professional societies. U.S. organizations frequently schedule meetings in Canada. Canadians frequently attend meetings within the U.S.[3]
— Canadian journals, particularly those issued by Canada's National Research Council, are strikingly attractive in design, and production quality. They tend to get noticed in displays of current journals. A look at the "Instructions for Authors" shows that many also have the attractive feature for authors of no page charges.

Yet, certain misconceptions may remain.

The first is that since Canada is still, in some American minds, a sort of British "colony," there is probably a British emphasis in journal pattern. (Informally noticing that there are many Canadian papers in American journals does not preclude the possibility that there are even more in British journals.)

The second is, that since Quebec is French-speaking, there just has to be a substantial percentage of Canadian scientific literature in Canadian journals that is inaccessible to linguistically limited Americans.

The third is that Canada is basically just one big Alaska-in-waiting, a kind of eventual member state of the United States. All good science coming from Canada automatically appears in American journals.

A CLOSER LOOK AT CANADIAN SCIENTIFIC PUBLISHING PATTERNS: WHY THE UNIVERSITIES MAY BE KEY TO FINDING WHAT IS GENUINELY CANADIAN AND YET NOT BASED ON OLD NATURAL RESOURCES

Can these assertions be supported? What sectors of the Canadian scientific community will tell us?[4] We feel that university output is key to understanding modern Canadian science. There are certain limitations on the power of the Canadian federal and Canadian corporate sectors to give us a feel for what is truly modern and truly Canadian:

— Canadian federal efforts have until very recently focused on resource-based industries: forestry, mining, oil, hydroelectric power, fisheries, agriculture. The success of Canadians in these fields, and of the Canadian journals that report their successes, is undisputed. But these otherwise valuable journals have limited appeal to U.S. audiences in modern hitech and biotech.
— Canadian corporate research is heavily influenced by U.S. ownership of many Canadian firms. Historically, most of the corporate research and development for transnational firms has been carried on in the States. Such research as is carried on within Canadian borders has a good possibility of being directed from without them.
— Canadian universities, on the other hand, are free from U.S. control, and indeed free from any strong control by Canadian federal authorities as well. The bulk of the universities are funded privately or by the provinces in which they are located. Such federal funding as has been made available tends to involve general scholarships in the basic sciences and engineering, and research in the modern laboratory sciences.

We have identified five important universities in five of Canada's major geographical and cultural climates. We followed their output for the years 1985-1987 through the "Corporate Index" of *Science Citation Index*.[5] The Maritimes are represented by Dalhousie University, Quebec by Laval, Toronto by the University of Toronto, the Prairie Provinces by the University of Alberta, and the Northwest by the University of British Columbia. We separately analyzed papers in hitech fields such as solid state physics, electrical engineering, and computing, and important biotech fields such as biochemistry, genetics, and microbiology. A number of facts immediately came to light.

As Figures 1 and 2 indicate, Canadians publish in a broad array of outlets. American outlets are generally the favorite across Canada, save as will shortly be seen, in Quebec. There are differences in hitech vs. biotech patterns, however. The U.S. society sector, particularly the American Institute of Physics, Association for Computing Machinery, and the IEEE, is far more dominant in the hitech sector, than any small cluster of biologically oriented U.S. societies are within the biotech sector. It should be noted that these hitech societies have a virtually unparalleled combination of reputation, manuscript capacity, and assortment in their extensive families of specialty and subspecialty journals. Life science societies are not so effectively gathered together under a few umbrella organizations.

The Continental European for-profit sector is second most common in both hitech and biotech fields. However, it should be noted that while the rest of these blocs are fairly stable, there has been some decline in the share in this sector in each of the three years. This is most notable in the biotech fields which started off with a 32% market share but are now down to the mid-to-low twenties in some cases. The British sector is third, closely followed by the largely not-for-profit indigenous Canadian sector.

Figure 3 indicates that hitech scientists at Laval send markedly

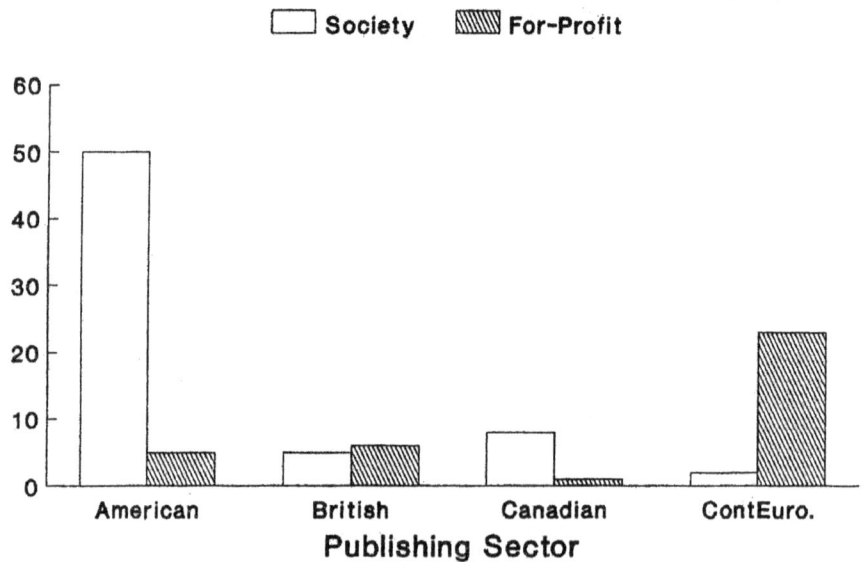

FIGURE 1. Outlets Used by Canadian Hitech Scientists

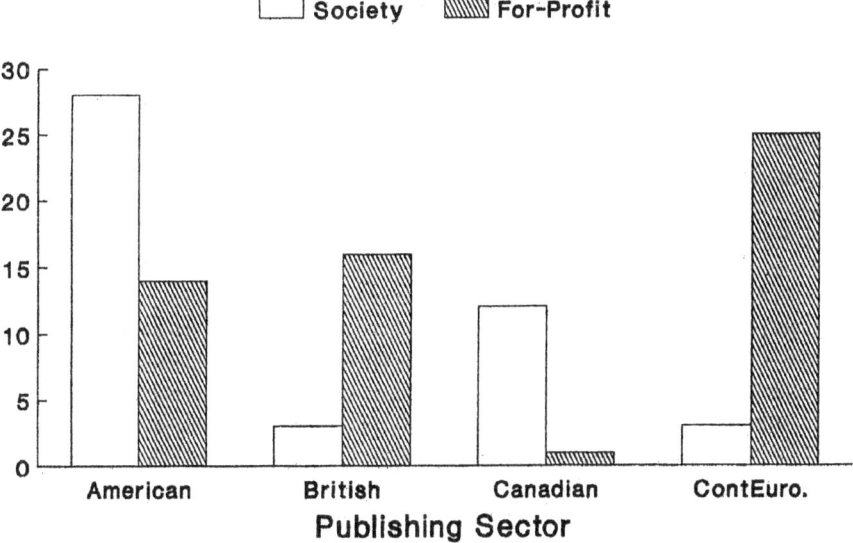

FIGURE 2. Outlets Used by Canadian Biotech Scientists

fewer papers to U.S. journals than do their Anglophone counterparts. They also emphasize Canadian society and Continental European for-profit journals more. Figure 4 shows us an even more striking differential in lower contributions from Laval scientists to U.S. biotech outlets. A heavy reliance on Canadian outlets is even more obvious. Moreover Francophone biotech scientists quite often turn to Continental European society outlets.

The role of language in these differences of pattern is interesting and complex. Canadian Francophone contributions to society journals from France, Belgium, and Francophone Switzerland are almost always written in French. But the fairly frequent contributions to Canadian journals from French, and sometimes Belgian and Swiss authors are written more often in English than in French! Most pertinently about 80% of the papers from scientists at Francophone Canadian institutions appearing in Canadian journals also appear to be written in English. Linguistically lazy Americans can expect to be able to read most papers in Canadian journals without any difficulty.

In terms of our initial suppositions it is safe to say that Canada is certainly not a British Colony in manuscript placement. And while the Canadian pattern is quite similar to that of Americans, the depth of involvement of Canadian scientists with Canadian journals is understandably higher and provides a diagnostically reliable differentiation from U.S. institutions. It is also clear that while Québecois scientists certainly contribute markedly less to U.S. titles than their Anglophone counterparts, most of what they do write is in English. If an American might be allowed to conjecture on a matter of some sensitivity, it appears that while French Canadians maintain more frequent scientific publishing contacts with their European counterparts than do other Canadians, this may reflect more nearly a sensible compromise than some sort of anti-Anglophone or anti-American sentiment. This pattern allows Francophones to maintain some of their continental European heritage—particularly the use of the French language that continues to be the medium of conversation and informal written communications in labs in Quebec and in much of Europe—while acknowledging in a business-like manner that, however unfairly, English has become the language of North

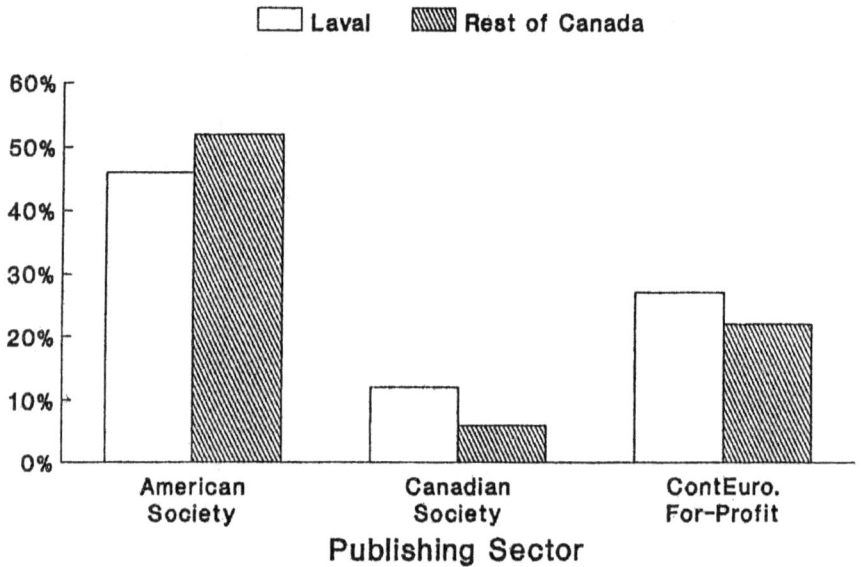

FIGURE 3. Laval's Differences in Hitech Outlets

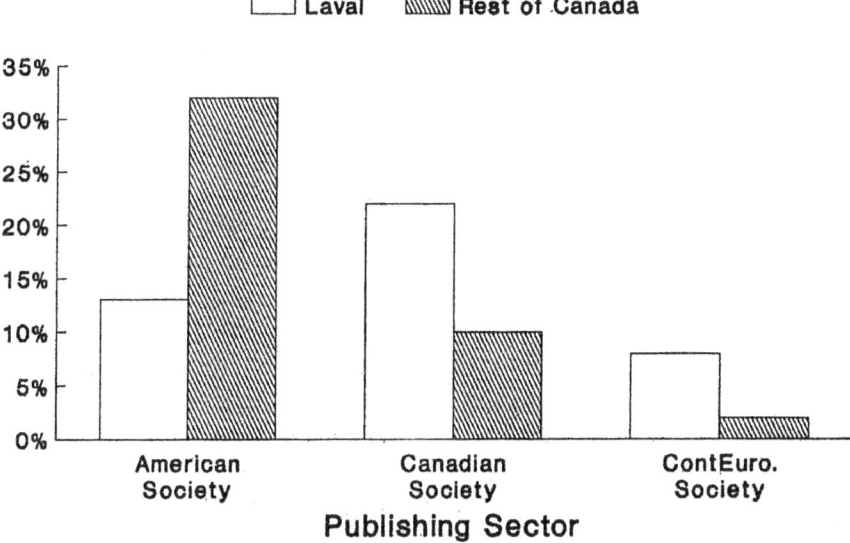

FIGURE 4. Laval's Differences in Biotech Outlets

American science in print. This compromise assumes a certain abandonment of an independent Québecois scientific identity, but replaces this with a somewhat greater commitment to definably Canadian scientific outlets. Canadian journals certainly make those who may choose to write in French more comfortable through the bilingual nature of their editorial instructions. This attitude of respect allows Francophones to exercise an option for the use of French, preserving a deserved sense of pride and dignity, even though for purely practical reasons, that option is currently less exercised.

This still leaves us with the question of whether the status of Canadian science journals suggests a kind of one way road to America for Canadian scholars with good papers. Does it suggest to Americans that they might just keep their own papers home or send them to the European for-profits? In short, is Canadian journal status just like one of the smaller European countries and most of developing Asia? Or do its journals have something special to offer Americans?

DISCOVERING ANOTHER ONE OF CANADA'S VALUABLE RESOURCES: ITS JOURNALS

In order to more closely answer these questions we directly examined several Canadian journals, and a number of their competitors. We set up a comparison of six sets of journals.[6] Each set contained for a given subject the leading American journal, the Canadian journal, the leading journal from one of the major British or Continental European for-profit houses, and a leading society journal from Continental Europe or Japan. Analyses for each title involved a sample including no less than 100 papers or three year's contents. The subject areas were mathematics, chemistry and physics, as well as biochemistry, microbiology, and genetics. Since there was a remarkable similarity of results among the subject sets, it was both accurate and space-saving to present the averaged results for the physical and life sciences in the figures that follow. (Indeed, the similarities of results for those two blocs could probably allow for generalizations on the combined blocs that that would be separately true for either of them.)

Probably the most widely respected and accessible indicator of quality of a journal is the impact factor reported for it within annual installments of *Journal Citation Reports*, a segment of *Science Citation Index*. When comparisons of impact factor are carefully made among journals of similar subject and function, the result is very likely to be reliable. For our tests, the leader was scored as 100%, with lesser impact factors within that subject graded as a percentage. By this test Canadian journals do rather modestly. See Figure 5.

Not too surprisingly U.S. society journals scored first in four of six individual subject comparisons and second in two. This clearly made American journals the overall leaders. Two Continental European for-profits garnered first places, resulting in their second place standing overall. Canadian journals came in third overall. Interestingly, their small margin of superiority over the individual national continental European societies was persistent.

A quick reading of these results suggests that the current Canadian path of exporting papers to America will continue for a long

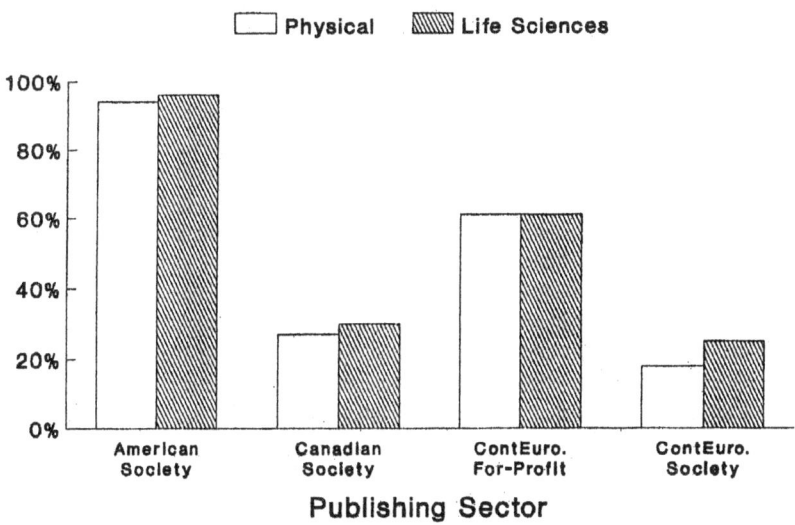

FIGURE 5. Average Score Over 6 Impact Factor Trials

time, and exporting to the European for-profits will continue in the short run. But a certain alarm bell should now go off in the reader's mind. Aren't the number of Canadian papers in the European for-profits declining? What might be the cause?

At least one cause may have been suggested when another measure of scientific journals was employed: relative price. See Figure 6. By this measure the European for-profits have the dubious honor of leading in five of six comparisons. American society journals came in second in five of the six comparisons for second place overall. Canadian journals and those of other individual societies cost essentially the same: about half as much as an American title and a third or less of a European for-profit. With such a sharp differential in price advantage, it is not hard to see why other outlets are gaining on the manuscript share of the European for-profits. Submitting to a journal your own library cannot afford to take is an awkward business that becomes more chancy as the scientist loses his feel over time for the papers it takes.

What about two other, interrelated measures of journal value ap-

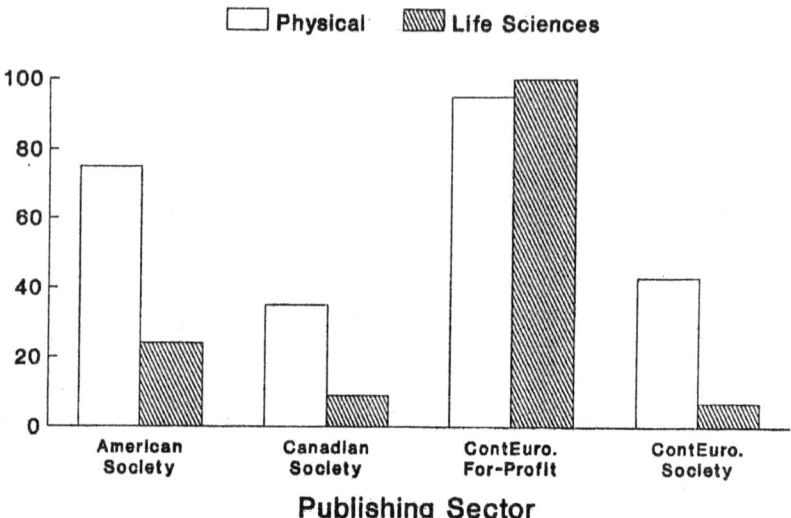

FIGURE 6. Relative Costs Over 6 Matched Sets

propriate to the special relationship that Canadians and Americans have in science? These are relative shares of manuscripts by American authors, and relative holdings of the journal by American libraries.

What is most remarkable about the share of U.S. papers in American journals is not that the bulk is American, but that such a substantial portion is not. See Figure 7. It would seem that Canadian authors are not the only non-U.S. authors flocking to American titles. What is even more striking is that the European for-profits do not hold a markedly higher level of U.S. authorship than do Canadian titles. It is fairly clear that at least proportionally, Canadian journals attract an equal American involvement. American papers are in fact, frequently the most common non-Canadian papers found in Canadian journals.[7] While the lead of Canadian life sciences journals over other individual national society journals is clear, the lead in physical sciences is not. It is skewed by the penchant of American mathematicians to publish in historically important European society journals.

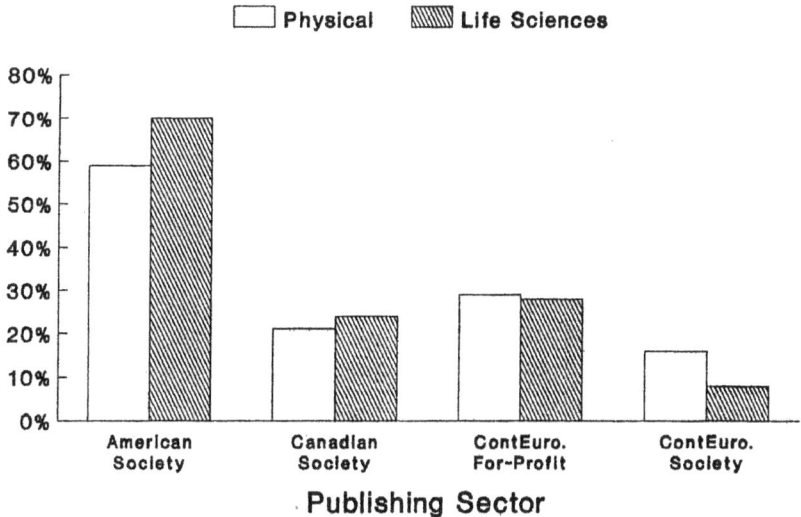

FIGURE 7. Average American Share of Articles in 6 Matched Sets of Journals

Just how available are Canadian publications in U.S. libraries? What level of exposure would either a Canadian or an American author in a Canadian journal enjoy relative to appearing in an American journal? As Figure 8 indicates, his potential audience would be second highest. Using holdings records from OCLC libraries as a broad, nationally-based sample, we can determine that Canadian journals in the physical sciences enjoy a clear lead over both the European for-profit and society titles. The lead is not so clear in the life sciences. This is partly because there are so many life sciences society journals to choose from that no consensus occurs on which particular journals are in second place, so to speak. It is certain from library holdings data that Canadian titles are at the least very competitive in this pack.

PRACTICAL IMPLICATIONS FOR AMERICANS

While it is certain that U.S. society titles represent the best outlets for American researchers and should be in every American library, it is just as certain that no American library could well serve

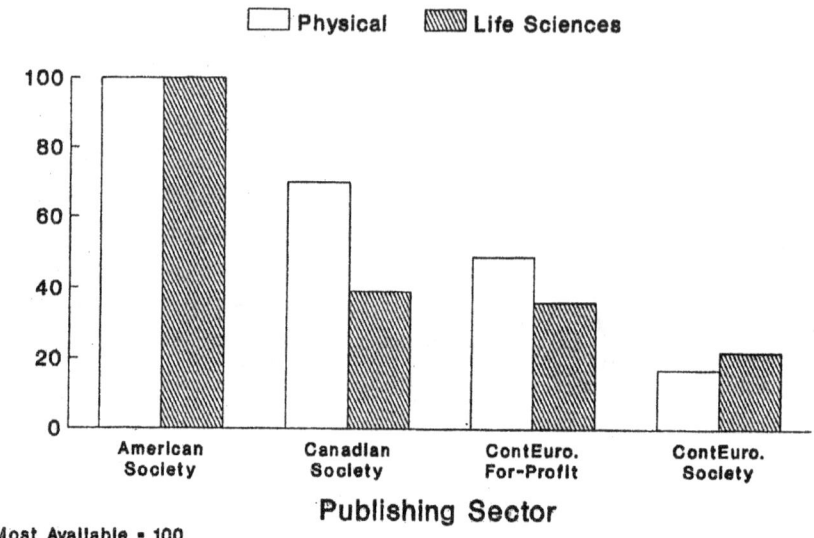

FIGURE 8. Comparative Availability Among U.S. Libraries

a publishing clientele with only U.S. society publications. For both coverage of important papers by colleagues and for outlets for their own manuscripts the clientele need other titles. The postwar dominance of European for-profits for this secondary market continues today in both Canada and the U.S., but the Canadian experience of a decline in involvement with these expensive titles may have a message for American scientific audiences. The day is coming when substantial numbers of American libraries will also have to cancel more European for-profits. Any librarians reevaluating titles should ask themselves and their clientele four questions:

1. Does the journal have a high rate (20% or better) of American papers? (Right or wrong, Americans feel that this is a measure of journal quality in many fields, and authors from all but the very strongest scientific powers tend to confirm it behaviorally by preferring such journals for their own best manuscripts.)
2. If the strong American presence is not there, does the journal at least serve to concentrate in a single journal — by official agreement or unwritten consensus — the very best work by members of several major Western European or competitive

Asian national societies? Is the journal, for example, a Euro-journal?
3. Is the journal widely held by U.S. college and research libraries? (Availability of a journal for interlibrary loan from a few prominent institutions does not constitute a widespread opportunity for exposure of a given paper to other readers nor allow your author to keep in touch with what the journal seems to like in its papers.)
4. Is the journal affordable from year to year? (If your library is having trouble sustaining a subscription, it is not likely a quirk, but symptomatic of what may be happening in many libraries.)

To date, it is clear that Canadian journals do 1, 3, and 4, at least as well as many comparable European for-profits, and surpass most other journals of individual national societies.

Of course, this study has limitations. More Canadian universities could be sampled. Different individual national societies or different European for-profits might be included in comparisons. The question of capacity is still unanswered: could Canadian titles singlehandedly absorb a migration of U.S. manuscripts towards them? Nonetheless, given the American crisis in paying for European for-profits, the onus of proof of clear superiority of the more general European for-profits that compete directly with Canadian titles now rests on those firms.

REFERENCES AND STATISTICAL NOTES

1. Table 40 of the most recent *Statistical Abstracts of the United States* reports that there are over 800,000 legal Canadian immigrants in the U.S. A conservative estimate from its section on technical and professional help suggests that there are over 10,000 scientific, engineering, and clinical professionals within this group. Canadian credentials in these fields are more readily transferable to U.S. professional jobs than are those in fields such as law or accounting. Interestingly, U.S. credentials in science, engineering, medicine, and even librarianship, are very much recognized in Canada, but both hiring preferences and lower income for the same job keep many Americans out of the Canadian market. American scientists are more likely to know — albeit unwittingly — someone who is in fact, a Canadian, in their daily work, even though like Donald Sutherland, Michael J. Fox,

and Peter Jennings, the "Canadianness" of Anglophone Canadians is rarely obvious to Americans.

2. Stankus, Tony; Rosseel, Kevin; Littlefield, William J. "Is the Best Japanese Science in Western Journals?," *The Serials Librarian* 14(nos.1/2):95-107. See Figures 1 and 2.

3. Examples of this can be found in our own profession. Both NASIG and SLA meet in Canada on a rotating basis.

4. An excellent and very extensive overview of Canadian science has recently been done by Earl V. Anderson. See "Canada Grapples with Its Science and Technology," *Chemical and Engineering News* 67(10):7-14 (March 6, 1989).

5. The study uncovered 3,663 papers: 1,720 in hitech, 1,943 in biotech. Growth in number of papers from year to year was very slow: approximately 32% came from 1985, 33% from 1986, 35% from 1987. While each of the five schools contributed a different amount (in descending order: Toronto, Alberta, British Columbia, Laval, and Dalhousie) each school's output was weighed equally. The percentages given to differing sectors of scientific publishing were calculated for each school, and then a group average was derived. As a practical matter, only Laval had a truly distinctive pattern. We attributed that distinction primarily to Francophone influence, although we realize that there are some who are primarily Anglophones on its staff, and that there are some who are primarily Francophone serving at the other schools.

6. Matched sets of subject journals are listed in the following sequence: U.S. Society; Canadian Nonprofit; European For Profit; Individual European or Japanese Society.

Mathematics = *Transactions of the American Mathematical Society; Canadian Journal of Mathematics; Inventiones Mathematicae; Commentarii Mathematici Helvetica.*

Chemistry = *Journal of the American Chemical Society; Canadian Journal of Chemistry; Angewandte Chemie-International Edition in English; Bulletin de la Societe Chimique de France.*

Physics = *Physical Review A; Canadian Journal of Physics; Physics Letters A; Nuovo Cimento B.*

Biochemistry = *Journal of Biological Chemistry; Biochemistry and Cell Biology; Biochimica et Biophysica Acta* (section on *Protein Chemistry and Molecular Enzymology*); *Journal of Biochemistry-Tokyo.*

Microbiology = *Journal of Bacteriology; Canadian Journal of Microbiology; Archives of Microbiology; Antonie von Leeuwenhoek Journal of Microbiology.*

Genetics = *Genetics; Genome; Molecular and General Genetics; Hereditas.*

We acknowledge that journals such as *Angewandte Chemie* are both society vehicles and yet distributed by European for-profit publishers. We used price as a deciding factor in how they should best be classified.

7. While Americans hold the overall title for non-Canadians in Canadian journals, the French and consistent exporters of papers like Japan and India follow closely behind with percentages of papers in the 10%-15% per issue range.

The Producer of the Article as Its Distributor: The Competitive Status and Prospects of the University Sector of U.S. Science Journal Publishing

SUMMARY. Many of the historical motivations for the founding of university press journals in the sciences have been diminished by advances in other sectors of publishing. Future prospects for this sector can be undercut by certain weaknesses that are still occasionally found. One is part-time management by full-time academics, another is some lack of sympathy or expertise in handling scientific materials on the part of professional managers. Nonetheless, a number of today's university-based journals are quite successful and offer price advantages over titles from for-profit houses. Financially pressed librarians promoting a revival of university science journals should realize that in order for these new journals to be economically viable and responsive to their scientific audiences, their managements—like the managements of successful science journals from other sectors—would probably have to make some choices that would make them less popular with librarians.

DOUGHERTY'S PARADOX

One of the most intriguing suggestions in the literature of complaints against the European for-profit science journal publishers concerns the following paradox pointed out by Richard Dougherty.[1] American universities give to European for-profit publishers tens of thousands of articles at no cost to those publishers, then buy them back in the form of subscriptions at enormous cost. Dougherty asks why more U.S. universities are not cutting out the expensive middleman and publishing these articles in domestic university press journals issued at a more modest cost. That such an obvious suggestion has not been aggressively followed up deserves an investigation.

THE HISTORICAL MOTIVATIONS FOR AN AMERICAN UNIVERSITY PRESS

The reasons for the establishment of university publishing houses in the U.S. include some of the following considerations:

- The states that granted charters to both public and private universities often mandated that these institutions disseminate useful knowledge to the general public, as well as educate the select few who actually matriculated. This was often accomplished through the publication, often further subsidized by the state, of irregular bulletins in agriculture and the "mechanical arts."
- Universities in cities served as meeting centers of educated men of leisure. The groups included alumni, local professionals, and after-hours faculty. Learned discussion groups evolved into journals for intellectuals. Since some science was part of the common core of a university education, it was part also of the content of either conversations or articles.
- Some university journals were designed as instructional tools, containing what amounted to tutorial papers and summaries of foreign scientific developments. The universities were a natural source of printed instructional material, and students were a captive audience for revenue that could be partly diverted to support journals. Moreover, foreign language scientific journals were neither widely available nor easily read by Americans even then. Capsule summaries were a unique service that only universities, whose strong component of foreign-born faculties and foreign-language-competent advanced students and librarians, could be reasonably expected to supply.
- Some university bulletins were built on the continental European model of reports of seminars or convocations. In these, the chairman or dean would preside over a series of talks to be later transcribed. Speakers were mostly senior faculty and distinguished visitors. Inaugural lectures by new faculty were included, as were the final dissertations of outgoing students.

— Individual, specialized facilities at universities frequently issued irregular bulletins intended for highly specialized audiences. In the last century, this meant bulletins from the principal teaching hospital, natural history museums, astronomical observatories, and field stations. The production quality and decorative aspects of some of these bulletins reflected a kind of institutional advertisement of the advanced scientific status and level of enlightenment of the school and pride in these facilities of distinction.
— There was a certain, nationalistic impulse among U.S. universities to field specifically "American" journals in virtually all the scientific disciplines as a counterpoise to the publications of the various royal societies from abroad.
— The last century produced a large number of colorful, strong-willed, scientific pioneers, who were generally university connected and who insisted on editing their own journal. Yale's *American Journal of Science* was for 50 years, subtitled *Silliman's Journal* after its founder and the founder's son, who, like his father before him, was a flamboyant scientist. Many university titles still prominently bear their founding editor's name on their covers.

ARE TODAY'S CIRCUMSTANCES AS FAVORABLE?

With all of these historical roots, it is surprising that there are not groves of prominent scientific journals located at U.S. universities, offering the fruits of scientific articles. But certain circumstances have altered the number and depth of their feeder roots, and this has affected the size and success of that grove nationally:

— While states still charter universities, and still expect them to perform some services for the general public, the university pamphlet is not one of the most common services any longer, save in agriculture. Today, universities emphasize services such as night schools, branch campuses, advising of state and local government, and contract research for local industries much more than semi-popular technical bulletins.
— The university-based intellectual or alumni journal survives, but not as a forum that contains much involvement of science,

or science faculty or scientifically-inclined alumni. First, the level of scientific background, interest, and working ability that can be assumed among university graduates is fairly low, in large part because of the substantial amount of mathematical background and technical language that today's science requires: a background avoided by most students not specializing in the sciences. Second, the science faculty members, having long recognized that their potential audience in these journals has shrunken, have emphasized publishing in specialized scientific journals, and pretty much limit themselves to that. Third, the publishing of alumni magazines has become a branch of the fund raising sector of a college, and tends to discuss issues like the financial viability of a school, the current admissions picture for alumni children, the status of a given endowment drive, where one's classmates are working today, etc. Only in literature and history do we tend to find the university "little press" generalist intellectual journal alive and well.

— There has been a huge expansion of the for-profit sector in educational publishing at all grade levels. It is far more common for an instructor to choose a title in use at several universities, than to mimeograph his or her own special text. Deprived of this source of hidden subsidy, journal presses at universities often foundered. For-profit presses further hurt some university presses that had a tutorial journal by introducing the "reader" composed of authorized reprints of articles from many scholarly journals, with commentary and translations. Once again, the question became one of avoiding the expensive duplication of efforts by having most instructors adopt a nationally available product. A further undermining factor lay in the for-profit publisher paying university faculty, who still wished to compile and edit new material, a better royalty than did the university for work on texts and readers. Universities frequently paid them nothing at all, taking faculty efforts to be part of their day-to-day jobs.

— Convocations and special seminars are still held at universities, some even largely staffed by a given university's faculty. But the role of the individual university in this *genre* has changed, with the university press having less of a proprietary hold on the printed proceedings. The school now functions as conference host more often than provider of speakers. This was partly motivated by the fact that with hundreds of universities, few individual universities could guarantee that sufficient reader demand for their own faculty's pronouncements existed so as to warrant printing them up. Indeed the natural way to develop a greater interest was to invite more and more speakers from outside the host institutions. Internal campus events became first regional, and then national meetings. Indeed many conferences have become based in city-wide complexes of hotels, much like ALA annual meetings. This has led to some curious circumstances in fields like Analytical Chemistry, where the (University of) "Pittsburgh" conference, as it it still called thirty years after its initial meeting, is now held in the Superdome in New Orleans. Proceedings of conferences are now also included as special issues of journals from many sectors of academic publishing, with the university presses not particularly dominant despite their historical head start. Dissertations of outgoing students are now handled by UMI's *Dissertations Abstracts* and on-demand reproduction. Initial lectures by new faculty are now regarded by both faculty and students as generally something to be improved upon, not memorialized.

— Bulletins from specialized facilities bulletins are still around, but the ownership and relative importance of those facilities have changed. First, the bulk of serious astronomical facilities are owned by consortia, and heavily subsidized by the federal government or foundations. Single university bulletins for these, with self-promotional undertones, no longer seems appropriate. Museums are still common on large university campuses, and irregular bulletins of very detailed or beautifully illustrated works are still their specialty, but the support for comparative anatomy, plant and animal classification, paleontology, and the like is not as strong relative to genetic engineering, superconductivity, or accelerator facilities today. Those new facilities do have technical reports, but sooner or later the information they contain goes into regular articles that are more widely read or into patents that can be quickly retrieved. Some university hospitals still publish their own journal, but few medical schools depend solely on a single hospital today. Each of up to a dozen hospitals has serious involvement in clinical training and research. Faculty develop a sense of loyalty not to the leading hospital, particularly if they do not do much work there, so much as to their clinical specialty. Submitting to another hospital's journal does not make as much sense as submitting to journals widely read by one's specialist peers.

— Americans still take an almost overbearing pride in American science, but they have already attached the adjective "American" to hundreds of journal titles. Given the longstanding leadership of the U.S. in many scientific fields, American universities and their presses no longer feel an urge to defend the national honor with the overkill of yet another "American" this or that. Indeed, a small intellectual or moral undercurrent is found on campuses that affirms that science belongs to all nationalities, and that nationalistic designations on scientific organs represents a kind of imperialism.

— Flamboyant personalities still abound among scientists on U.S. university campuses, but few still demand the right to establish their own university press journals as a means of stamping their mark on the field. Rather than personally edit a journal of a hundred papers per year, today's celebrity scientists will publish fifty to a hundred papers a year in the journals that define their field.

To a substantial degree, the decline of the university press in science journal publishing is a result of the success of the university's scientific graduates.

— The graduates of schools like Johns Hopkins have gone on to create Johns Hopkins' most serious academic rivals in both professional programs and in university publishing.
— The society journals that compete with university titles are underwritten by society members who are graduates of those universities.
— The pressure from university administrations upon faculty to

produce more papers has sustained the rise of the for-profit segment of journal publishing that has absorbed those papers.

Moreover, some university journals remain susceptible to certain weaknesses in the academic's way of doing business:

— Journals that were editorially in the hands of a faculty member working alone for all practical purposes got the part-time treatment that his or her schedule allowed. Alternatively, journals that were in the hands of an entire department were tied up in endless arguments over contents and procedures. Under either regime, regularity and thickness of journal issue frequently suffered.
— Many university journals never paid for themselves, and indeed many academics disdained handling business matters. Hopelessly addicted to subsidies, university press journals were often unable to bear reductions in university support in times of general financial stress on campus.
— Some universities have become so large and so balkanized that individual academic departments or research institutes have bypassed their own university presses to either publish on their own or have struck up deals with the for-profit sector. While deals with societies have generally gone very well, some independent departmental journals have folded because of an insufficient critical mass of publishing expertise, while some for-profit firms have effectively diluted the university identity of the publication. With each defection or lost opportunity, the resident university press itself loses some economy of scale.
— Few scientists have gone on to head university presses. The lack of a sympathetic voice in this sector of publishing has resulted in two biases. First, university press journals in the humanities and social studies numerically overwhelm scientific titles in stark contrast to scholarly publishing in the other sectors. Second, many university presses have come to emphasize book publication, a format much favored by authors in the humanities and social studies, but of substantially reduced importance in the sciences.
— University fund raising in the U.S. has ironically emphasized

the construction of new buildings, and the establishment of endowed chairs with which to staff them, but rarely has included money for the provision of a trust to secure the existence of high quality scientific journals in which the fruits of that construction and hiring are displayed before the world.

Nonetheless, there are some highly successful university journals of science around, some continuing in defiance of all odds. The times demand an examination of their performance, particularly as compared to competitors in other sectors.

WHICH DO BETTER? UNIVERSITIES WHICH FIELD SEVERAL TITLES, OR THOSE MANAGING ONLY ONE OR TWO?

The *1987 Index Guide and List of Journals Covered for Science Citation Index* disclosed 43 university-based titles from the United States. Our first task was to detect any "families" consisting of three or more titles from the same university, to see how they perform in certain citation measures relative to universities with only one or two titles. Our initial theory was that universities that handled several titles, whether through their university press or through coalitions with other publishing sectors, still tended to have more successes. Five universities qualified for "family" status: Chicago, Johns Hopkins, MIT, Rockefeller, and Yale, accounting for 24 titles. Twenty-four other schools accounted for the remaining 29. Two citation measures were employed. Both involved the impact factor, a quality indicator that is essentially average citations per recent paper.

As a first step we identified the subject field of each journal, and determined the impact factor leader for that field. We then compared it to the impact factor of the university press title, and expressed the result as a percentage of the leader. Families of university journals had their percentages further averaged for a family average. Those university titles that were not part of a family had the same procedure followed except that all non-family percentages were then averaged together.

The results are clear. (See Figures 1 and 2.) The mean percentage

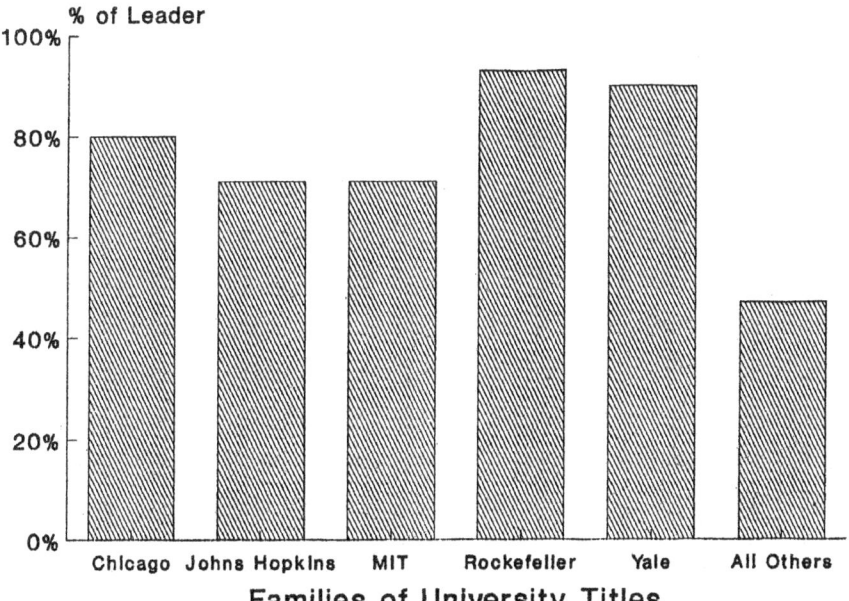

FIGURE 1. Average Impact Factors

scores for multi-title universities range from 71% to 93%. The average for the rest was 47%. Both groups had impact factor leaders. The multi-title group of five schools had 13, while the remaining 22 schools accounted for four.

Another approach was to rank the journals much like children in a class. For example a child who is second in a class of five could be given a score of 80 on a hundred point scale. Impact factors were once again used as rank indicators. This time the scores for the multi-title group of 5 schools ranged from 80% to 99%. The comparison group had 67%. The gap narrowed, but is still significant.

It is arguable that schools like Chicago, Johns Hopkins, MIT, Rockefeller, and Yale represent a scientifically unbeatable team. But schools like Berkeley, Cornell, Duke, Princeton, and Michigan, all non-family entries in our comparisons, are certainly elite as well. It is safe to say that there is at least some basis for crediting the notion of a superior performance when a more experienced, or more heavily committed, or more scientifically sympathetic press management is involved.

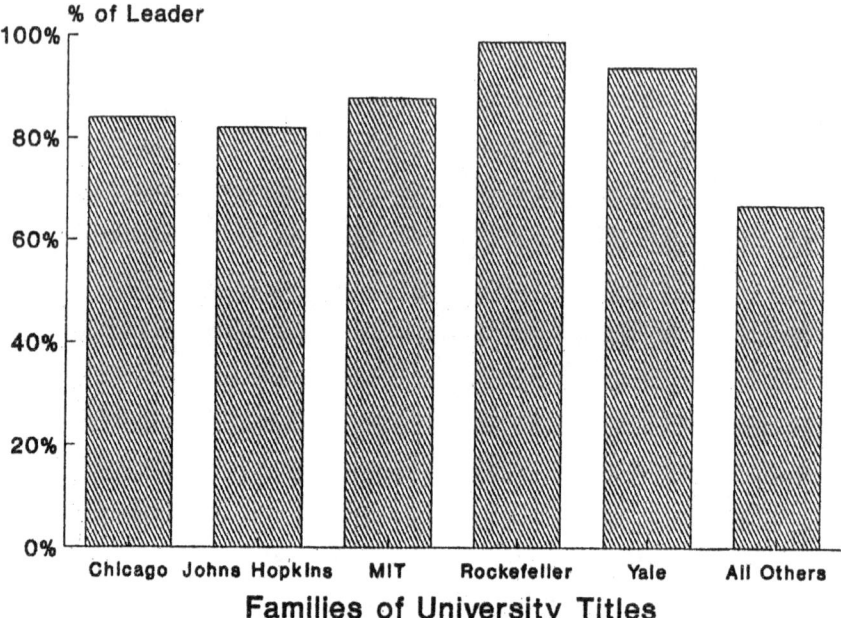

FIGURE 2. Average "Class Rank"

COMPARING U.S. UNIVERSITY PRESS PERFORMANCE AGAINST EUROPEAN FOR-PROFIT COMPETITORS

Twenty of the 42 university titles had direct competition from the European for-profit sector. We compared impact-factors, a quality indicator based on average rates of citation to recent articles. As Figure 3 indicates the European for-profits won six of the contests, and the American university titles, fourteen. The margin of victory for the university titles was almost 50%. This would seem decisive, save that in their victories, the European for-profits had even larger margins, 67%. The European for-profits are not constitutionally of low quality, they are merely being beaten by a very high quality U.S. competitor most of the time.

Another comparison, cost of subscription, is truly of no contest. Every U.S. university press title was substantially cheaper than its

European for-profit counterpart, costing only about a third as much. See Figure 4.

Figure 5 displays a natural corollary. U.S. libraries tend to take American university press titles at a substantially higher rate than the European for-profit competitors of those journals. Using OCLC holdings records, we noted that in fifteen of the twenty comparisons, the U.S. title was more widely circulated. The margin was some 67% greater circulation. Five European for-profits beat out the American titles with an average margin of 40% more locations.

WHAT IS NEEDED TO EXPAND ON TODAY'S SUCCESS STORIES?

Dougherty's dream seems desirable: the current university press participants seem so successful. What is holding them back from greater success? In the author's opinion, several steps need to be taken before new journals are launched:

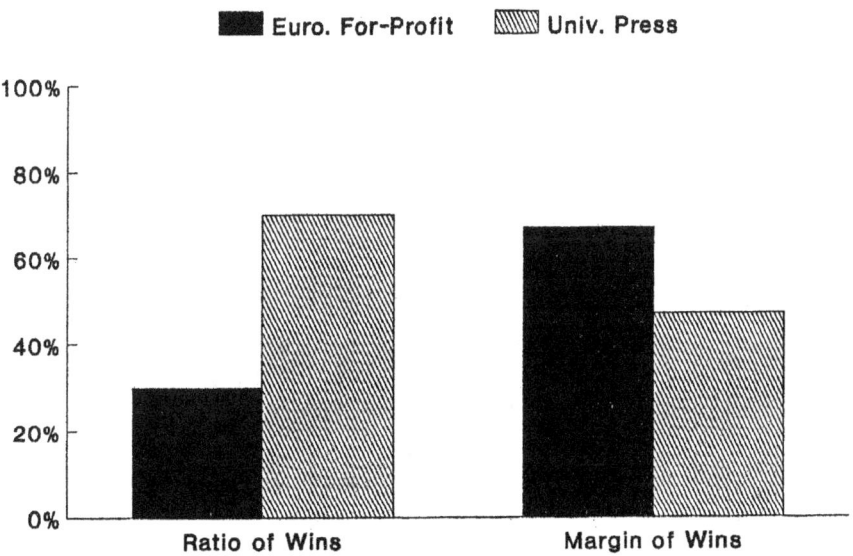

FIGURE 3. Impact Factors from Competing Sectors

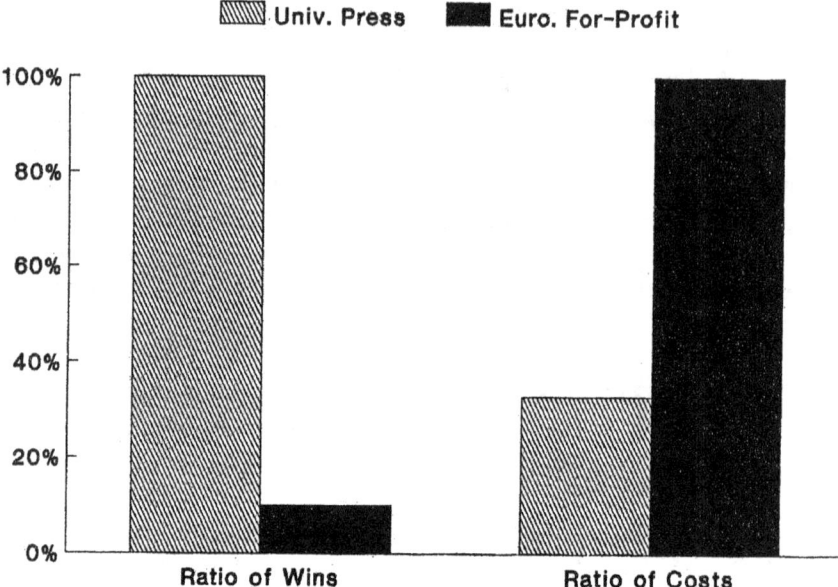

FIGURE 4. Costs from Competing Sectors

— Professional managers must have control over deadlines, production, distribution, and cash management. Let the faculty editors control the choice of content, but let there be content delivered on time! As a shield against fluctuations in university subsidies, journals should be expected to pay for themselves within a few years.
— If the editorial control is largely in the hands of a single academic department, that department should have a national reputation for both the quality of its own papers and for fairness in dealing with papers from outside that institution. As a practical matter, it is often wise to let local faculty serve as first readers of papers and then let outsiders on an editorial board serve as second and third referees. This gives the journal the advantages of both speed and fairness. Duty on the editorial board by home campus scientists should be a matter of agreed-upon language in their contract and included in their performance evaluations. No one should be coerced into serving, but nei-

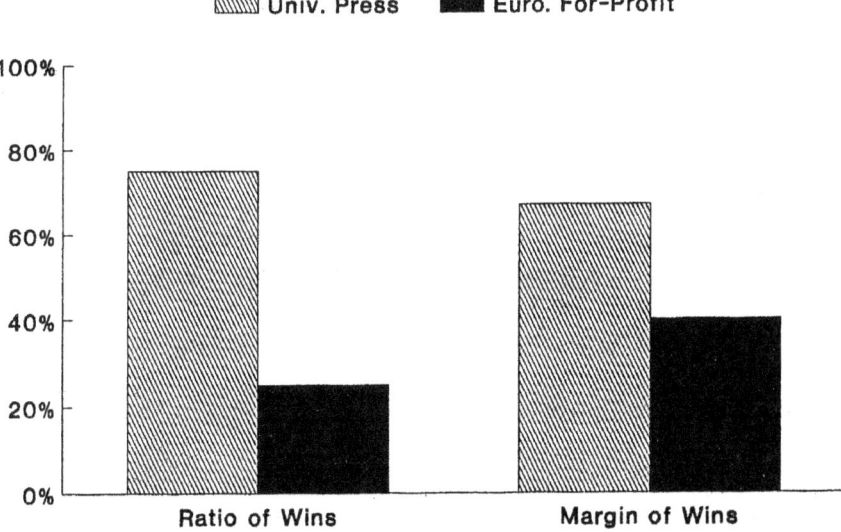

FIGURE 5. Holdings in U.S. Libraries Compared

ther should any name be included on the masthead automatically or for purely cosmetic reasons. Being listed should mean being seriously involved.
— Consortial arrangements can work under two circumstances. When the parties involved are few, they must be both rich and administratively committed for the long haul. When the parties are numerous, the lack of performance of one or two members is more likely to be annoying than fatal. There should be no absolute restriction on authorship from member institutions save that the papers are of sufficient quality. The misplaced notion that one cannot publish in his own journal, particularly ironic if the works are very good, contains the seeds of journal suicide. Of course, hogging of the space by one institution to the exclusion of the others is at least tactless.
— Deals with societies to co-publish a journal seem to be particularly advantageous. There are added benefits when, instead of starting yet another journal in a crowded field, a university press takes over a struggling title from a society. The usual

tradeoff is that the society has the subscribers but not the stability of production, distribution, and financial management necessary for smooth operation. Costs can be spread out over several titles when dealing with a university press with more than one title.

WILL SUCCESS AMONG SCIENTISTS SPOIL THE UNIVERSITY PRESS JOURNAL FOR LIBRARIANS?

A secret fear of some librarians is that should university press journals lose their amateur status and act in a business-like manner, they will soon take on some of the undesirable characteristics of titles from other sectors of publishing. Librarians will have to endure some compromises if they are to have truly viable university titles, and encourage the expansion of this sector:

— While librarians would prefer fatter issues rather than more frequent issues — fewer issues are easier to track and process, and have lower postage costs — they should accept increased frequency if it is honestly sustainable. They despise irregular and/or dubiously doubled-up issues.
— Librarians should probably support improvements in the variety of features included in a journal, even at some added cost. In exchange there should be an abandonment of frequent title changes, and renunciation of a functional fission of the journal into a newsletter, a brief communications vehicle, a review papers edition, a separately sold convention program with abstracts, etc. It is both cheaper and more convenient for the library to pay a little more for a single omnibus journal than to handle several separately issued daughter journals, even if the combined cover price initially equals only that of the consolidated mother journal. Librarians have come to realize that such initial "bargains" tend not to stay that way. On the other hand, librarians must realize that if they resist the division of the journal along subject subspecialties, it is extremely likely that the alert and flexible for-profit sector will seize the oppor-

tunity to satisfy the subspecialists. The library community will probably end up taking more and more expensive subspecialty journals from the for-profit sector, if it does not respond to this scientifically natural urge.

—Librarians should prefer to have no page charges for authors as a kind of subsidy, as opposed to allowing special prices for individual subscribers—a favorite demand of societies in collaboration with publishers. The depth and ultimate strength of loyalty to a journal probably derives more from its being a competitive outlet rather than a cheaper piece of personal reading. (Time tends to enhance dependency on library holdings over personal holdings, anyway.) After a few years of coping with an accumulation of loose back issues, the wise scientific researcher realizes that he or she is likely to have to use the library after all in order to find past papers. Moreover, a lower price for libraries helps the future of the journal by making it more successful with younger scientists, graduate students, the small liberal arts colleges that serve as graduate school talent incubators, and with the Third World—all subscribers with fewer resources and less adventurous spending habits than established scientists and very large graduate schools. All of these represent future sources of the manuscripts that are every bit as necessary as the subscriptions to sustain a viable journal.

Probably the most important take-home lesson for librarians is that not even university press titles will represent a free lunch. Librarians stand to gain some cost advantages, but must be careful not to penny-wise carp about inevitable cost increases or undercut the journals—as they have so often done in recent years—by interlibrary photocopying beyond fair use. If they are truly serious, librarians must put reliable subscriptions where their mouths are.

REFERENCE

1. Dougherty, Richard M., and Johnson, Brenda L. "Periodical Price Escalation: a Library Response," *Library Journal* 113, no.9(May 15,1988):27-29.

THEME THREE

Technology and Competition are Improving Today's Science Journal

I regularly receive extremely useful hints on processing journals from my colleagues in serials. I am often informed about price increases from cross-town librarians before these increases ever show up on a jobber's printout. But I get too many puzzled looks when I ask my professional friends their reaction to some important changes, whether of new features or new subject orientations in the journals themselves. This is certainly not because my colleagues are uninterested or fundamentally incapable of appreciating them. It is just that actually opening up the journals slows down the check-in and pay-out that still constitutes so much of their day-to-day routine. I am unusually lucky in that the division of labor at my particular institution allows me to stop and actually smell the roses of my profession: the science journals themselves. If my colleagues had been given a similar grace from heaven, they too might have hit upon the answers to a question they ask me about all the time: how is it that the stodgy system of print journals stays in business in an age of computerization. The answer I have hit upon is two-fold. First, the print journals have co-opted computerization. Second, scientific journals are a lot less stodgy than is commonly thought. These are the themes of the two papers in this bloc.

Desktop Publishing and Camera-Ready Copy Science Journals

SUMMARY. Desktop processed manuscripts are well on their way to dominating camera-ready-copy science journals. The spread of this technology over time (1984-1987) and distance (author's country) is plotted. An analysis of over 1,000 papers in four major journals finds fewer flaws in the desktop entries than is common with conventionally prepared typescripts. In today's allegedly paperless information age, mutual interests will sustain this form of print journal. Desktop authors have greatly enhanced control over the appearance of their articles. Publishers get improvements in overall graphic quality at no added cost. Manuscript turnaround will further accelerate at little added cost for either publisher or author with increased use of telefaxing.

The camera-ready-copy approach to journal composition has long functioned to speed publication and hold down production costs for some scientific periodicals. In this method, the publisher requires authors who submit manuscripts to follow a rather rigid format in the matter of length, margins, and section headings with particular emphasis on a neat and cleanly typed document. The publisher's graphics department then directly photographs the document to make printing masters, thereby obviating the need for formal typesetting. In 1959, Pergamon's *Tetrahedron Letters* and Academic's *Biochemical and Biophysical Research Communications* were experimentally introduced as nimble junior partners of the well-established, typeset *Tetrahedron* and *Archives of Biochem-*

This article is reprinted from *The Serials Librarian*, Vol. 15(1/2) 1988.

istry and Biophysics. Both have since gone on to become among the most cited journals in the world. Today, there are more than 200 similarly produced titles. Indeed, most are no longer junior partners of any typeset journal, and stand on their own as members of an accepted genre.

The advantages of these journals do come at a cost in appearance and print clarity. For a long time little seemed possible by way of improvement. The wider use of well-maintained electric typewriters with single-use blackcarbon ribbons represented the state of the art, and gave satisfactory, if not beautiful, results. Clearly in any issue, some manuscripts were more attentively prepared than others, but readers understood that editors, despite pleas from their printers, were reluctant to delay papers of good content for the sake of optimum graphic quality.

This tradeoff may become less frequent in an age of desktop publishing.[14] By desktop publishing is meant the preparation of manuscripts that are products of microcomputers with appropriate software, coupled with small printers other than typewriters. Use of this technology in camera-ready-copy journals has variously promised (depending upon its generation of sophistication):

- clearer, more even printing
- more choice of typeface or font
- margin justification
- automatic centering of titles and section headings
- ease of manuscript correction or figure insertion
- running totals for pages, lines or words (an important factor in most of these brief communications journals)
- a generally crisper, more professional presentation

This paper examines how the products of this technology have fared in competition with conventional typescripts and reveals the extent to which esthetic and readability shortcomings have been removed.

GATHERING THE DATA

Four journals were chosen for their use of the camera-ready format, their international contributorship, and their importance in scientific collections. In addition to the two historically important journals mentioned in the introduction, *Manuscripta Mathematica* from Springer and *Analytical Letters* from Marcel Dekker were chosen. Samples of issues were rated for the years 1984-1987, emphasizing papers appearing in the fall of each year. The goal was to have approximately 100 papers from each journal each year, although fluctuations in numbers of papers gave varying results for which there were easy statistical adjustments. In 1984, 373 papers were examined, in 1985, 363, in 1986, 375, in 1987, 234 (fewer than usual owing to the incomplete year).

Manuscripts were sorted into those of traditional preparation and those that gave evidence of desktop publishing. Both groups were rated according to Jansson's guidelines[5] for the presence of three flaws:

Smearing. For traditionally prepared manuscripts this generally was a matter of filled-in letters and indistinct boundaries between letters or numerals in words or formulas. Desktop manuscripts also had problems with fuzzy words or phrases owing to the slightly unsynchronized double-striking some daisy wheel printers used when authors sought to have a desirably dark manuscript.

Voids. For traditionally prepared manuscripts this generally was a matter of worn type or uneven typing pressure. Conversely for desktop manuscripts this could involve ambiguous or misshapen letters or numerals owing to inadequacies in early dot-matrix printers, particularly in vertical and diagonal dot arrays.

Faintness. For traditionally prepared manuscripts this involved for the most part either an inappropriate typeface (many picas featured on electric portables are simply too delicate) or inadequacy of ribbon freshness or darkness. For desktop manuscripts this was in general a matter of poor equipment tuning. In both cases this flaw had serious repercussions for readers working from photocopies of issues from the library. It might be argued that publishers can correct for failings in either mode of production by simply increasing photographic exposure time. As a practical matter, however, few publishers process their plates for an issue one paper at a time. Rather, they photograph many papers, side-by-side, in a large grid, at the same time. Overexposing to salvage a faint manuscript tends to cause the appearance of smearing in appropriately dark neighbors so that publishers avoid it.

In 1984 there were 95 flaws, 90 in 1985, 89 in 1986, and most surprisingly, 119 in 1987. Examples of flawed manuscripts are given in Figure 1, and examples of good manuscripts are given in Figure 2. All examples are kept anonymous as to author, country and journal source.

ANALYZING THE RESULTS

Figures 3 and 4 should be viewed in tandem. They tell the story of the march between 1984 and 1987 of desktop manuscripts from an 8% to a 55% share of all published manuscripts and of the decline in number of typescripts from 92% to 45%. The surprise in both cases is the gap between share of total papers and share of mistakes. Not only are desktop manuscripts increasing in number but at the same time their flaw rate is decreasing disproportionately. Conversely, typescripts, which depend on no new technology, and which might therefore be expected to maintain only the share of flaws that their market share suggests, are in fact full of unexpected errors. Why is this happening?

An answer might be found in Figure 5. This figure indicates where the desktop and typewritten papers are coming from. The U.S., Canada, and Western Europe are already predominantly desktop in output. Japan and its newly industrialized neighbors Korea, Hong Kong, Singapore and Malaysia, still send proportionally more typescripts, but this situation is changing rapidly. Together, the West and competitive Asia account for 80% of the more flaw-prone typescripts. This seemingly large figure, however, is really the result of greater publication activity there than in the rest of the world. The share of errors these account for is actually smaller than might be expected.

It is in the Third World and the Soviet Bloc that the most surpris-

A

A novel system for the determination of ammonia based on the chemiluminescent reaction between hypochlorite and luminol is presented. The technique of flow injection analysis was employed to automate the system. Ammonia reacts with hypochlorite to form monochloramine in basic solution which decreases the observed chemiluminescence intensity. Several interferents are identified, and the reasons why they interfere are discussed. The effects of interferents are minimized through the use of a double-tube dialyzer where the ammonia is diffused across the dialyzer membrane into a recipient stream of hydrochloric acid.

B

INTRODUCTION

Although many organic reagents have been employed for the spectrophotometric determination of osmium and palladium, little attention has been paid to develop a method that can determine the two ions simultaneously. Moreover, most of the methods proposed have not found wide application because of the complexity of operations.

In a recent paper[1], a simple, sensitive and rapid spectrophotometric method has been developed for the determination of palladium(II), using allyl thiourea (ATU for brevity) as reagent. A detailed study of the Pd(II)-ATU system has been described. The

C

fonden, erweisen sich die aus 2,2-Dichlorvinyl-ketonen (Acylket 1 und sekundären Aminen leicht erhältlichen 2-Acyl-1-chlor-vorteilhafte Synthese-Edukte [5]) (Schema 1). Sie reagieren beoluen unter Einleiten von HCl verblüffend glatt zu 2,4-Bis-)pyrylium-chloriden 2, X = Cl; dabei wird eine Acylgruppe in Po id entbunden [6]. Die wasserlöslichen Produkte sind zweckmäßiger hlorate (X = ClO₄) oder Tetrafluoroborate (X = BF₄) zu isolier terisieren [7]. Auf diesen Wege gewonnenes 2a, X = BF₄, stimmte 4-Dimethoxy-6-methyl-pyrylium-hexafluoroantimonat nach Lit.[7c] iporat ¹H-NMR- und UV-spektroskopisch überein.

FIGURE 1. Three actual camera-ready-copy articles from our survey with flaws. "A" has smearing. "B" has voids. "C" is too faint. Compare these samples with those of Figure 2. Both sets were reproduced here with exactly the same exposure time and intensity.

A
Two sex pheromones of the American cockroach Periplaneta americana, perip planone B, which enter into the corresponding different receptors,[1,2] have be Persoons et al.[1] The former has been also detected by Nishino et al.,[2] Of the the stereostructure of periplanone B has been unambiguously determined as 1.[3] the structure (2) of periplanone A has been proposed by Persoons et al., on the spectral data together with some chemical evidence.[4] In 1986, however, Haupte reported on the isolation and structure of an epoxygermacrone (3), a common p periplanone A and periplanone B, and named it as periplanone A,[5] although its are completely different from those of Persoons' periplanone A. On the other

B

TABLE 1
DECOMPOSITION OF NITRO RADICAL ANIONS

Radical Anion	k's, 1/sec	
	DMF	AN
1-Nitronorbornyl (I)	0.37	0.36
1-Nitroadamantyl (II)	0.48	0.35
2-Methyl-2-nitropropyl (III)	2.5	0.65
2-Methyl-2-nitrobutyl (IV)	2.4	0.64
2,4-Dimethyl-2-nitropentyl (V)	17	4.0
2,4,4-Trimethyl-2-nitropentyl (VI)	(600)	47

C
MATERIALS AND METHODS
 Cell Cultures: Swiss 3T3 Mouse Fibrobla Dulbecco's Modified Eagles Medium containing 10% CO_2, 95% air. Confluency and morphology of the ce inverted microscope. Cell viability was assessed by
 Uptake of Vitamin K into Cells: Cells wer /well). Prior to addition of vitamin, the medium was 2 ml Earle's balanced salts solution with $NaHCO_3$ (medium (MEM), for at least one hour. The medium other test compounds were dissolved in DMSO and setting of 35% full scale for 30 seconds using a Fish titanium microtip. Experimental media containing te at 37°C in a controlled 5% CO_2 atmosphere for the period, the medium was aspirated and the cells were ml) to remove non-specifically adhering residual vita removed by scraping with a rubber policeman into 1 procedures were repeated and the pooled cell suspe 15 minutes (Sorvall GLC-2B). The supernatant was performed by a modification of procedures previousl from biological tissues (7). Briefly, the pellet was su containing 10 mg/ml BSA and extracted twice by vol The chloroform (bottom) layers were removed with.

D
Lemmas 5.1 and 5.2 may now be combined. The convergence of simple truncation, and estimates the A_0 has compact inverse.

Theorem 5.3. For each i such that $\lambda_i(A) < \lambda_{\nu+1}^0$,

$$|\lambda_i(A) - \lambda_i(A_n^\nu)| \leq (\tau - \lambda_1^0)\alpha_1\delta_M[\hat{A}$$
$$+ (\tau - \lambda_1)\alpha_2\delta_N[\hat{A}R_n] + \alpha_3$$

were $M = U_0^\tau$ and $N = R(E_{\tau^-}[A^\nu]$ with $\tau = \lambda_{\nu+1}^0$.

6. APPLICATIONS. In order to apply the precedin eigenvalue problems, we first introduce a convenie $\| u - Q_n u \|$ in terms of the spectral projections of Now Q_n is the orthogonal projection in N onto $R($ $\{p_k\}$ are chosen so that the vectors $\{\hat{A}p_k\}$ are ortho

FIGURE 2. Four actual camera-ready-copy articles from our survey showing good visual quality. "A" is a conventional typescript. "B" is from an early dot matrix printer. "C" and "D" represent competing state-of-the-art systems. Compare these samples with those of Figure 1. Both sets were reproduced here with exactly the same exposure time and intensity.

Desktop

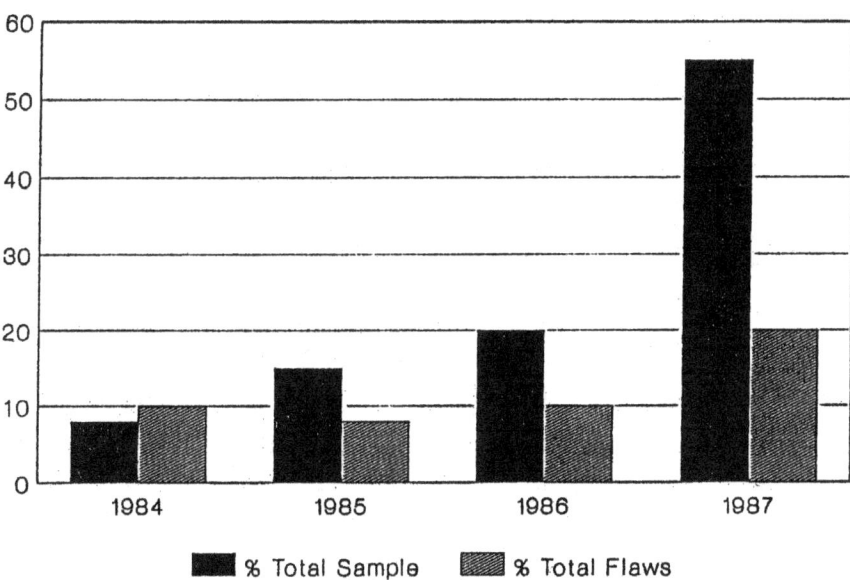

FIGURE 3. The rise of desktop manuscripts. Note the relatively diminished share of desktop flaws despite their growth, especially in comparison with Figure 4.

ing imbalance occurs. This group accounts for only 5% of the desktop manuscripts, but produces a surprising 20% of the typescripts. A reexamination of entries from these areas confirms them as primary sources of actually flawed documents. It may well be that these countries can neither afford the newer technologies nor the maintenance of their existing typewriter stock. This sad tale is not surprising for much of the Third World. A country struggling with famine is scarcely likely to focus for any length of time on the quality of the few camera-ready-copy manuscripts that its scientists produce. But it is remarkable that the Soviet Union and its allies, a bloc that even political critics admit is far from famine and represents an enormous reservoir of scientific talent, is showing deficiencies that place it behind some Asian countries. This finding would not come as a surprise to Brandin and Harrison, authors of the bestselling *The Technology War: A Case for Competitiveness*.[9] They

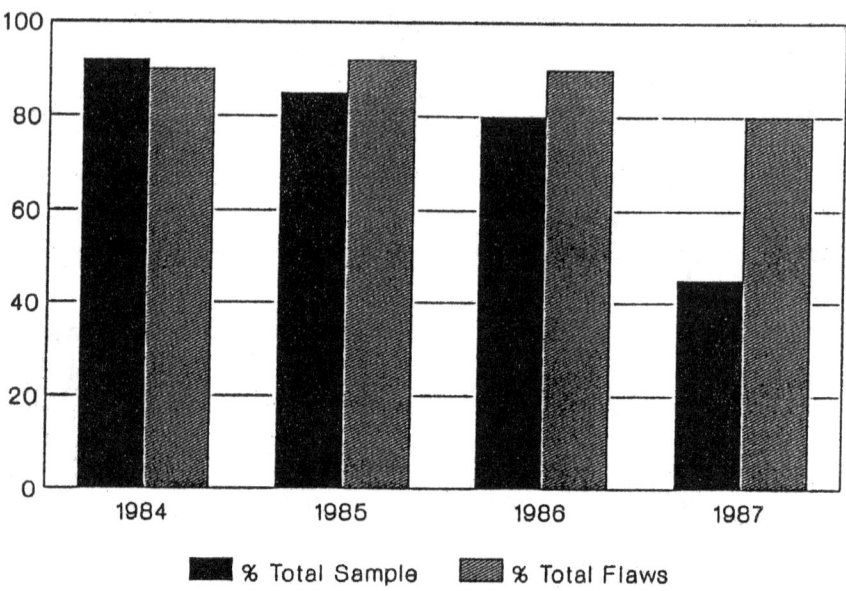

FIGURE 4. The decline of typewritten manuscripts. Note that, in contrast to Figure 3, typewritten manuscripts seem to account for a growing share of flaws.

argue that Soviet attentiveness to security police objections hampers the ownership and networking of personal computers, even as some Asian economies have grown 180% over the last 20 years largely by encouraging this phenomenon. Perhaps *glasnost* and *perestroika* will bear fruit in improved information flow and crisper documents.

A LOOK AT THE FUTURE

Will the trend toward desktop manuscripts continue? Several factors suggest that it will:

— The scientifically developed Western alliance sets the trend for the rest of the world. The inequitable distribution of technology around the world does not stop the West from pursuing more advanced research than is possible elsewhere. Nor will

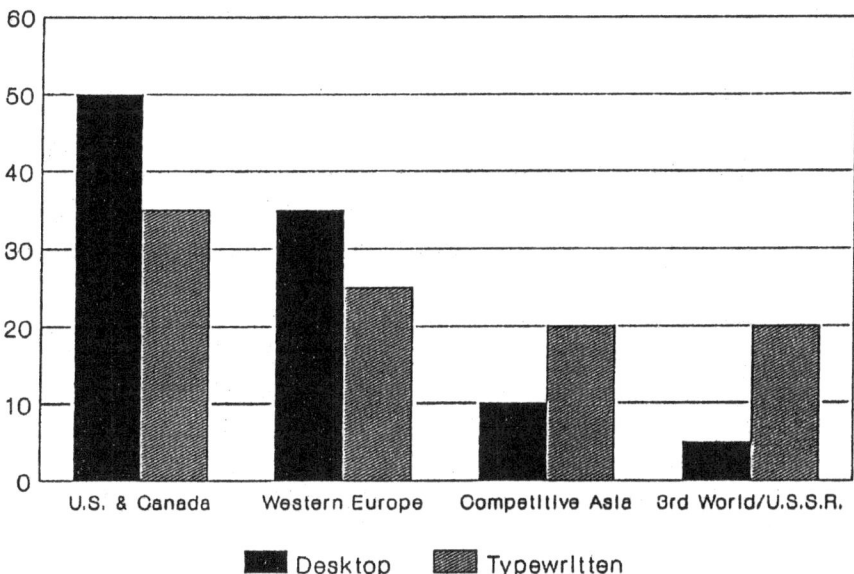

FIGURE 5. The developed West accounts for most of the less flawed desktop manuscripts. The Third World and Soviet Bloc allies tend to have proportionately fewer desktop manuscripts, and an inordinate and increasing number of the more flawed typescripts. Japan and the newly industrialized Asian countries are converting to desktop manuscripts at about twice the speed as the latter two groups.

the more general scarcity of micro-based word processing retard its application in camera-ready-copy journals out of some sense of fair play.
— Publishers of camera-ready-copy journals find it in their interest to encourage desktop manuscripts. When these are well prepared, they answer the criticisms of esthetics and legibility at no cost to the publisher. Moreover, they allow the publisher to maintain the advantages of quick manuscript turnaround time and low production costs at a time when science publishers in particular are under increasing pressure from librarians to hold down costs[6-8] and from scientific authors to speed up publication schedules.

—The notion that publishers soon will simply skip dealing with the paper copies of the article altogether and merely run submitted floppies or diskettes into a master typesetting microcomputer deserves serious consideration. Book publishers are already using similar arrangements. But it is not clear that what will work in the case of a single author item of straightforward prose requiring only a few typefaces will also work in that of a scientific journal in which articles appear each year by hundreds of authors and in which many typefaces and symbols are used. There still remain problems of licensing and compatibility of software, hardware, and peripherals, especially when the variety of graphics, symbols, and typefonts is large. Moreover, compatible workstations for not only the publishers but for all the editors and referees must be provided. Finally, while much desktop publishing equipment is standardized to a certain degree (e.g., in the use of ASCII for text), acceptance of standards is not sufficiently widespread given the cosmopolitan pool of contributors to journals that accept camera-ready-copy.

There is by contrast an enormous economy, acceptance and flexibility in graphics, symbols, and print, done in black on $8\ 1/2 \times 11$ inch white paper by any means the author chooses that will get past the editors. Such manuscripts can be photographed easily by just about any publisher's technician. Indeed the most likely technical event to impact on camera-ready copy journals in the near future is the telefaxing of manuscripts to editorial offices, and their subsequent dispersal to referees in a similar manner. It is likely that general purpose, high resolution facsimile machines will be widespread soon, and that pressures for compatibility will mount steadily as scientists are joined by the legal, commercial, and journalistic communities in pressing for them. None of this will obviate the need for the preparation of manuscripts of good quality. Nor will it make existing desktop equipment obsolete. The visual qualities that make for a good "fax-able" document are the same as those needed in camera-ready-copy journal production. It is likely, moreover, that this technology will speed up already fast manuscript turnaround times. When this happens, the already considerable appeal of camera-ready-copy journals for authors will be heightened and publishers will be encouraged to field new titles.

REFERENCES

1. Stanley J. Wszola, "Introduction to the Desktop Publishing Issue," *Byte* 12, no.5 (May, 1987):148. The first of several useful papers in that number of the journal.
2. George A. Stewart, and Jane M. Tazelaar, "Introduction to the Printer Technologies Issue," *Byte* 12, no. 10 (September, 1987):162. The first of several useful papers in that number of the journal.
3. Dusty R. Pedersen, "World Class PC," *PC World* 5, no.10 (October, 1987):232-247. A survey with ratings of current equipment.
4. Robert Palais, "Mathematical Text Processing," *Notices of the American Mathematical Society* 33 (January, 1986):3-7. The first paper in a series running through 1987 on the toughest manuscripts in Science to handle via desktop publishing.
5. Lars Jansson, "Print Quality: The Factors Influencing Print Quality and Ways to Measure It," *Byte* 12, no.10 (September, 1987):199-207.
6. Tony Stankus, "The Year's Work in Serials: 1986," *Library Resources and Technical Services* 31, no.4 (October-December, 1987):306-320. No less than 15 papers decrying journal costs are reviewed.
7. J. Lubans, "Scholars and Serials: Will Electronic Journals Save Us from the Heartbreak of Scholarly Drivel, the Embarrassment of Book Budget Bankruptcy, the Halitosis of Salami Publications, and the Morbid Obesity of our Collections?," *American Libraries* 18, no.3 (March, 1987):180-182.
8. Robert L. Houbeck, "If Present Trends Continue: Responding to Journal Price Increases," *Journal of Academic Librarianship* 13, no.4 (September, 1987):214-220.
9. David H. Brandin and Michael A. Harrison. *The Technology War: A Case for Competitiveness*. New York: Wiley, 1987. See pages 5-6, and 192-197.

Competition as a Force in the Evolution of Science Journal Format and Publishing Schedules: A Case Study from Cell Biology

SUMMARY. The advance over the last twenty years in the reporting and storing of original research that has been most readily accessible to the average scientist around the world has not been electronic or laser optical in nature. It has been the improvement in the speed of issuance and capacity for text and image of some conventional journals that have gone over to large format. The need for a leading journal in each subject field to adopt such changes is emphasized. A spirit of competition spurs other titles to keep up. Critics of print journals and print journal prices should be careful to note that there may be significant differences in efficiencies and information value between "before" and "after" generations of the same title.

HOW DID JOURNALS IN A GIVEN FIELD COME TO LOOK THE WAY THEY DO TODAY?

Pick up an assortment of current issues of journals that share a common discipline. Physically examine them. Are they all the same height and width? Do they all seem to have the same issue thickness? Do they all seem to come out on a monthly or quarterly basis? Are all equally illustrated? Do they have similar typography? Is there a use of many colors, or do black and white predominate? In some fields there is likely to be a surprising uniformity. In others there is likely to be sharp contrasts. Is there an explanation for how either uniformity or variety came about? Have these features changed over time in a way that allows for an understanding based on history? This paper suggests that journals within the same field change formats and production schedules as one means of competing.

This paper postulates that in any group of journals over time, a leader will emerge which seems to be more highly regarded by the clientele. Follower journals notice what the leader does, including the leader's practices in format and production schedule, and then generally move in similar directions. This leads to a gradual improvement in those followers, and tends to force the leader into sustaining its advantage. This keeps a cycle of modest improvements going, and represents a kind of gentle evolution of format and production schedules. The customer benefits, the librarian easily copes.

Occasionally a new entry into the field might establish a deliberately distinct pattern. This is a high risk move for both the newcomer and the existing group of journals. The newcomer risks having too few journals follow its lead, and can end up appearing eccentric, rather than progressive: a mutant out of place in an already healthy environment. The conventional circle of journals risks being considered old-fashioned by a clientele that finds the radical change highly desirable: codgers no longer up to the demands of a changing environment.

Both the newcomer and the established assortment are also mindful of costs. There is "startup" in the first case and "changeover" in the second. This paper suggests that this causes two behaviors. First, new competitors cannot risk all their money only by being different, they have to cover their bet by doing some conventional things better as well. Second, most of the established assortment will attempt to compete by improvements in their conventional way of doing things until they are certain that the new approach is successful, and the revenues lost by *not* changing to the radical look are greater than the costs of a makeover.

If the format or production strategy of the new title is sufficiently different and sufficiently successful, the literature of the whole field will take on a substantially new look. Old and new generations of journal issues will look quite different from each other. The intervening era of flux in format and publishing schedule is a time of violently "punctuated evolutionary equilibrium," and is one of the causes of a wide variety of formats and schedules in journals in the same subject field. This situation still offers benefits for the adventurous and savvy among the clientele, but offers pitfalls for librarians who have not come to understand the process.

WHY THE LITERATURE OF CELL BIOLOGY IS A GOOD STARTING POINT FOR AN EVOLUTIONARY STUDY

Cell biology has been one of the dominant specialties in the life sciences since the turn of the century. The discipline is central to academic biochemistry, molecular biology, virology and much biotechnology. Virtually all surgical pathology is based on analysis of diseased cells and most anatomy research in medical schools is based on electron microscope studies of normal cells. Journals of cell biology are understandably ubiquitous in libraries of science, medicine, and nowadays even in technical firms with a genetic engineering future. Many librarians have access to — and should have an interest in — journals in cell biology.

Twenty years ago each new volume of a given cell biology journal pretty much resembled its predecessors in format and publishing schedules, and indeed, even competing titles resembled one another fairly closely. Today most competing cell biology journals also resemble one another strongly, but no longer closely resemble their static forebears. These journals have changed in response to certain pressures — changes and pressures that many librarians continue to be unable to interpret as a periodically necessary life-renewing flux, and resent as being disruptive of the good old days. Without an understanding of this phenomenon, librarians who manage serials collections in science will be continuously caught off guard by shifts in check-in procedures, shelving requirements, and to some degree by price increases, and will miss the point.

"The format and scheduling strategies that cell biology publishes attempted so as to cope with these pressures may not have been entirely foreseeable then. Today, however, an examination of the demands they faced may tell us much about what strategies seem to work better than others, both in cell biology and possibly in other fields." This paper argues that, to a large degree, the present uniformity of format in cell biology came from emulation of a highly successful newcomer to the standard set of key cell biology journals. The new look in cell biology journals that has resulted represents a significant improvement.

THE PRESSURES ON CELL BIOLOGY JOURNALS: ACUTE BUT NOT UNIQUE

Virtually all scientific fields face demands which shape certain aspects of their format and production schedule. In cell biology, these have become particularly strident:

More Space for More Manuscripts To Be Published

Cell biology has never been out of scientific fashion since its founding. It has enjoyed both steadily increasing funding and new recruits at the Ph.D. and M.D. investigator levels. More money and more talent naturally lead to more work being done and more papers being submitted. Not only has the federal government been supportive, but much of the research funding from the major voluntary foundations for heart, lung, muscle diseases and cancers supports cell labs. Moreover cellular biologists have not allowed new findings in molecular genetics or virology to deprive them of money, recruits, or manuscripts. The sites of the action of genes and viruses are within the cell, and many cell labs have become training sites in the newer disciplines. Papers in those fields, as well as in biochemistry, continue to be welcomed into cell journals. The American experience of avoiding obsolescence and co-opting new fields has been repeated abroad. By the early 1960s, not only had the great research centers of Britain and the Continent fully recovered from WWII, but new centers in Japan and economically advancing Asia were opening for the first time. Both Europeans and Asians were eager to have their work published in outlets favored by Americans, further pushing the demand for more space.

Moreover, there is at least one school of format taste that finds the thick, substantial issue a reassuring sign that the journal is fulfilling its role as an archive, preserving as much as is possible for succeeding scientific workers to consult. Some would argue that failure to provide enough space encourages the expansion of existing rival journals or the founding of new rivals.

The down side of accepting too many manuscripts, however can include the development of a reputation for being too easy, an increase in the backlog of unpublished articles, journals that are too thick to handle and daunting to keep up with, and cost increases. **A strategy that nonetheless emphasizes adding more pages can be termed the "fat issue" approach.**

More Allowance for Illustrations, Especially Photos of Microscopic Slides

The whole system of argumentation and proof in cell biology is dependent on visual evidence. With the exception of cell physiology where certain chemical measurements are paramount, the bulk of advances in cell biology have involved identification of cell structures and the changes they undergo in life processes. There has been tremendous advances in microscope engineering to go along with the demand for better visualization. Not only has the traditional light microscope been improved and modified in dozens of ways, including the use of time-lapse photography, but the power of electron microscopy has been startling. Observation of finer details and the acquisition of new perspectives through improvements in staining, mounting, or shadowing are frequently reported.

Computer graphics have added another impetus to the demands for more illustration allowances. Complicated tables, long verbal passages, and even some of the older hand-composed graphs have given way to clear, highly illustrative graphical representations. Line drawings done in ink have often been replaced by computer-assisted perspective art-work etched by laser. Indeed, it is now no longer uncommon to see computer-enhanced photos of slides with interpretive or schematic computer detail blended into the figure.

Journal publishers have been intellectually understanding of the demand for more illustration space, but face constraints owing to the cost of slicker paper for photos, increased total pages, and the need for more skilled layout technicians at the plant. The efficient integration of text, tables, and photos in meaningful and space-efficient sequence is not an easy task. **Nonetheless a strategy that emphasizes a highly illustrative approach can be termed, crudely, but not entirely inaccurately, the "pretty issue" ap-**

proach. Not surprisingly, some critics feel that such an approach shows a certain lack of respect for scholarly prose style, and is open to abuse. They first see the serious journal sliding down to a popularization like *Scientific American* and then down to something like a comic book, with colored pictures.

Increased Speed of Publication of Submitted Manuscripts

Scientists are frequently frustrated by waiting several months to a year for the actual appearance of a manuscript in print. Having worked hard to be the first to report a finding, they now stand in line with their manuscript, while hundreds of other months-old papers appear before them. Blame for slow appearance is divided equally between the editors, who pick and prod the referees to come to an acceptance or rejection decision, and the publishers, who set the page limits for each issue, and thereby determine the number of papers that will appear on schedule.

The careers of both scientists and journals may share a paradox. As scientists become more prominent they tend to be sent more manuscripts to referee. Much like the journals themselves, they are forced to choose between making faster decisions, which leaves them open to the charge of arbitrariness, or forced to make the backlog worse as each manuscript awaits more measured individual attention. The usually suggested remedy, more frequent issues, increases postage and staff costs. It commonly takes as much time for the publisher's production supervisors to "put to bed" 24 issues of a single journal, providing a single income, as it does to handle two twelve issue journals, providing two incomes. The cost for **"frequent issue"** approach journals tends to reflect this.

HOW DO WE MEASURE SUCCESS? HOW LIKELY IS IT THAT FORMAT OR PUBLISHING SCHEDULE PLAY A ROLE?

One of the hardest problems in comparing the outcomes of differing format and production strategies is to arrive at a workable measure of their success in the overall performance of the journal. This paper will report "Total Papers"[1] and "Least Lag"[2] as intermediate measures of success, derived at least in part from strategies of fatness,[3] frequency,[4] and prettiness.[5] "Impact Factor" (essentially per paper quotability by specialists in the subject) as reported in the *Journal Citation Reports* volume of *Science Citation Index* annual cumulations will be used as a global indicator of which journals are ahead in scientific esteem or success.

It is of course undeniable that the scientific content of a journal is more important in its impact factor than the nature of its format or publishing schedule. Likewise the perceived prestige of the sponsoring authority can initially play a large role. However, it is unlikely in many scientific fields that papers of good content, will over long periods, appear in journals that have poor formats or are chronically backlogged. Scientists have no incentive to choose unattractive and less timely publication of their work, particularly when better outlets are available. Moreover as both this case study and common sense suggest: it is too improbable that all the changes that one sees over time in an individual journal edited by Nobel class scholars are just whimsical or that the patterns shared by journals in a field are merely the result of coincidence.

In examining changes that we will interpret as deliberate strategies, we must ask ourselves:

— Is it more important for a journal issue to be "fat" than "frequent," or vice-versa?
— Does being "pretty" correlate or conflict with success?
— Does success in terms of least lag in one time period cause the journal to be so swamped with new papers in a subsequent span that it bogs down the journal?
— Does a journal have to be a leader in all format and production measures in order to be the leader in impact factor?

In the following section we will measure journals in terms of placement points earned over the time spans under study. A journal that is in first place in a field of three journals in a given year for some characteristic is said to score three points. The title in second place for that characteristic scores two and so on. These placement points are summed for each title and the totals earned during the time span are compared among the competitors. For convenience sake, and because the individual totals will vary according to the number of competitors and years in the timespan, the leader's score is uniformly set at 100% in our graphs, and the follower journals at the percentage they earned. A percentage for a follower journal that is close to 100 indicates that in some years, it may have itself held the leadership, and is suggestive of a close competition in the journal characteristic under study. A low percentage for a journal is indicative of a strategy that does not emphasize this characteristic. While impact factors are available for each year during any time span, the last impact factor for the time span under study has been chosen for a basis of comparison. This is appropriate in the sense that the success of any changes in format or production schedule can be best judged as the result of accumulated, multiple reactions from the clientele. The impact factor itself is the result of quotations of articles over the two most recent years.

From time to time we will report averages of actual peak performances,[6] demonstrating the quantitative drift towards improvement that the evolutionary process is expected to provide.

1969-1973:
THE ERA BEFORE CELL

Three journals dominated general cell biology during the 1960s and early 1970s. Each had a different home base of editorial control, but competed for subscriptions and manuscripts internationally. In practical terms every U.S. library that took one of these titles, was very likely to have the other two.

The *Journal of Cell Biology* was the youngest journal in our study (1962), but had a "Headstart" program built into its parentage. It was officially sponsored by the leading U.S. group in the field, the American Society for Cell Biology, and produced and distributed by one of the leading U.S. university presses, Rockefeller. The *Journal of Cell Science* was the senior member of the "Big 3," with a heritage going back to the 1852 founding of the *Quarterly Journal of Microscopial Science*. Its pedigree was also very strong. The sponsor was the leading British life sciences society, the Company of Biologists, in conjunction with Cambridge University Press, certainly a worthy competitor for Rockefeller. *Experi-*

mental Cell Research was of intermediate age, with a 1950 founding. It represented a joint Euro-American strategy. The bulk of the editors would be based in Europe, and indeed were headquartered at the Karolinska Institut in Stockholm, site of the Nobel Prize Award announcements in Physiology and Medicine. A minority of the editors, as well as the majority of financial backing came from the U.S., under the auspices of Academic Press, the leading American for-profit publisher in the sciences. The journal served as the organ of the International Society for Cell Biology, and, as with all three journals, the principal language of publication was English.

How did the journals compare in formats and publishing schedules? All journals seemed effectively standardized at a six inch by nine inch dimensions[7] from the year of their individual founding. All had essentially unchanging covers on each issue in spare academic style. They uniformly featured traditional typography and relied, with extremely rare exceptions, solely on black and white line drawings and photographic plates for illustrations. All of these factors were held in common among the three titles and from year to year. There were, however, some differences of interest for our study. See Figures 1 through 3.

The *Journal of Cell Biology* effectively placed second in three areas of format: issue thickness (ranges between 212-278 pages),

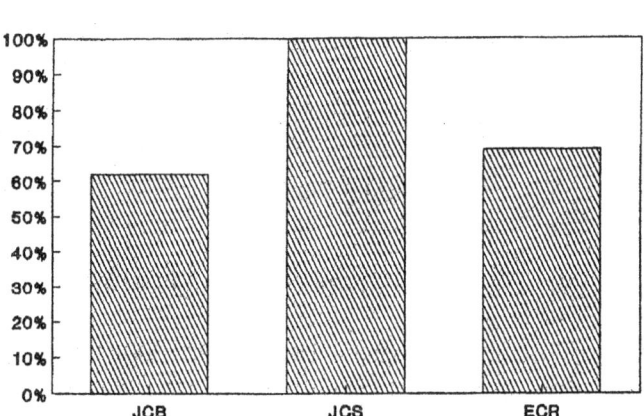

FIGURE 1. Fat Issues

1969-1973

FIGURE 2. Frequent Issues

1969-1973

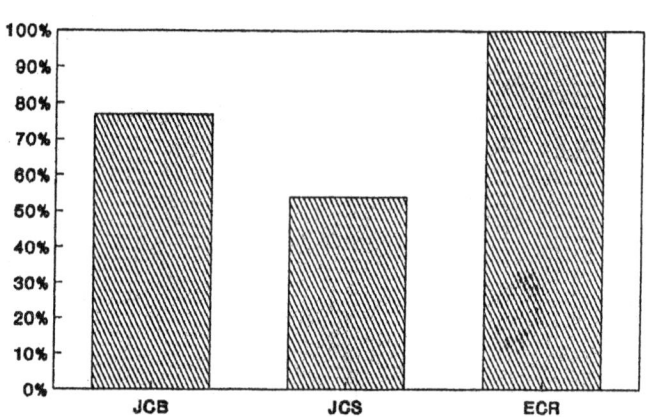

FIGURE 3. Pretty Issues

illustrations per 100 pages (ranges between 85-111), and frequency (monthly).

The *Journal of Cell Science* clearly placed all its format eggs in one basket: issue thickness. It became the first journal to regularly range over 300 pages an issue. And while it is true that it had demonstrated some resolve to speed up by changing from a quarterly journal, it nonetheless remained the least frequent with only six issues. Its density of illustrations (ranging from 61-106) was also the lowest.

Experimental Cell Research had an early lead in frequency with an announced schedule of 14 issues a year (two in March and October, otherwise monthly). But in three of the five years of this study span, it simply doubled up one or more of the issues, decreasing this advantage. However this doubling enabled it to effectively tie the *Journal of Cell Biology* for individual issue thickness (191-293 pages). In another close race with the *Journal of Cell Biology*, it claimed first place in illustrations (ranging between 101-119).

The two more broadly based strategies of the *Journal of Cell Biology* and *Experimental Cell Research* served them well in the intermediate measures of success. See Figures 4 and 5. The *Journal of Cell Biology*, with a lag time of approximately six months beat the seven month lag of *Experimental Cell research* and the 8-12 month lags noted in the *Journal of Cell Science*. *Experimental Cell Research* with its high frequency and moderate thickness gained the total papers lead (341-446 annually).

Which of these two mixtures was most effective in the overall prize of impact factor? As it turned out, the *Journal of Cell Biology*, with its edge in speed, clearly overcame *Experimental Cell Re-*

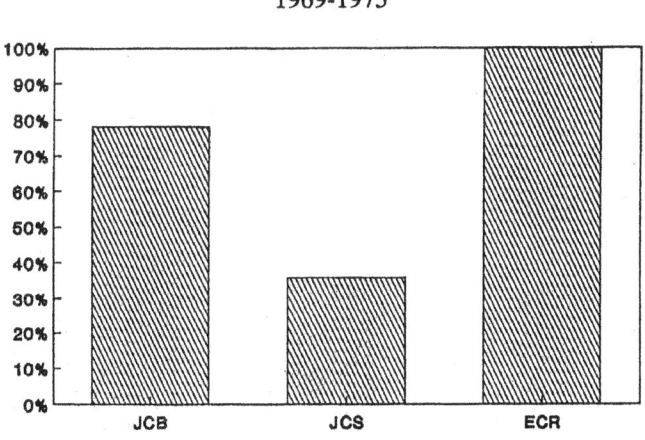

FIGURE 4. Total Papers

search's lead in bulk. See Figure 6. Almost as surprisingly, the stodgy *Journal of Cell Science* with its measured, archival approach did essentially as well as *Experimental Cell Research*.

This impact factor gap would set *Experimental Cell Research* and the *Journal of Cell Science* on their way to format and production

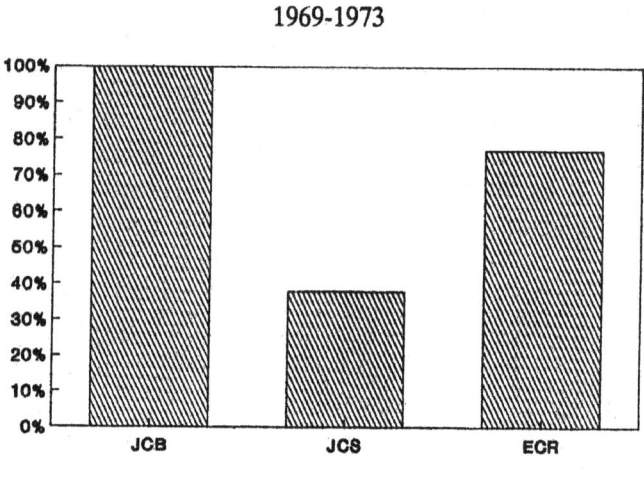

FIGURE 5. Least Lag

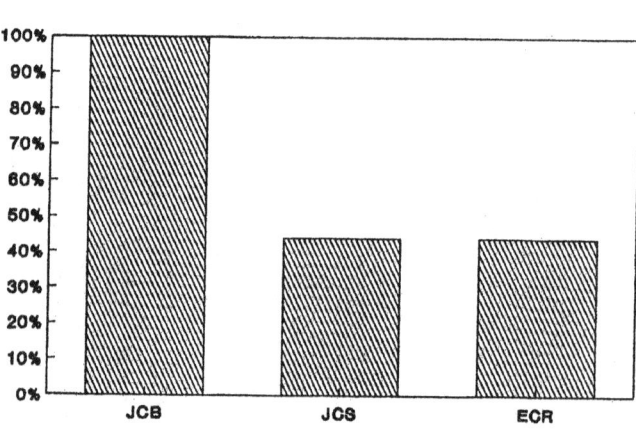

FIGURE 6. Impact Factor

reform to either catch up to the *Journal of Cell Biology* in speed or attempt to attract a following based on some enhancement in another area.

1974-1980:
AS THE OTHERS CHASE
THE JOURNAL OF CELL BIOLOGY
AROUND THE RACE COURSE
CELL ARRIVES AND CHANGES THE TRACK

Without losing any of its issue thickness in 1969-1973 terms, *Experimental Cell Research* greatly improved the reliability of its issue frequency, the 14 issues were more dependable. Moreover it increased its density of illustrations by 15%.

The *Journal of Cell Science* also improved its illustration situation by 16%. But it displayed two diametrically opposed behaviors on countering the *Journal of Cell Biology*'s advantage in lag time. For the first three years, it added three more issues annually, for a peak total of nine issues. Then however, it apparently thought better of it, and reverted to its original typecasting as archive of record. After the highly novel approach of polling its library subscribers[8] by mail ballot, it not only went back to six issues, but had each arrive already hardbound, with issues regularly ranging between 400-500 pages.

The *Journal of Cell Biology* did not rest on its laurels. It expanded the average issue and average density of illustration by approximately 10% each. Only its highly dependable monthly appearance remained the same.

The results of this competition gave cell biology three highly improved journals: and this leads to our first display of evolutionary progress. See Figure 7. Despite an increase in every measure of bulk and complexity, including total papers, lag times decreased a month for each journal in the survey. The *Journal of Cell Biology* went down to almost four months, *Experimental Cell Research* went down to almost five months, and even in its hardbound format the *Journal of Cell Science*, reached down to seven months. In many instances, a given issue of any of even the second or third place journals in the 1974-1980 format was the superior of leading

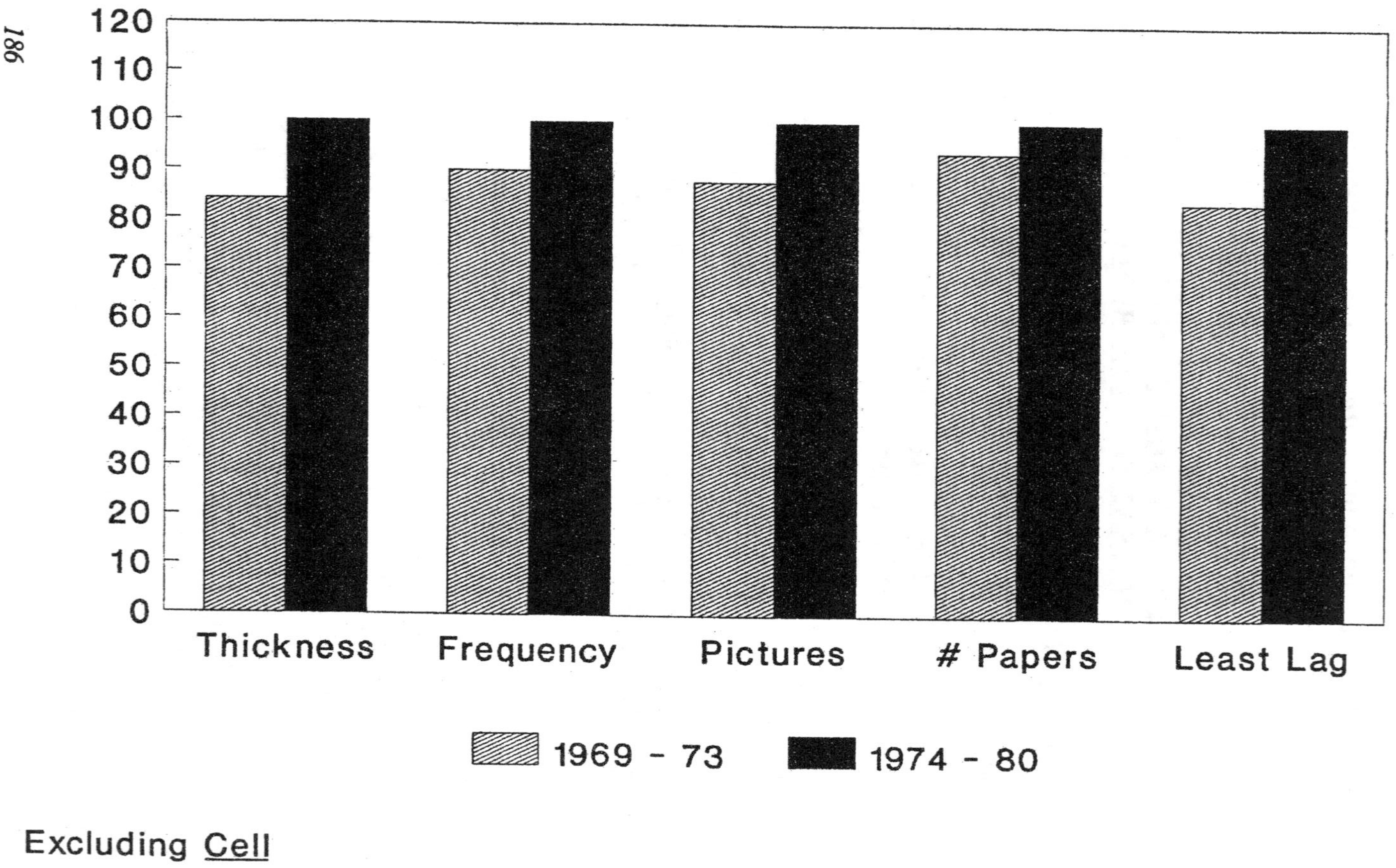

FIGURE 7. Peak Performance of Leading Cell Biology Journals Excluding Cell

examples from the 1969-1973 period. Because the *Journal of Cell Biology* kept up with its traditional rivals, it effectively maintained its lead in the race. The problem was, as Figure 8 indicates, a whole new player *Cell*, had since arrived on the scene and altered the track.

Cell looked very different and acted somewhat differently from the customary cell biology journal. First, it was in 8 1/2 × 11 inch format. Second, it had constantly changing, highly illustrative covers, many of which were in color. Third, it started off with a rather slender page count, some of which was attributable to its newness. However, much could be explained by the greater efficiency of larger pages in space actually covered by print as opposed to the whiteness of the border and inter-column regions. Fourth, some of its illustrations tended to be larger, an obvious advantage of its format. More subtly, more creative configurations of text and illustrations were now possible, given the greater field on which layout designers could work. Fifth, the typography was fresh. Sixth, there was the brashness of the editor in proclaiming *Cell* "the journal for exciting biology." There had been nothing like this since 1969 when *Cytobios* announced that it was the "prestige journal" of cell biology, and then promptly faded into relative obscurity, perhaps as a punishment from cell biology's Olympians for such *hubris*. Sev-

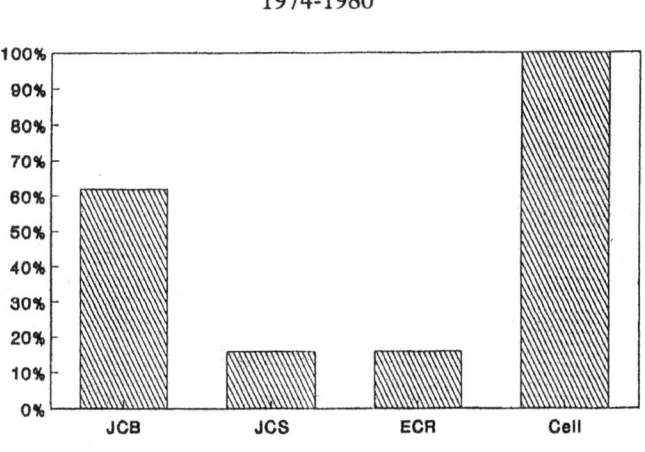

FIGURE 8. Impact Factor

enth, the journal developed a reputation for having its highly colorful editor-in-chief personally and very rapidly screen out valid but "unexciting" manuscripts.

Yet *Cell* was not entirely from another planet. It was firmly anchored to one of the finest scientific schools on earth, MIT, in the person of its editor, a large proportion of its early contributors, and the sponsoring press. In fact, it seemed to have learned its format efficiency lessons from existing journals in biochemistry like the *Journal of Biological Chemistry*, which had long gone over to the larger format, as had the journal of the anointed life sciences elite, the *Proceedings of the National Academy of Sciences*. Two multiscience journals, avidly followed by cell biologists, *Science* and *Nature*, not only shared this format, but had gone over to highly illustrative jackets (and often highly illustrative articles) for each weekly issue.

Within the cell biology literature proper, as Figures 9-13 show, *Cell* quickly positioned itself at or near the top of strategies most closely associated with the conventional leader, the *Journal of Cell Biology*. It too, emphasized frequency over thickness, and employed its illustrative possibilities heavily. While by no means weak in total pages after its startup, it absolutely dominated least lag, with manuscripts appearing within three months of acceptance in

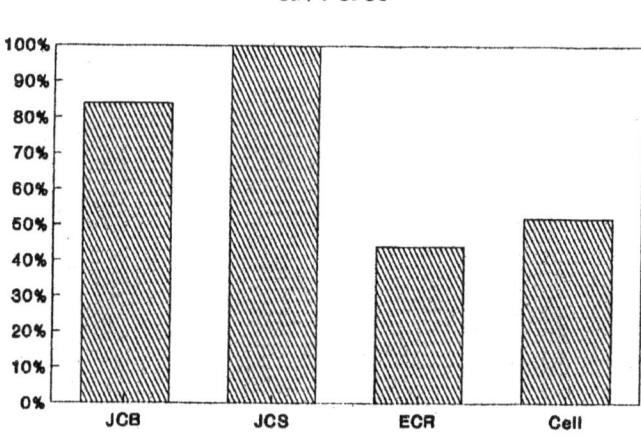

FIGURE 9. Fat Issues

each and every issue. Was this hybrid of new look and old strategies an evolutionary freak or a fit competitor to be copied? It would meet its first real "survival-of-the-fittest" test as yet another seriously sponsored journal would join the group.

1981-PRESENT: MOLECULAR AND CELLULAR BIOLOGY ARRIVES READY TO RUN THE OLD RACE, ONLY TO FIND ALL THE VETERANS ON THE NEW TRACK

The American Society for Microbiology had envied the success of journals in cell biology in coopting good papers in topics that could have just as readily been handled within its own extensive family of solid specialty journals. Confident of its ability to manage problems of production and distribution, it saw an opportunity to venture a new journal in a field already undergoing quite an upheaval. This would enable the society to stem any hemorrhage of papers or young talent, and indeed make new converts in a dignified way. Correctly, it assembled an editorial board and a group of preliminary contributors of first rank.

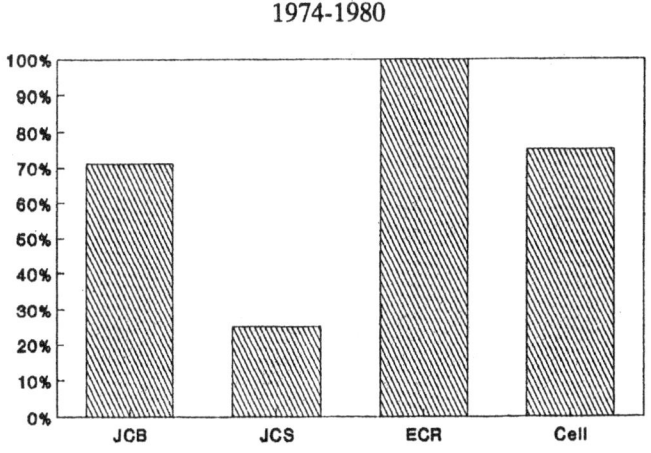

FIGURE 10. Frequent Issues

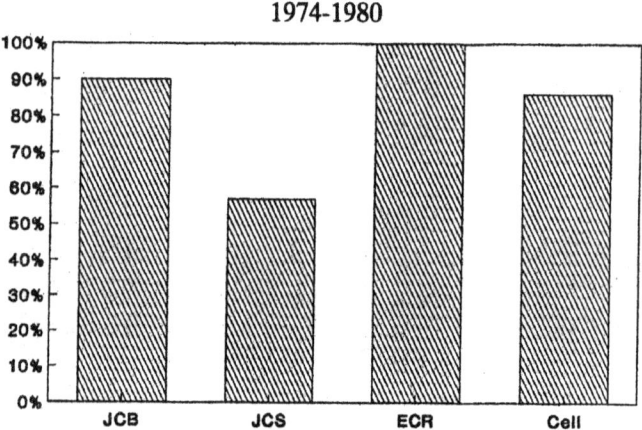

FIGURE 11. Pretty Issues

FIGURE 12. Total Issues

Perhaps not so wisely, the first seven pages were devoted to a daunting list of rules and restrictions on manuscript submission. While many of these made sense and essentially appealed to those who may have been offended by *Cell*'s freewheeling manuscript processing style, they set a conservative tone that was reinforced by the new journal's old, literally graying format. Perhaps the new

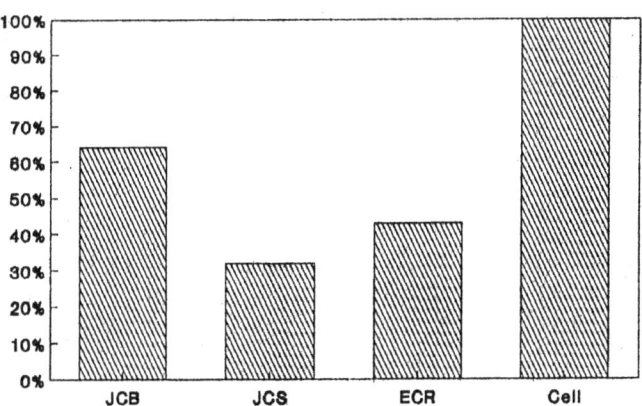

FIGURE 13. Least Lag

journal was out to emulate the traditional leader, the *Journal of Cell Biology*. This would have made sense, since the format used in the other A.S.M titles was quite similar to the venerable *Journal of Cell Biology*. The only flaw was at virtually the same time, the *Journal of Cell Biology* switched whole-heartedly to the large "Cell" class format.

By 1984 not only *Molecular and Cellular Biology*, but the entire family of A.S.M. journals, would find itself following suit. By that year the *Journal of Cell Biology* had already used the new format to solidify its position as the most densely illustrated journal in cell biology. By 1985, the covers of the *Journal of Cell Biology* featured new photographs for each issue. By 1986, many of these were in brilliant color. In what has to be the ultimate breakdown of resistance, the *Journal of Cell Science* in 1987, not only went to large format, but had stunning color photography on its covers. In the next year, it finally hit a twelve issue frequency and went for a speed-based strategy. Only *Experimental Cell Research* held on to its old format,[9] and in fact, reduced frequency to twelve monthly issues.

But *Cell* scarcely stood still. At about the same time that the *Journal of Cell Biology* was making its changes, and *Molecular and Cellular Biology* was makings its appearance, *Cell* picked up its frequency to the seemingly quaint number of thirteen. This made it reminiscent at first of the old fourteen issue strategy of *Experimental Cell Research*, and did not at first seem to provide a great deal of advantage over a twelve issue schedule. The underlying goal became clear, when in 1986, each issue of *Cell* divided, yielding cell biology's first biweekly. *Cell* has also explicitly renounced a fat-issue approach, with the editor effectively saying that there was an inverse ratio between the thickness of an issue and the scientists willingness to actually read it. Having seemingly conceded the total illustration prize to the *Journal of Cell Biology*, *Cell* appears to be moving slowly in the direction of color: in the 1984 sample approximately 15% of the plates within the journals itself were in stunning color.

As Figure 14 shows, these moves helped keep *Cell* well ahead of the competition. There is some movement in the issue thickness and frequency graphs (see Figures 15 and 16). As mentioned earlier, the *Journal of Cell Science* and *Cell* are, by the end stage of time covered by this graph, actually moving down (ranging down to about 150-200 pages an issue) relative to both the *Journal of Cell Biology* and *Molecular and Cellular Biology* (both of which now have issues ranging from 400-500 pages). Likewise *Experimental Cell Research* is moving down in frequency to 12 issues just as the *Journal*

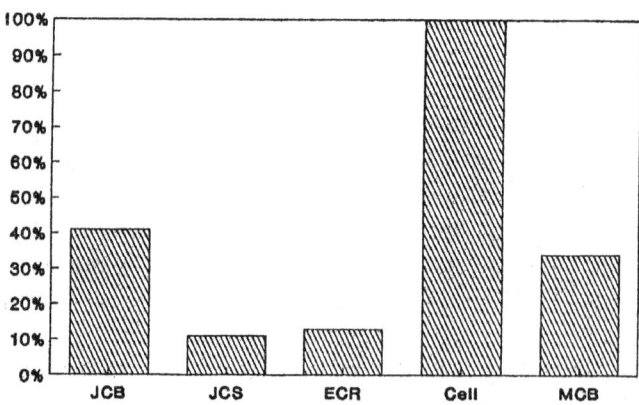

FIGURE 14. Impact Factor

of Cell Science is moving up to it. Curiously, *Molecular and Cellular Biology* is not increasing in illustration as quickly as might be expected. See Figure 17. It may be assuming the conservative niche held formerly by the *Journal of Cell Science*. It has the old thickness (if in the new format), but has shown itself capable of very respectable lag times. See Figures 18 and 19.

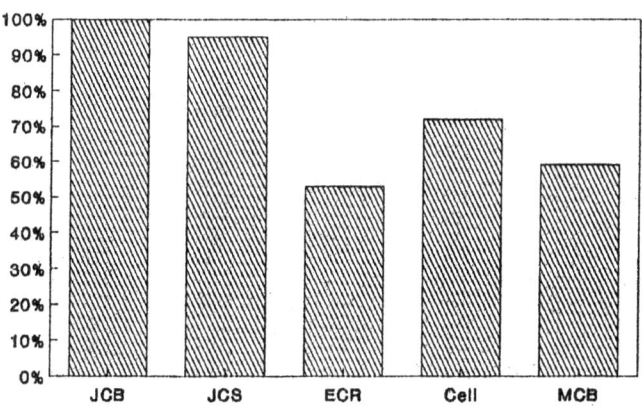

FIGURE 15. Fat Issues

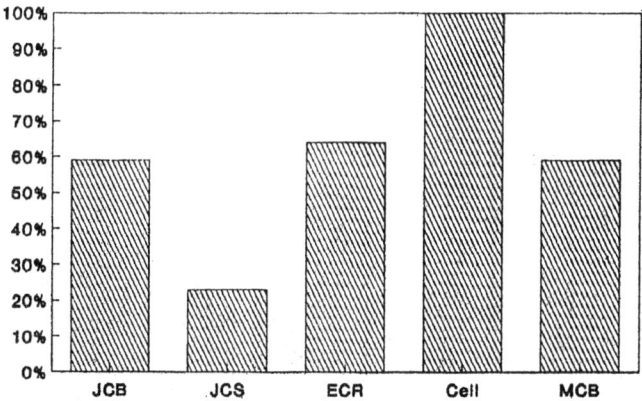

FIGURE 16. Frequent Issues

For all this movement, there have in fact been signs of the attainment of something like an evolutionary equilibrium in format, with two matters undecided. See Figure 20 for an evolutionary status report.

The first matter is optimum frequency. It is likely that *Cell*'s

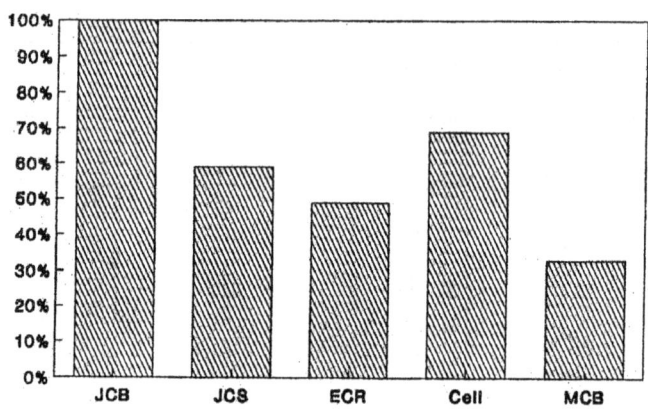

FIGURE 17. Pretty Issues

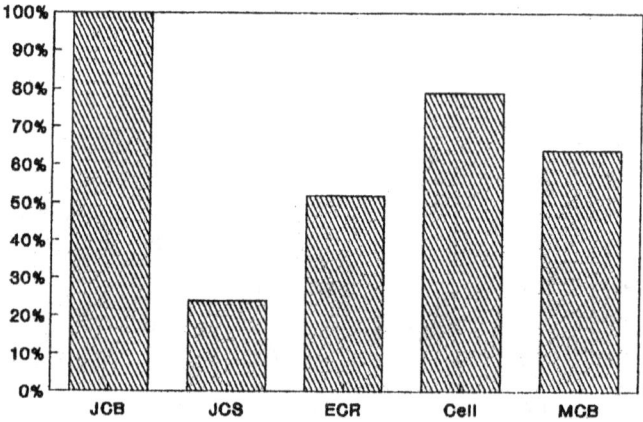

FIGURE 18. Total Papers

1981-Current

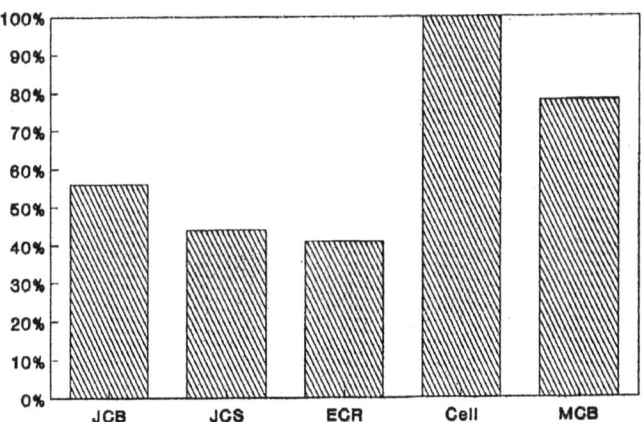

FIGURE 19. Least Lag

approach will win out eventually as subscribers to the *Journal of Cell Biology* and *Molecular and Cellular Biology* die of stress-induced heart attacks trying to lift current issues. Seriously, we are probably approaching the maximum thickness of slick pages held together by most of today's single-issue bindings.[10] (The people back at the old *Journal of Cell Science* probably recognized this when they offered hardbound issues.) One tradeoff for the increased cost of more frequent issues is more advertising space. It is not unrealistic to suggest that twelve to fourteen more back covers alone would pay the postage.

The second matter is the use of color. The immediate evolutionary future is not so clear because color's use in regular journal articles, even within *Cell*, cannot yet be taken for granted. Not surprisingly the "Instructions for Authors" in *Molecular and Cellular Biology* specifically ask authors to avoid it. Some journals assess surcharges for those manuscripts which propose to use it. There may be an underlying prejudice operating against such manuscripts in the refereeing stage. The most obvious barrier would seem to be financial, but the real problem may be attitudinal. Scientists must first be convinced that illustrations that use color are not merely decorative, but use the color to offer additional information. It will

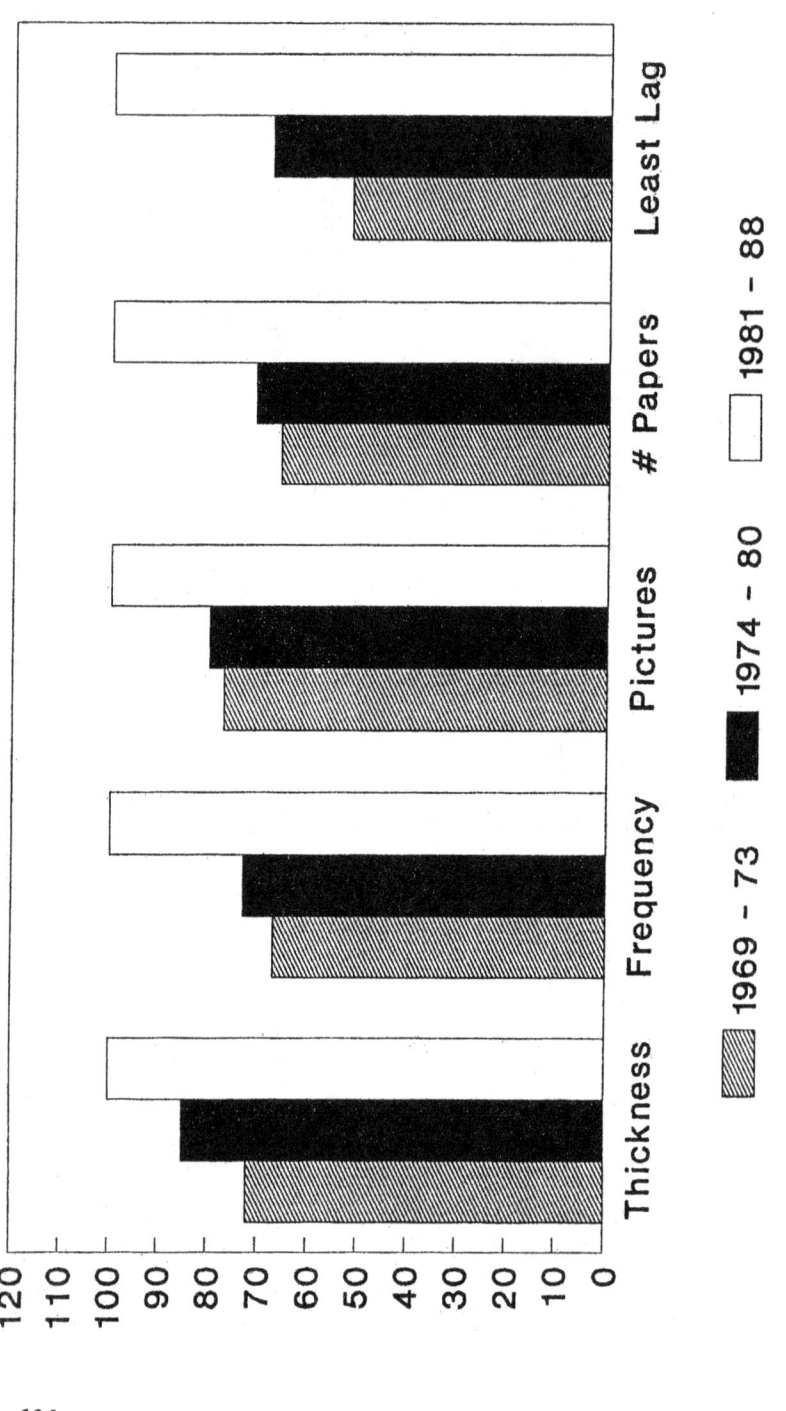

FIGURE 20. Peak Performance of Leading Cell Biology Journals
Including <u>Cell</u> & <u>MCB</u>

take money and courage to widely incorporate color into the mainstream of cell publications. A leader in the use of color is needed. One will probably be found, and when that happens, the field will evolve once again.

NOTES

1. Figures for total papers were taken from *Journal Citation Reports* or direct inspection.

2. Lag times were determined from the first issue of each year, usually January. The *Journal of Cell Science* started with February for a number of years, but adjustments were made for this. Since not all journals accepted brief communications, which do have a somewhat shorter turnaround time, our samples stressed regular articles, which are common to all the journals in our study. This may make for somewhat larger lags than others might calculate. Interestingly, most issues examined shared a common recipe of lag times: a few papers that seem to be a bit older than the others (as if they belonged in an earlier issue, but didn't quite make it), the bulk of articles which seem to have been accepted within a few weeks of one another, and a few lucky papers that were a month younger (perhaps selected because of extra merit or because their length fit better than another article that had waited longer).

3. The thickness of the average issue was calculated by dividing the total number of pages by the actual number (not the announced number) of issues. Because of the commutative law, this gave us effectively the same result as averaging the actual page counts of each issue.

4. Frequency was determined by direct inspection of regular issues. Supplements, commemorative, and conference issues were not included.

5. All line drawings, graphs, tables, diagrams, clusters of extensive formulas with special notation, computer images, spectra, and photographic plates were counted as illustrations. Over time the proportion of photographs grew, particularly in the *Journal of Cell Biology*. Camera-ready-copy graphs that the author himself had joined in display were counted as a single figure. Illustrations that covered an entire page were counted as two items. Photographic mosaics or composites were judged individually. If a sequence showed substantial change or had differing details highlighted in each frame or segment, each component was counted. On the other hand, side-by-side comparison figures designed to show that the results were repeatable time after time, or that two different methods gave the same results, were counted as one figure. The first 100 pages of the first issue of each year were used.

6. We emphasize peak performances because competition is based on beating your rival's top score. True competitors rarely claim, for example, that they beat your average effort.

7. The old *Journal of Cell Science* had slightly different dimensions resulting from differences in the size of standard British paper stock.

8. Yes, I confess. I voted for the less-frequent, fatter, hardbound issues. I hadn't read this paper yet.

9. *Experimental Cell Research* has several incentives to eventually change to large format apart from competition from the group of cell biology journals studied. First, its sister journal from Academic Press, *Developmental Biology* from the sister society, the International Society for Developmental Biology, has already gone over, and features *Cell* class color jackets and some color illustrations. Second, a rival continental journal, the *European Journal of Cell Biology*, from the rival European Cell Biology Organization, has gone over to large format and is doing quite well. Part of the problem may be that Academic has pretty much let not only the editorial control, but the printing itself, be done in Sweden, where the sense of competition between publishers is not so keen.

10. The thickness of current issues of some American Society for Microbiology publications has surpassed the most recent *Sears* catalog. Of course phone books in large cities are still thicker, but the paper used for them is meant to quickly soak up glue in the binding and ink on the page. Such light, uncoated paper would not be able to support high quality illustrations.

Index

Academic Press 57,86,198n.
   Annual Reviews series 42
   Asian research published by 110,124
   camera-ready copy journals 161
   journal cancellation analysis 71,72,73,
      75,76,77,78,79
   subspecialty journals 80,82,83
Acta Academia Sinica 122
Advances in Chemical Physics 42
Advances in Mathematics 42
Advances in Photochemistry 42
Agricultural and Biological Chemistry
      125-126
Ajinomoto 93
Alan R. Liss 124
Alumni magazines 145-146
American Institute of Physics 110,116,132
American Journal of Physiology 124
American Journal of Science 145
American Society for Microbiology 125, 189,191,198n.
Annual Reviews Incorporated 42
Applied and Environmental Microbiology 125
Archives of Biochemistry and Biophysics 124,161-162
Asia. *See also* individual countries
   camera-ready manuscript submissions
      164,167
   manuscript placement patterns 105-127
      biotechnology research 109-116,117, 123-126
      collection strategy implications
         116-126
      economic implications 105-108
      hitechnology research 109-122
      indigenous journals 121-122,126
      for-profit journals (Europe), 110-116, 117,120-121,123,125,126
      for-profit journals (U.K.) 110-116, 117,120,121,122

      for-profit journals (U.S.) 110-116,117, 120-121,123-124
      scholarly society journals (Japan) 110-116,117,120-121,125-126,127
      scholarly society journals (U.K.) 110-117,124-125
      scholarly society journals (U.S.) 110-117,124-125
Association for Computing Machinery 132
Astronomy and Astrophysics 86
AT&T Bell Laboratories 14

Bell Laboratories 14
Berkeley University 42
Bibliometrics 16n. *See also* Impact factor analysis
Binding 6
Biochemical and Biophysical Research Communications 124,161
Biochemical Journal 125
Biochemistry 124-125
Biochemistry International 124
Biochimica et Biophysica Acta 123
Biomedical journals. *See also* specific biomedical journals
   editors' publication rates 21-27
Biomedical sciences
   National Academy of Sciences members' authorship patterns in 32, 47-48
   following Academy election 31,33,35, 37
   paper sponsorship 47
   review papers 39-40,41,42,43
   undergraduate journal use patterns in 9,10-14
Biotechnology. *See also* Life sciences
   Asian manuscript placement patterns 109-116,117
   collection strategy implications 123-126
Biotechnology and Bioengineering 124
Blackwell 57

Boycott, of foreign journals 51-52
BRS 86
Bulletins, university-published 145,147-148

California Institute of Technology 13-14
Cambridge University Press 180
Camera-ready copy journals 161
  desktop publishing and 162-171
  future trends 168-171
  manuscript quality 163-168,169
  publication schedules 169
Canada
  scientific manuscript placement patterns 129-142
    Canadian journals 132,133,134, 135, 137,138,139,140
    for-profit journals 132,133,134, 136-137,138,139,140,141
    impact factor analysis 136-141
    implications for librarians 139-141
    language of publications 133-135
    scholarly society journals 132-135, 136-137,138,139,140
    university output 130-135
Canadian journals
  Canadian research published in 132,133, 135,136,137,138,139,140
  Japanese research published in 96,97
Cancellation, of scientific journals 70-74, 75,76,77
  journal editor's involvement 25-26
  new journal funding and 92-93
  reasons for 5-8
  Soviet Bloc journals 101
  subspecialty journals 81-82,85
  Third World journals 101
Cancer research 91
Cell
  Asian research published in 123,124
  illustrations 187,188,190,192,194,195
  issue size 187,188,192,193,194-195
  manuscript quality 187-188
  publication schedule 188-189,191-192, 193
Cell biology journals. *See also* titles of specific cell biology journals
  format/publication schedules 175-198
    format uniformity 175-176
    from 1969-1973 180-185
    from 1974-1980 185-189
    from 1981 to present 189-197
    impact factors 176-178
    issue size, 176-177,181,182,185,186, 187,188,192,193,195,196,197n.
    photographs/illustrations 177-178, 181-182,185,186,187,188,191,192, 193,195,196,197
    publication schedules 178,182-185, 186,188-189,191-196
Cell Physiology 124
Centers for Disease Control 14
Chapman Hall 110
Chemistry, Japanese research in 91
Citation rate. *See also* Impact factor analysis
  science journal cost relationship 6, 16-17n.
Claiming 6
Communications on Mathematical Physics 86
Company of Biologists 180
Comparative Biochemistry and Physiology 123
Computer graphics 177
Conference proceedings 146-147
Cornell University 10,13-14
Corporate-sponsored research
  Canadian 130-131
  Japanese 93,102-103n.
Cost, of scientific journals 5
  camera-ready copy journals 169
  citation rate relationship 6,16-17n.
  electronic publishing and 92
  for-profit journals 70,92,137,138
  manuscript publication schedule and 178
  subspecialty journals 75,76-77,79,88
  scholarly society journals 137,138
  university press journals, 152-153,154, 157
CRC Press 43
Cytobios 187

Dainippon Pharmaceuticals 93
Dalhousie University, scientific publication output 131,142n.
Databases, online 92
Dekker 163
Desktop publishing
  camera-ready copy and 162-171
  future trends 168-171
  manuscript quality 163-168,169
  publication schedules 169
  definition 162
Developmental Biology 198n.

DIALOG 92
Dissertation Abstracts 9,147
Doctoral degree, scientific journal use
  correlation 9-12
  professional affiliation and 12-14,15
Duke University 14
DuPont 14

Editors
  of Annual Reviews Incorporated 42
  of Eurojournals 58
  manuscript publication schedule and 178
  research publications of 19-27
    decreased publications 19-20,22,23-24
    as "gatekeepers of science" 21
    increased publications 20,22,23-24,26
    journal assortment 22,23,24-25
    libraries' response 25-26
  of subspecialty journals 76,81
  of university journals 145,149,154-155
Electronic publishing. *See also* Desktop
    publishing
  journal subscription cost and 92
Elsevier 57,58
  Asian research published by 110,123
  journal cancellation analysis 71,73,74,
    75,76,77,78,79
  subspecialty journals 80,82,83,84,86
EMBO Journal 57
Eurojournals 55-67
  characteristics 55-59
  editors 58
  evaluation 60-66
  impact factors 62-65
  Japanese research published in 93-99,
    100-101
  predecessor journals 56-57
  Springer-Verlag and 86
  Third World research published in 63-64
  U.K. journals comparison 62,63,67n.
  U.S. journals comparison 62,64-65
  U.S. research published in 64-65
European Cell Biology Organization 198n.
European Heart Journal 57
European Journal of Biochemistry 57
European Journal of Cell Biology 198n.
European Journal of Clinical Investigation
    57
European Journal of Medicinal Chemistry
    57
European Journal of Physiology 57

European Journal of Respiratory Diseases
    57
European Neurology 57
Europhysics journals 59
Europhysics Letters 57
Experimental Cell Research 180-181
  illustrations 183,190,194
  issue size 183-184,188,193
  publication schedule 183,185,189,191,
    192-193

FEMS Letters 57
Fujitsu 93

"Gatekeepers of science" 21
Gene 123
General Electric 14
Genetics 99-100
Grants 79,88

Harcourt, Brace, and Jovanovich 86
Harvard University 10,13,14
Hitachi 93
Hitechnology. *See also* Physical sciences
  Asian manuscript placement patterns
    109-116
  collection strategy implications 116-122
  Canadian manuscript placement patterns
    131-135
  Hong Kong, manuscript placement patterns
    105-106
  biotechnology 112,115,116,123,125,126
  hitechnology 112,115,119,121-122
Hospitals, journals published by 145,
    147-148
Humanities, university press journals 149

IBM 14
Impact factor analysis
  Annual Reviews 42
  Canadian manuscript placement patterns
    136-141
  definition 150
  Eurojournals 62-65
  Japanese manuscript placement patterns
    93-101,103-104n.
  university press journals 150-152,153
Institute of Electrical and Electronic
    Engineers (IEEE) 110,116,123-124,
    132
Institute of Electrical Engineers (IEE) 110,
    119

International Journal of Biochemistry 123, 124
International Society for Cell Biology 181
International Society for Developmental Biology 198
IRL 57

Japan
  manuscript placement patterns 93-101
    corporation-sponsored research 93, 102-103n.
    in European journals 93-99,100-101
    impact factors 95,98-100,101, 103-104n.
    implications for libraries 101
    in U.S. journals 93-101
    scholarly society journals 110-116,117, 120,125-126,127
  scientific research activity 91
Japanese Technical Abstracts 92
Japanese Technical Information Service 92
Japanese Technical Literature Act 92
Japan Information Center for Science and Technology 92
Japan Technology Online 92
Johns Hopkins University 148,150,151,152
Journal(s). *See also* Scientific journals; titles of specific journals
  academic departmental 149
  new, funding of 92-93
Journal Citation Reports 136,179
Journal of Bacteriology 125
Journal of Biochemistry-Tokyo 125-126
Journal of Biological Chemistry 124-125, 188
Journal of Cell Biology 180,191
  Asian research published in 124
  illustrations 182,183,185,190, 191,192, 194,197n.
  issue size 181,183,185,188,192,193
  publication schedule 182,183-184,185, 189,191
Journal of Cell Science 184-185
  illustrations 185,190,191,194
  issue size 182,188,192,193,195
  publication schedule 182-183,185,189, 191,192-193
Journal of Cellular Physiology 124
Journal of Fermentation Technology 125-126
Journal of General and Applied Microbiology 125-126

Journal of General Microbiology 125
Journal of Organometallic Chemistry 84
Journal of the Physical Society of Japan 99
Jovanovich, William 86

Karger 57,58
Karolinska Institut 181

Laval University, scientific publication output 131,132-133,135,142n.
Letters journals 34-37,38,39,40
Library science, research publications in 6
Liebert 124
Life sciences. *See also* Biomedical sciences; Biotechnology
  Canadian manuscript placement patterns 136-141
  Eurojournals 60-63
  Japanese manuscript placement patterns 95,97,99,103-104n.
  Japanese research 91
  National Academy of Sciences members' authorship patterns 31
Lincoln, Abraham 29
Liss 124

Manuscripta Mathematica 163
Marcel Dekker 163
Massachusetts Institute of Technology 150, 151,152,188
Mathematics
  Japanese research 91
  National Academy of Sciences' members authorship patterns, 31,32,33,35,37
  paper sponsorship 47
  review paper authorship 40,41,42
Mathematische Annalen 85
Mathematische Zeitschrift 85
Maxwell, Robert 86,121-122
Mayo Clinic 13
McGraw-Hill 86
Medical degree, scientific journal use correlation 9,10-12
  professional affiliation and 13-14
Molecular and Cellular Biology 189-191, 194-197
  illustrations 193,194,195
  issue size 192,193,195
  publication schedule 193
Molecular and General Genetics 99,123
Multispecialty journals 35,38,39. *See also* titles of specific journals

Munksgaard 57,58,65
Mutation Research 123

Nagoya University 93
National Academy of Sciences of the
    United States of America (NAS)
    academy members' publication
    patterns 29-49
  in biomedical science 31,33,35,37,
    39-40,41,43,47-48
  in mathematics 31,32,33,35,37,40,41,47
  new academicians' patterns 32-33
  in physical sciences 31,32,33,35,37,40,
    41,43,47
  Proceedings of the NAS authorship
    patterns
    biomedical papers 47-48
    letters journals and 34-37,38,39,40
    multispecialty journals and 35,38,39
    review papers and 37-43,44,45
    specialty journals and 35-37,38,39
    sponsored papers 33-34,43-47
    subspecialty journals and 38,39
National Institutes of Health 14
National Research Council (Canada) 130
Nature
  Asian manuscript 123
  editorial centers 92
  format 188
  National Academy of Sciences members'
    manuscripts 36
NEC 93
Nobel Prize 30,181

Online databases 92
ORBIT 86
Organometallics 84
Osaka University 93

Page charges 25
  scholarly societies 77,102n.
  university press journals 77,157
People's Republic of China, manuscript
    placement patterns 106
  biotechnology 116,117,123,126
  hitechnology 116,117,121-122
Pergamon 58
  Asian research published by 109,110,
    121-122,123,124
  camera-ready copy journals 161
  journal cancellation analysis 71,73,74,
    75,76,77,78,79

subspecialty journals 80,82,83,84,86
Physical Review B 99
Physical sciences
  Canadian manuscript placement patterns
    136-141
  Japanese manuscript placement patterns
    95,99,103-104n.
  National Academy of Sciences members'
    authorship patterns 31,32,33,35,37
  paper sponsorship 47
  review papers 40,41,42,43
Physica Status Solidi 99,100
Physics journals 59,91
Plenum
  Asian research published by 110,124
  journal cancellation analysis 71,73,74,
    75,76,77,78
  subspecialty journals 80,82,83
Polyhedron 84
*Proceedings of the National Academy of
    Sciences*
  Asian research published in 123
  format 188
  authorship patterns
    letters journal authorship and 34-37,
      38,39,40
    multispecialty journal authorship and
      35,38,39
    review paper authorship and 37-43,44,45
    specialty journal authorship and 35-37,
      38,39
    sponsored papers 33-34,43-47
    subspecialty journal authorship and 38,39
Professional affiliation, undergraduate
    journal use correlation 12-14,15
Publication schedules
  camera-ready copy journals 169
  cell biology journals 178,182-185,186,
    188-189,191-196
  university press journals 156
Publishers. *See also* names of specific
    publishers
  of camera-ready copy journals 169-170
  Eurojournal affiliations 58,65-66
Publishers, for-profit
  European
    American for-profit publishers versus
      69-89
    Asian research published by 110-116,
      117,120-121,123,125,126
    Canadian research published by 132,
      133,134

journal cancellation analysis 70-74,75, 76,77,81,82,85
journal cost 70,92,137,138,152-153, 154
subspecialty journals 25,72,74-89
U.K. 110-116,117,120-121,122
university presses versus 143-144,146, 152-153,154,156-157
manuscript publication speed and 178
U.S.
   Asian research published by, 110-116, 117,120-121,123-124
   European for-profit publishers comparison 69-89
Purdue University 14

Quarterly Journal of Microscopial Science 180

Referee
   manuscript publication schedule and 178
   of telefaxed manuscripts 170
   of university press journals 154
Research centers
   Eurojournals and 58,61-62
   multinational 58
Review journals 37-43,44,45
Rockefeller University 150,151,152,180
Roux's Archives of Developmental Biology 57

Scholarly society (ies), Eurojournal endorsement by 56-58
Scholarly society journals
   Asian manuscript placement in 110-119, 120,124-126,127
   Canadian manuscript placement in 132-135,136-137,138,139,140
   cost 137,138
   page charges 77,102n.
Science 36,123,188
Science Citation Index 61,93,136,179
   Corporate Index 109,131
Scientific journals. *See also* titles of specific journals
   students' use of 5-17
      subsequent educational attainment and 9-12
      subsequent professional employment and 12-14,15
Sciences, student enrollment decrease 7

Scientific American 178
Scientists
   as journal editors 19-27
   subspecialty journal use by 21
SDC 86
Serials librarian, lack of scientific training 6
Silliman's Journal 145
Singapore, manuscript placement patterns 105-106
   biotechnology 112,114,123,125
   hitechnology 112,114,119
Social sciences, university press journals 149
Society for General Microbiology 125
South Korea, manuscript placement patterns 105-106, 123
   biotechnology 110,111,123
   hitechnology 110,111
Soviet Bloc journals
   camera-ready copy 164,167-168,169
   cancellation 101
   Japanese manuscript placement in 100
Specialty journals. *See also* titles of specific journals
   National Academy of Sciences members' publication in 35-37,38,39
   subspecialty journal comparison 83-89
Springer-Verlag
   Asian research published by 110
   camera-ready copy journals 163
   Eurojournals 57,58,65,86
   journal cancellation analysis 71,72,73, 74,75,76,77,78,79
   subspecialty journals 80,82,83,84,85,86
Stanford University 13,42
STN 92
Students, scientific journal use 8-16
Subspecialty journals, 74-89. *See also* titles of specific journals
   advantages 77-79,81
   cancellation analysis 71,73-79,81-82
   cost 75,76-77,79,88
   definition 74-75
   disadvantages 75-77
   editors 21,23,24-25,26,76,81
   National Academy of Sciences members' publication in 38,39
   quality 77,81,83-84
   scientists' use of 21
   specialty journal comparison 83-89
   university press journals 156-157
Swedish Royal Academy 30

Taiwan, manuscript placement patterns 106
  biotechnology 111,112,113,123
  hitechnology 111,113
Tanabe 93
Taylor and Francis 110
Technical processing, of science journals 6
Telefaxing, of manuscripts 170
Tenure 21
Tetrahedron Letters 161-162
Third World
  camera-ready copy manuscripts 164,167, 169
  journals 101
Tokyo University 93

United Kingdom
  for-profit journals 110-116,117,120,121, 122
  scholarly society journals 110-116,117, 118-119
U. S. Department of Defense 14
University Microfilms International 92
University of Alberta, scientific publication output 131,142n.
University of British Columbia, scientific publication output 131,142n.
University of California at Berkeley, students' scientific journal use 10, 13-14
University of Chicago, journals published by 150,151,152
University of Illinois, students' scientific journal use 10,13,14
University of North Carolina at Chapel Hill, students' scientific journal use 10

University press journals
  book publication and 149
  cost 152-153,154,157
  decline of 145-150
  editors 145,149,154-155
  European for-profit journals versus 143-144,146,152-153,154,156-157
  historical background 144-145
  impact factors 150-152,153
  issue size 156
  multiple versus single titles 150-152
  new journal development guidelines 153-156
  page charges 77,157
  publication schedules 156
  referees 154
  societies as co-publishers 155-156
  subspecialty journals 156-157
University of Toronto, scientific publication output 131,142n.
University of Wisconsin, students' scientific journal use 14

Washington University of St. Louis 14
White, Herb 51-52
Wiley
  Asian research published by 110,124
  journal cancellation analysis 71,73,74, 75,76,77,78,79
  subspecialty journals 80,82,83

Yale University, journals published by 150, 151,152

Zeitschrift fuer Verebungslehre 99

For Product Safety Concerns and Information please contact our EU representative GPSR@taylorandfrancis.com
Taylor & Francis Verlag GmbH, Kaufingerstraße 24, 80331 München, Germany

www.ingramcontent.com/pod-product-compliance
Lightning Source LLC
Chambersburg PA
CBHW070606300426
44113CB00010B/1427